DEDICATION

Grace Jordan McFadden, my wife
Rashida Hannah McFadden, our daughter

Contents

PREFACE

JOHN McFADDEN

Now more than ever before, world events are shaped by racial, ethnic, and cultural issues. This book is written amid media reports from Somalia, Bosnia-Herzegovina, Eastern Europe, and the United States of rising racial tension, hatred, and violence related to "ethnic cleansing." We hear accounts of the president of the United States making Cabinet appointments that seek to reflect society in terms of race, ethnicity, and sex. The continuing atmosphere of belligerency in the Middle East reminds us of the complex of bigotry and animosity stemming from religious, ethnic, and cultural differences as much as it reflects the economics of oil and geopolitics. In such a perplexed world, mental health professionals can easily be overwhelmed by cultural encapsulation. Many of the macro problems of the world find their expression in the microcosm of the counseling profession. Counselors cannot be expected to solve the greater problems of the world, but they cannot be exempted from seeking new and unique solutions to problems of clients that emanate directly from the greater struggle.

This book focuses on new and renewed roles. Competencies for these roles call for effective professional counseling to manifest itself in a transcultural environment. We must be able to look beyond the current field of cross-cultural and multicultural counseling and develop skills and knowledge relevant to international interaction of multiple languages, races, ethnicities, and life-styles.

Current problems across the Atlantic and Pacific may continue to confront the world community. How can we resolve the problems peacefully and prevent them from recurring unless we understand the perceptions and cultures of the groups involved? How can we ameliorate the harm caused by the purveyors of hate and disrespect without understanding the differences between peoples? We can enumerate many persisting and emerging problems of substance abuse, crime, violence, and the like. We find it essential to deal with these issues of human behavior and development within the complex of ethnic and cultural diversity. Counseling toward such complexities clearly requires cultural competence, professional maturity, and understanding of specific problems related to the client's culture and history as well as the client's unique behavioral development. This book is intended to provide insight for some approaches to appreciating, celebrating, and promoting diversity in anticipation of greater professional proficiency and peaceful coexistence of peoples.

Transcultural Counseling: Bilateral and International Perspectives introduces in part I theoretical approaches and models for transcultural counseling. Part II advocates techniques and paradigms recommended for counseling individuals from diverse cultural backgrounds. Part III outlines issues of evaluation, assessment, and curriculum trends in educating transcultural counselors. This publication challenges each of us to see cultural and ethnic diversity as an opportunity for professional changes leading to greater proficiency and effectiveness.

Acknowledgments

I gratefully acknowledge the dedicated support staff of the office of the Benjamin E. Mays Professor, Saagu Zeleke, for scholarly and editorial review, Christie D. Linguard for research and computer support, and Amanda B. Thompson for technical and clerical assistance. Appreciation is extended to participants in the stylistic counseling seminars at the University of South Carolina: Henry Bracey, Chun-Chi Chen, Sandie J. Ellis, Paula D. Gaffney, Sohail S. Khwaja, Ronald D. Miles, Patti F. Rixx, and Randolph B. Rowe. Professor Roger D. Herring of the University of Arkansas at Little Rock, Professor Tracey L. Robinson of North Carolina State University, and F. Sharon Lindsay and Hao Hai Shi of the University of South Carolina are gratefully recognized for their professional reviews during the writing of this book.

W. Mark Hamilton, associate executive director, Carolyn C. Baker, acquisitions and development editor, and other professional staff of the American Counseling Association provided continuous support and encouragement. To these persons, I extend special thanks.

This book would not have been possible without the enormous breadth of experience and research expertise of each contributor. The editor, therefore, wishes to extend humble thanks to these scholars.

Contributors

Nuha Abudabbeh, PhD, executive director, Naim Foundation, Washington, DC.

Kenneth L. Beals, PhD, professor, Department of Anthropology, Oregon State University.

Maria J. Beals, PhD, adjunct professor, Graduate School of Professional Psychology, Pacific University, and licensed psychologist in private practice in Corvallis, Oregon.

Douglas M. Chay, MSW, group counselor, William S. Hall Psychiatric Institute, Columbia, South Carolina.

Herbert A. Exum, PhD, professor, Department of Counselor Education, and associate dean, Research and External Affairs, North Carolina State University.

Ellen S. Fabian, PhD, assistant professor, Department of Counselor Education, Counseling Psychology, and Rehabilitation Services Education, The Pennsylvania State University.

Tony A. Gore, MD, senior deputy commissioner, Division of Clinical Services, South Carolina Department of Mental Health.

Frederick D. Harper, PhD, chairman and professor, Psychological Education Department, Howard University.

Edwin L. Herr, PhD, distinguished professor of education and associate dean for academic programs and research, College of Education, The Pennsylvania State University.

Farah A. Ibrahim, PhD, associate professor, Department of Educational Psychology, University of Connecticut.

David A. Kahn, MS, clinical counselor, Bruce Hall Alcohol and Drug Treatment Center, Florence, South Carolina.

Maxie C. Maultsby, Jr., MD, professor and chairman, Department of Psychiatry, Howard University.

John McFadden, PhD, Benjamin E. Mays Professor, Department of Educational Psychology, University of South Carolina.

Quincy L. Moore, PhD, assistant professor and director, Office of Academic Support, Virginia Commonwealth University.

Margaret K. Nydell, PhD, director, Arabic Language Project, Diplomatic Language Services, Inc., Arlington, Virginia.

John Joseph Peregoy, PhD, adjunct assistant professor, Department of Counseling Psychology, Denver University, and director of Counseling, Diversity, and Educational Services, Littleton, Colorado.

J. Ronald Quinn, PhD, professor of counselor education and dean, School of Graduate Studies, South Carolina State University.

Hilel B. Salomon, PhD, associate professor of Chinese history, Department of History, University of South Carolina.

Winifred O. Stone, PhD, associate professor of ethnic studies, associate dean, Graduate College, and director of Graduate Studies, Bowling Green State University.

Jia Wenhao, MA, associate professor, Foreign Language Department, Shanxi University, Taiyuan, People's Republic of China.

INTRODUCTION

JOHN McFADDEN

Transcultural counseling is a relatively new profession that attempts to respond to beliefs, needs, and other circumstances prevalent among people of different cultural, ethnic, and economic backgrounds (d'Ardenne & Mahatani, 1989). One wonders why such an essential perspective on counseling is considered new, particularly in the United States, a nation that has opened doors to people of diverse cultures and multiple ethnic and racial origins for years. The answer is that everyone was assumed to adopt mainstream perspectives and mesh into existing socioeconomic practices and opportunities (the "melting pot" ideology). In fact, however, each ethnic group chooses to perpetuate and cherish its own customs, history, and values within the melting pot, reflecting the pluralistic nature of American society. One is likely to find considerable variations within such a social mix. It is these variations and the problems they are likely to pose in counseling that our transcultural counseling approaches address in this book.

Assimilation, in which minority cultures adopt customs, values, and mores of the majority culture with the aim of achieving accepted, is a seductive idea. Such a view simply strengthens the myth of the melting pot, which may be true as long as one is not of color. Race, an indelible mark that sets one group of people apart from others, is the key variable in any counseling environment. No matter what one does, one can never change one's identity. Nor should one try to change identity simply to gain acceptance by other groups. Unfortunately, attempts have been and continue to be made to change others to fit the frame of the dominant societal group. Traditional counselors have been encouraged to match clients with existing resources and perspectives. Attempts to blend unlike social groups not only fail to achieve the goals of mainstream society, but have also led to cultural deprivation of those who abandon their way of life to gain majority acceptance. The transcultural counseling approach, emphasizing active and reciprocal processes in an environment acceptable to everyone concerned, is designed to bridge cultural gaps between social groups. The method not only encourages counselors to work across diverse cultures but also empowers those involved to travel through and beyond all cultural barriers, empathizing and experiencing cultural meshing via transference and countertransference processes (d'Ardenne & Mahatani, 1989), thus setting a stage for transcultural therapy for people of different cultures. The ability to face increased complexity and to work across and through cultures is the major theme reflected by transcultural counselors who labor to provide a caring environment that transcends cultural, ethnic, racial, and national boundaries to develop mutual understanding between peoples. Draguns (1991), for example, describes transcultural counseling as "the method of using cultural knowledge and skills creatively to help others live and survive satisfactorily in a multicultural world." Transcultural counseling strives to challenge counselors to use their knowledge and resources more flexibly and to provide effective counseling across cultures.

It is important to clarify that we are not implying that a transcultural counselor is an expert in any of the cultures he or she deals with or that a counselor adheres to any particular school of thought. Rather, transcultural counseling endeavors to develop open-mindedness on issues pertaining to the clients' value system. Counselors who plan to deal with issues involving plural societies should have flexible approaches at their disposal to effectively respond to their clients' needs.

The tendency in recent years has been to develop and broaden the transcultural concept of counseling by encouraging interested professionals to develop and enhance a scheme to maintain mutual understanding between counselors and clients. The consensus of counselors who deal with multiple cultures is that counseling can no longer be effectively administered from only one or two cultural perspectives. As Draguns (1991) states, training procedures, in the past as today, have provided and facilitated possibilities for mainstream consumption: Middle-class counselors have been equipped to work with middle-class clients. Such a narrow focus needs to change in favor of a broader approach to create a basis for understanding appropriate intervention. The transcultural notion of counseling also addresses issues of traditional interests and tends to strike a balance between issues for those with a mainstream frame of reference and those with other value systems.

Counselors have traditionally approached their clients with a set of stereotypes, especially when the client is of a different race, color, culture, or ethnicity. Stereotypes affect human behavior, and they determine perceptions and thus affect interactions between individuals, groups, society, and peoples of different backgrounds. Research supports the belief that stereotypes have pervasive effects on any communication. Stereotypical interaction obviously results in prejudiced decisions. Asante, Newmark, and Blake (1979) found tangible support for the negative effects of stereotypes in all forms of communication. Racism is believed to hinder counseling because it is laden with stereotypes. In other words, stereotypes are reflected in what one does and thinks. Actions based on race relations are usually preceded by prejudices and followed by discrimination. Stereotyping, therefore, leads to a self-fulfilling prophecy that produces a fixed mental picture that, once adopted, becomes highly resistant to change. Traditional counseling procedures have apparently been grossly contaminated with such preconceived ideas and methods in which social practices by clients from unfamiliar backgrounds are viewed as inferior. Counselors need to manage and transcend such preconceived concepts. To be effective professionals, they should analyze and relinquish subjective perceptions. The transcultural counseling approach stands for self-examination leading to the creation of symmetrical relations between counselor and client, which leads to a better understanding of the ways others view themselves and avoids self-righteousness.

The most important objective of the transcultural counseling approach, therefore, is to create a trusting relationship between counselor and client for successful interaction. Trust is essential in laying the firm basis for constructive communication before counselors can enhance their working relationship. The helper can only establish trust by making explicit what is already implicit to the parties involved, that they represent different cultural backgrounds.

To establish credibility, transcultural counselors must modify their style and be consistent with clients' expectations. Adapting oneself to fit the needs of others is a challenging task. For example, counselors trained in the United States have been exposed to skills and techniques that primarily reflect Western ways of life and concepts that place much emphasis on individualism. Transcultural counseling tells counselors to be open while being aware and ready to adopt as well as employ diverse methods and strategies that promote access to cultural values alien to them. Knowing a client's value orientation is useful in identifying and implementing appropriate treatment strategies. In essence, as counseling and human development specialists, we must understand that we are uniquely qualified to make an impact and take effective measures in this era of great confusion caused by variable life-styles. Confusion and shifts in political, social, and economic problems that have never been greater present themselves in every aspect of our lives; they require more professional help than is presently offered. As counselors, we need to review and learn from literature of the magnitude of such upheavals. The transcultural counseling model strives to empathize with social perspectives and relate to human development nationally and internationally by constructing broader parameters for cross-cultural understanding and appreciation (Gunnings & Stewart, 1989).

Pedersen, Draguns, Lonner, and Trimble (1989) identify the importance of modifying the communicative style of the counselor to accommodate clients from clients from different cultural backgrounds. Pedersen speaks of the need for counselors to adjust themselves to interact more constructively with clients. Our transcultural counseling effort must focus far beyond national borders. As the number of persons who leave their home culture in search of jobs and other opportunities continues to grow, education and new life among foreign cultures, and interaction and communication among people of different backgrounds, have come to be the norm rather than the exception. World travel and international politics create the demand for a more open society, which creates needs and opportunities for transcultural counseling.

Participants in intercultural experiences find numerous problems when dealing with an unfamiliar environment. Communication across cultural boundaries is difficult. Differences in customs, behavior, and values result in problems that can only be managed through effective transcultural interaction. When working with persons from different cultures, we may commit errors by being unaware of others' problems, often because we lack cultural self-awareness.

In Japan, order and harmony among persons in a group—be it a family or a vast corporation—are more valued than the characteristics or idiosyncrasies of any member (Harris & Moran, 1979). Although such feelings are not foreign to people in the United States—or to any other society in the Western world—Americans tend to stress individuality as a value and assert individual differences when they seem justifiably in conflict with the goals or the values of the group. The transcultural counseling approach attempts to understand such cultural differences and develop a reciprocal approach between counselor and client. It allows a give-and-take environment to develop in the communicative process. Transcultural counselors feel that this communication is a circular interaction that involves all parties under scrutiny. It is a dynamic process that counselors need to understand before they begin counseling.

THEORIES, APPROACHES, AND MODELS FOR TRANSCULTURAL COUNSELING

Having briefly established the general purpose of this book, I will now focus on the concepts and theories to be developed to interface with the transcultural counseling model in a multilateral context. In addition, I wish to clarify that this book is written to show that different existing theoretical approaches could be extrapolated to meet the emerging needs of the transcultural counseling scheme in various counseling environments. Although transcultural counseling may represent a recent trend for some readers, I have reserved chapter 1 of this book for historical approaches to this emerging emphasis in the discipline of counseling. Both evolution and trends are addressed in part I.

The construct of a worldview is proposed as an essential force toward ensuring that traditional and developing theories are effective in the practice of transcultural counseling. To break away from our historically confined environment is to expand our worldview and to enhance our sensitivity toward cultural introspection. The existential worldview theory, described in chapter 2, provides the framework for a comprehensive training model to assist in transcending the limits of cognitive or affective approaches projected by models focusing on culture-specific variables and knowledge of cultures alone or in combination (Ibrahim, 1991).

Chapter 3 introduces the stylistic model for transcultural counseling, a technique developed in response to the needs for counseling in pluralistic societies (McFadden, 1986). The approach has three dimensions:

- The *cultural-historical* dimension relates specifically to the culture of a people and how their history has evolved over time. The counselor should possess some knowledge of the client's culture.

- The *psychosocial* dimension relates to the psychological framework of how one's psyche influences one's scope of development. The counselor should understand the ethnic, racial, and social group's performance, speeches, or behaviors to communicate meaningfully.

- The *scientific-ideological* dimension is based primarily on a plan of action: The stylistic approach will be most useful in the newly emerging approach to counseling in dealing with problems related to regional, national, and international environments.

The transcendent approach for transcultural counseling focuses on the learning process wherein the counselor employs teaching, motivating, and setting examples to capture the client's perception in order to change the client's life-style. The technique in transcendent counseling is directive and action-oriented (Harper & Stone, 1986). It involves advising, approving, confronting, encouraging, giving, and other techniques that can be useful in transcultural counseling. However, counselors need to understand the group with which they are working before using this technique because ignorance of the group's culture can easily lead to misunderstanding and miscommunication. Chapter 4 develops the transcendent technique in a manner that corresponds with transcultural counseling requirements.

Systems theories and family counseling have a strong foundation and support within the transcultural counseling community. Multiple family counseling has a number of practitioners who find it useful in helping individuals and families become who and what they want to become. Chapter 5 is devoted to a discussion of the concepts, goals, techniques, and prospects of transcultural family counseling with a systems approach.

Historical, structural, and *experiential* are common paradigms of system theory that deal with the family therapeutic technique (Nichols, 1984). The historical approach to family systems for transcultural counseling is concerned with persons in a system and their attachments to the past that affect current and future behaviors, whereas the structural process focuses on current patterns of interaction believed to maintain the problems that families might present. The aim here is to reorder the family system. The experiential aspect of this mode of therapy provides an intense affective experience for family members so that their self-actualizing tendencies will be liberated. Transcultural counselors find it beneficial to understand the family system technique and extrapolate and compare it in a diverse environment. Transcultural counselors in a bilateral and international situation need to realize that they are coping with the psychological and emotional subsystems and demarcation within society. Quite often, however, Western society assumes that educational and vocational guidance, as developed through mainstream viewpoints and experience, should be valid elsewhere either as it is or with readily made modifications. Chapter 5 concentrates on developing the aforementioned trend and the need to adjust that thinking for a transcultural counseling atmosphere.

The application of rational behavior therapy as an approach to transcultural counseling to help people of diverse sociocultural backgrounds has advanced markedly in recent years. Central to behavior modification is the assessment of functional relationships between clients' behavior and their environment. Thus, cultural factors should be evaluated carefully in the context of functional analysis (Maultsby, 1984). According to Krasner (1982), the functional view, in concert with situational analysis, examines the adequacy of intervention programs from a broad social and cultural perspective. Chapter 6 advocates the influence of that cultural perspective and the need for counselors to understand the basis of environmental influences on personality development before they attempt to intervene in a transcultural counseling setting.

CULTURAL PARADIGMS

Part II concentrates on description and analysis of various cultural parameters. The aim is to synthesize traditional and persisting tendencies in the counseling world with current social, political, and economic developments in the international environment. I believe that the current state of world affairs would be greatly improved if we assertively and positively resolve to understand cultural differences; I believe that society is experiencing a breakdown in communication because of the lack of comprehension of diverse ways and patterns of thinking and doing.

Part II addresses cultural differences of the various counseling case studies related to the unique life-styles of particular groups of people. Unlike good manners, culture is not something possessed by some and not by others—it is possessed by all human beings and is in that sense a unifying factor. Although we all share some aspects of culture in such things as processing our food, albeit in slightly different form, the diversity in human behavior is explained quite uniquely because we belong to various cultures. To facilitate intercultural relations and limit distortions, as counselors, we must move beyond our own cultural heritage into the world that is changing so rapidly. The analyses in this part of the book attempt to clarify that we should not be so locked into our own cultural way of doing things as to be unable to share other cultures. Humans create culture not only as an adaptive mechanism to their biological or geophysical development but as a means of contributing to social evolution. They also have social institutions—home, school, church, and government—that provide cultural contexts and affect behavior; counselors can work with these institutions to create social awareness.

PROFESSIONAL ISSUES

As transcultural counseling expands and becomes more widely advocated, issues, policies, and trends will emerge. In an effort to affect these developments, part III provides insight into evaluation and assessment measures for transcultural counseling and also addresses a span of challenges for consideration in counselor education programs. Global dynamics affect research and practice in counselor preparation, interlocking old ties and new opportunities in the field of counseling.

As Corey (1990) notes, culturally encapsulated counselors (those who substitute stereotypes for the real world) disregard cultural variations among clients and dogmatize technique-oriented therapy. Encapsulated individuals maintain a cocoon by evading reality and depend entirely on internalized value assumptions about what is good for society. Such professionals are trapped in one way of thinking, assuming that their perspective is universal. They would often encounter resistance from some ethnic clients. Transcultural counseling by its very nature is diverse. It advocates flexibility and a willingness to modify approaches to meet the client's needs. It must be clear to our readers, nevertheless, that we do not imply that our approach is the sole method to be used across the board in counseling. We desire to emphasize that transcultural counseling is effective in understanding the situation within which we work before reflecting or sharing internalized behavior. Thus, we believe that the transcultural counseling approach can be developed in ways that will enrich all counseling endeavors for the future.

REFERENCES

Asante, M. K., Newmark, E., & Blake, C. A. (Eds.). (1979). *Handbook of intercultural communication* (pp. 189–194). Beverly Hills, CA: Sage.

Corey, G. (1990). *Theory and practice of group counseling* (3rd ed.). Pacific Grove, CA: Cole.

d'Ardenne, P., & Mahatani, A. (1989). *Transcultural counseling in action* (pp. 2–11). Newbury Park, CA: Sage.

Draguns, J. G. (1991). Cross-cultural psychology in 1990. *Journal of Cross-Cultural Psychology, 22*, 6–7.

Gunnings, T. S., & Stewart, C. S. (1989). *A clinical theory for systemic counseling: The development of a perspective.* Paper presented at the meeting of the Meridian Professional Psychological Consultants, Michigan State University, East Lansing, MI.

Harper, F. D., & Stone, W. O. (1986). A multimodal model of multicultural counseling. *International Journal for the Advancement of Counseling, 9*(3), 251–256.

Harris, P. R., & Moran, R. (1979). *Managing cultural differences* (Vol. 1, pp. 126–149). Houston: Gulf.

Ibrahim, F. A. (1991). Contribution of cultural worldview to generic counseling and development. *Journal of Counseling and Development, 70*(1), 13–19.

Krasner, L. (1982). Behavior therapy: On roots, contexts, and growth. In G. T. Wilson & C. M. Franks (Eds.), *Contemporary behavior therapy: Conceptual and empirical foundations* (pp. 11–62). New York: Guilford Foundation.

Maultsby, M. C. (1984). *Rational behavior theory.* Englewood Cliffs, NJ: Prentice Hall.

McFadden, J. (1986). Stylistic dimensions of counseling minorities. *International Journal for the Advancement of Counseling, 9*(3), 209.

Nichols, M. P. (1984). *Family therapy concepts and methods* (p. 97). New York: Gardner.

Pedersen, P. B., Draguns, J. G., Lonner, W. J., & Trimble, J. E. (Eds.). (1989). *Counseling across cultures* (3rd ed., pp. 79–106). Honolulu: University of Hawaii Press.

PART I

THEORIES, APPROACHES, AND MODELS FOR TRANSCULTURAL COUNSELING

CHAPTER 1

HISTORICAL APPROACHES IN TRANSCULTURAL COUNSELING

JOHN McFADDEN

Counseling incorporates a process of service rendered to those in need of help by trained professionals. This service is presumed to help receivers understand themselves in relation to undesirable situations of which they are a part. In other words, counseling helps clients understand the world and confront real-life situations.

Throughout their lives, people seek assistance from others when they find themselves unable to cope with problems (Brodin, 1988). The help required may range from specific technical knowledge of how to perform various technical tasks to other behaviors involving caring, sharing, and displaying empathy toward persons experiencing personal problems. Helping people understand themselves in relationship to the world requires special effort and commitment from everyone involved. Society generally looks for help from peers or counselors to cope and deal with its problems. Counselors use different methodologies in combination with different personality characteristics to assist those in need during counseling sessions.

Counselors specialize in particular areas. For instance, school counselors receive special training to help students understand themselves and use their knowledge to make choices about future careers. Counselors also use various systems approaches to help families deal with marriage relationships and other family-related

3

problems, as society has come to realize that for many families familial difficulties arise not only from economic depression but also from strained family ties. Too often, Band-Aid approaches to problems serve as short-term solutions by intervening during emergency situations, but they cannot provide the lasting solution of preventing the disintegration of families (Burns, 1983). Social workers, having sought answers to social problems through socioeconomic models, have recently sought psychological help and understanding (Brodin, 1988) as part of the solution for their clients' difficulties. Throughout time the analysis of socioeconomic factors sought by sociologists as major causes for social ills has needed supplementing by psychological study of the family in particular and society in general. Accordingly, organized counseling, featuring specially trained professionals, began to take shape in the 1960s and 1970s.

A brief background on the development of the counseling profession, particularly in the United States, will be presented in this chapter. This chapter explores the types of problems people bring to counselors and the need to understand the philosophical underpinnings of the profession and its emphasis on serving mainstream society. The chapter will also develop the transition from a traditional approach to a more comprehensive perspective of multicultural/cross-cultural approaches that preceded the transcultural concept of counseling. Finally, the chapter summarizes the general trend in the counseling profession relative to the growing dimensions of multicultural and transcultural perspectives.

WORLD VIEW ON COUNSELING: A TAXONOMY OF TERMS

Achieving consensus among counseling professionals regarding terminology that accurately depicts their job description is a challenge in itself. A specific term may not communicate the idea it was intended to convey. Theories, concepts, and terms may have different meanings, depending on the context in which they are used. Likewise, nomenclature related to a multicultural learning environment varies. Language varies according to variables such as counselor, client, observer, time, place, culture, gender, socioeconomic reference, and ethnicity.

With these ideas in mind, the author has developed a taxonomy of key terms applicable to the world view on counseling as presented in this publication (Figure 1). The list of terms and concepts is intended to heighten the sensitivity and insight of counselors and counselor-educators as they expand their awareness and enhance their effectiveness in transcultural relations. Because of the pluralistic teaching/learning environment and societal interaction among persons of different ethnic, racial, cultural, religious, social, and economic groups, this list is an invaluable resource for students, counseling professionals, and others. The global chart and taxonomy

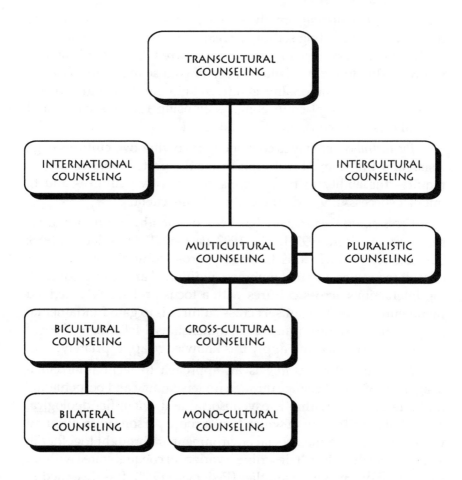

FIGURE 1. World View on Counseling.

of definitions are intended as a practical guide for educators and practitioners in their research and professional work.

Monocultural counseling involves a helping relationship between a counselor and a client with similar cultural backgrounds and developmental experiences. Counseling within cultures is predicated on the assumption that persons who share a common culture and history relate more effectively to each other in a counseling setting. Some professionals believe that using monocultural counseling as a sole focus promotes separatism, but an opposing viewpoint is that monocultural counseling can enhance growth and development of clients.

Bilateral counseling involves two points of reference that are brought to a counseling setting to create the basis for momentum to evolve during a counseling encounter wherein the client is able to resolve a dilemma. In this taxonomy of counseling terms, *bilateral* refers to ethnicity, nationality, gender, religion, and other groupings. An effective bilateral counseling relationship requires parity and mutual trust between counselor and client.

Bicultural counseling is counseling involving two cultures (e.g., Asian and Brazilian). Biculturalism for the professional counselor requires the ability to bridge gaps between two cultures and to interact successfully and efficiently with the client.

Cross-cultural counseling has been defined by a number of researchers (Axelson, 1992; Locke, 1992; Parham, 1989; Pedersen, 1988; Sue & Sue, 1990). In this taxonomy, cross-cultural counseling is considered a specialty that embraces individual and group counseling interactions across cultures with a focus on narrowly defined therapeutic areas. To counsel across cultures is to gain fundamental insights into the cultural-historical dimensions (McFadden, 1986) of the client's existence and apply this knowledge appropriately.

Multicultural counseling is an approach to facilitating client insight, growth, and change through understanding and perpetuating multiple cultures within a psychosocial and scientific-ideological context. It is a situation in which two or more persons with different ways of perceiving their social environment are brought together in a helping relationship. It describes a variety of coequal states without comparing one group to another (Pedersen, 1988). It is designed to provide one of the necessary steps in gaining an overview of cultural groups. It will help the reader identify characteristics of cultures, make comparisons between the dominant culture and the culturally different groups, make comparisons among culturally different groups, and use that information to develop strategies or interventions for clients (Locke, 1992). It is believed that—far from undermining the search for unity, identity, and purpose—the multicultural enterprise has the potential to strengthen it.

Pluralistic counseling parallels multicultural counseling in that the pluralistic nature of society is used as a basis for building interactions with clients. Many distinct cultural, ethnic, social, and religious components of society are taken into consideration through pluralistic counseling. The constructs a counselor uses in this counseling contain inherent factors of cultural coexistence of numerous groups and subgroups.

International counseling is concerned with the nature of international education, multilingual communication, and survival in an interdependent world that is becoming increasingly more competitive. It is a medium for helping clients recognize the significance of acquiring knowledge and skills to function in a globally interdependent society. International counseling recognizes in its principles that great numbers of our citizens deal with problems and decisions arising from relationships with people in other parts of the world. Thus, it is incumbent upon counselors to prepare themselves and help clients also to be equipped to cope and live in an evolving world.

Intercultural counseling is a mode for diagnosing and analyzing issues and problems confronting clients embedded in a multilateral/culture-based orientation, thus enhancing cultural understanding among clients and counselors and providing clients with a sense of self-help. Intercultural counseling is a counterpart to international counseling in that it subscribes to a worldview encompassing nations and people around the globe. It maintains a United Nations perspective and allows for client-counselor communication with a number of cultures affecting the counseling interview and dependent upon the scope and sequence of the interaction.

Transcultural counseling epitomizes for this taxonomy a level of cultural transcendency with a transnational perspective. Transcultural counselors are able to understand and elevate themselves above the idiosyncrasies of a particular cultural group. A model for transcultural counseling contains prerequisites for understanding and mastering other cultures in both an academic and an experiential sense. Transcultural counseling is having the ability and expertise to transcend cultural differences so that active interfacing with other cultures and populations considers cultural identity and contextual assimilation. It subscribes to the principles of client empowerment, strength, and functionalism.

Worldview is how a person perceives himself or herself in relation to the surrounding world: nature, institutions, other people, and so forth.

LITERATURE REVIEW

Understanding counseling requires comprehending the philosophies embedded in the counseling process. There are those who ignore the philosophical aspect of counseling when dealing with the profession. The earliest humans saw natural laws and explained phenomena in mystical terms. Philosophical thought viewed life as here and now and dealt with it in terms of interest in pleasure, wealth, and power. To a group of Greek philosophers known as the Sophists (Burns, 1983), life had no meaning beyond what people put into it. Contention over such philosophical perceptions has developed into concepts later referred to as *Christian Ideals,* as opposed to non-Christian ones.

Social development has evolved from many different kinds of interpersonal interactions. The experience from these interactions plays important roles in social and psychological growth and development. *Counseling* and *psychotherapy* are terms that have become interchangeably applicable to social interactions in which one of the interacting members, usually referred to as the *counselor* or *therapist,* assumes responsibility for contributing to personality development of others (Brodin, 1988) and cognitive power and stability. Gunnings and Stewart (1989) argued that systemic counseling attempts to improve those personal and social interactional functions by restructuring the style of interpersonal relations. To maintain consistency in the interactional process, Gunnings points out, therapeutic strategies must be prepared to emphasize the dynamics of such interactions between people and their environment. In other words, emphasis must be placed on exchanges between symptomatic behavior and environmental dynamics that can create problems.

Research emphasizing systemic models indicates that locating the nature of problems within person-environmental interactions encompasses both personal and environmental characteristics. It is important to work to minimize or even eliminate elements that interfere with communication. One idea that needs careful examination is the perception that all problems can be tackled by equipping helping professionals with majority-value orientations and perspectives. Assimilation, in which minority cultures are expected to adopt the customs, values, and mores of the majority culture, is a seductive idea (Gunnings & Stewart, 1989). Such an assumption only appeals to the myth of a great "melting pot." There is no such melting pot. Unfortunately, counseling professionals have been exposed to such perceptions that illuminate certain characteristics reflecting a particular environment dominated by a given majority group. The one indelible mark that sets minorities apart from each other is the issue of race. Attempts by majority counselors to blend minorities into mainstream ways of life and thinking patterns continue to falter.

Counselor training programs in the past have frequently approached minorities using a monocultural assumption that implies negative stereotypes of minority values and life-styles (Sue & Sue, 1990). Effective counseling requires mutual understanding between those sending and receiving communications. Otherwise, a breakdown in communication can occur between those who seek to help and those who are supposed to receive help. Professionals of note in the counseling practice have frequently expressed grave concern over misunderstandings that usually lead to failures in communication as major impediments to counseling (Sue & Sue, 1990; Vontress, 1981). Such misunderstandings arise from failure to appreciate diverse cultural and racial views that have been the basis of ethnic alienation or an inability to develop trust and establish much-needed rapport among plural societies (Sue & Sue, 1990).

Most theories of counseling, as mentioned above, are influenced by practitioners who make assumptions about goals and the means to achieve them. As Atkinson, Morten, and Sue (1989) have indicated, counseling and psychotherapy have traditionally been conceptualized in Western, individualistic terms. Counseling in the

United States in particular has traditionally projected a middle- and upper-class focus. Values and characteristics expressed as goals or processes have primarily focused on the privileged social group whom Sue and Sue (1990) refer to as the YAVIS syndrome: young, attractive, verbal, intelligent, and successful. Such preference clearly discriminates against the elderly, the indigent, and the culturally different. The social influence during an interaction, explicit or implicit, ranging from toilet training a child to convincing people to stop smoking, is targeted at changing the views, attitudes, and behaviors of clients without examining the counselor's self-being in contrast to the clients' cultural values. The counselor uses his or her social power to influence client attitudes (Sue & Sue, 1990). In the Sues' view, using social influence as a means to analyze counseling not only shows empirical validity but also concentrates on processes applicable to all approaches.

The preceding argument implies that minorities hold worldviews different from the view of the majority. Ibrahim (1991) calls it "our philosophy of life" or "our experience with social, cultural, environmental, philosophical, and psychological dimensions" (p. 9). According to Sue and Sue (1990), worldviews not only include our attitudes, values, opinions, and concepts, but they also affect how we think, make decisions, behave, and define events. Numerous counselors are indifferent to cultural diversities when they interact with clients. They respond to clients' needs in accordance with their own values and worldview, without regard for other values and worldviews.

It is quite gratifying to observe recent literature addressing the need to develop cultural sensitivity. Ponterotto and Casas (1987) as well as Atkinson et al. (1989) appear to endorse the idea that diverse racial groups require techniques different from those employed for mainstream clients. Many observers of the emerging multicultural counseling model contend that majority clients respond better to directives. Those observers believe that counseling approaches that are directive or active (participatory) rather than passive (nonparticipatory) are more effective.

Understanding mainstream experiences and being able to relay them to other groups require open-minded approaches and commitments from persons who are open to accepting persons from different backgrounds in parity. To date, there have been few systematic attempts to tear down the walls of cultural separation and hatred and construct bridges across cultural barriers to facilitate communication and encourage better understanding. On the contrary, prejudice against and exclusion of the culturally different have been as American as apple pie. This nation has for years allowed ethnic minorities to suffer segregation and degradation in the cities while affluent America winked its eyes en route to its suburban safe haven. The price for such gross negligence is reflected everywhere today in increased violence, bitterness, and inevitable destruction. Such a class structure obviously increases opportunities for some and limits possibilities for others. Intellectual development has become the instrument for dominance used by the privileged class to suppress others and perpetuate differences between cultural, ethnic, and social groups.

Discrimination is defined as "treatment or consideration of, making a distinction in favor of or against a person or thing based on the group, class, or category to which something or someone belongs rather than on individual merit" (Odom, 1989). Odom contends that politics provides a showcase in favor of discrimination, implicitly allowing the dominant and affluent group to prevail. Actions of discrimination are conspicuous and are naturally rejected by those discriminated against. Class conflicts are problems not only in our society but throughout social history. The gap in educational achievement levels between minority and majority children is clear from kindergarten through high school to university (Parham, 1989). In addition, minority students are more likely to be suspended and expelled than their majority counterparts (Sue & Sue, 1990). There seems to be a sustained feeling that society is less interested in the plight of minorities.

A pervasive assumption within the profession of counseling is that the definition of *normal* is universal across social, cultural, economic, and political lines. Arguments against the established norm as a universal standard for behavior are usually criticized as potentially destructive of the social fabric. Behavior changes according to the situation, the cultural background of the person being judged, and the time frame during which the behavior is being observed. It is important for transcultural counselors to understand such differences and to be enriched with diverse perceptions so that they transcend the boundaries of their own self-reference to examine issues based on the cultural outlook of their clients.

As Hall (1976) indicates, mainstream counselors have been too dependent on abstract concepts, assuming that others will understand the abstraction as they do. A general notion within Western culture favors individualism. To most Americans, for example, independence is valuable and dependence undesirable. In other words, individuals should not depend on others, nor should they allow others to depend on them. Yet there are many cultures throughout the world in which dependency is considered not only healthy but also necessary. Describing the concept of *amae*, a special relationship between a mother and her eldest son in Japanese culture, Pedersen (1988) states that, while young and dependent, the son is being prepared for the years ahead when his mother will be old and dependent on him. In Japanese society, therefore, the concept of dependency becomes a measure of the relationship between individuals and everything they represent in life. Such concepts and ways of thinking are important to understand before one sets out to help multicultural social groups. The masses of counselors have been trained in a context in which dependency is devalued. If counselors fail to change such assumptions (Pedersen, 1988), they are unlikely to be able to communicate appreciably with those from other cultural backgrounds. In an era of increasing pluralism and interdependence generated by miracles of modern technology, counselors should recognize the limits of a closed, biased, and culturally encapsulated (Pedersen, 1988) approach that strives to promote domination by an elite group. Many have recognized the need to move beyond parochial concerns of monoculturalism and look at the world comprehensively. Recognition of such limits has gradually introduced counseling professionals to a new perspective on counseling. Unfortunately, this recognition has not been transformed into implementation.

As counselors increase contacts with other cultures and nations, they experience exposure not only to other ways of life but also to opportunities to learn a great deal about themselves. Such encounters challenge them to examine their heretofore unquestioned assumptions and views about themselves and their environment. The challenge to examine themselves and their narrow-based views opens up an opportunity to look at the world through a different window. In the meantime, this challenge creates growth experiences by raising the level of minority consciousness to a point where minority groups have begun to confront majority perspectives not only in law and politics but also in counseling. Such challenges have led to what Atkinson et al. (1989) view as "the crossroads of a major choice in the counseling profession." Ethnocentricism has been the traditional perception, expressing superiority of the Euro-American world in contrast to all other worlds. As I noted earlier, it was this road that led to the development of traditional theories of counseling and psychotherapy and influenced a majority of the counseling professionals to date. The time has come to challenge monoculturalism in favor of multiculturalism and beyond.

TRANSCULTURALISM

Multicultural/transcultural awareness is an ongoing process not limited to any unique population or group. Multicultural awareness recognizes all varieties of cultural and individual identities. Pedersen (1982) provides a comprehensive description of the multicultural training process in reference to personality development. Pedersen contends that as we become more aware of ethnographic, demographic, and socioeconomic differences, we understand diversity and identity better.

Research indicates that attempts to prepare persons for communication across cultures have ranged from laissez-faire—letting them learn from their own experiences and mistakes—to directive and explicit training for specific skills. Technical competence, although required to teach skills, is insufficient without the interpersonal link essential to establishing effective communication between counselor and client. Literature evaluating cross-cultural/multicultural counseling programs has increased in popularity for the last two decades, and transculturalism is an extension of multicultural concepts to deal with issues at a more comprehensive level beyond national and international frontiers. Among several paradigms, the *cultural awareness* model assumes that for persons to function successfully in an alien environment, they must master principles of behavior that exist across cultures. Counseling across cultures must be extended to deal with issues at the international level. According to Locke (1992), the word *international* sparks mixed images, some exotic and some familiar to the professionals involved. Many would view the unique or unfamiliar as frightening and unacceptable. For example, in spite of diverse socializing processes of the people living in the United States, there is a common thread running through the cognitive system of mainstream America that can be observed by the majority through their monocultural lens.

Counseling is a profession that deals with culture in a generic sense, and circumstances for counseling vary with the nation where the counseling process is applied. In other words, differences within and among cultures should not be feared or suspected but must be valued and appreciated. The emphasis in transcultural counseling is on encouraging those whose work brings them in contact with many different cultural communities (d'Ardenne & Mahatani, 1989). As world cultures differ, so should counseling approaches and styles around the globe. As Locke (1992) states, the dominant cultural values of mainstream society in the United States, a nation characterized as direct, open, and honest in interpersonal interactions, could conflict with values held by others where communication is indirect and persons are reluctant to open up to those outside their immediate families. Pedersen (1982) believes that indigenous approaches to mental health in non-Western cultures must be taken more seriously instead of adopting the "shaman view," a stereotypical notion of curiosity and fascination with indigenous healer's techniques. In reality, one should try to integrate indigenous techniques with other mental health services. Studies on cross-cultural psychiatric evaluation and diagnosis (World Health Organization, 1979) have indicated a more careful assessment of culture beyond the unique, dramatic, and more conspicuous manifestations to a near-to-home phenomenon of everyday life.

For instance, African Americans face unique psychological, cultural, and economic stresses caused by racism exercised by mainstream society, in addition to problems common to many other Americans. Strong social support systems distinguish those family members who are able to cope with various common and unique problems. One such social support system is personal and group contacts through which the individual maintains social identity and receives emotional support, material aid and services, information, and social contact. Among many social support systems available to African Americans historically have been the church and the kinship network. The importance of these variables is consistent with the ancestral (African) values of spirituality and concern for others. The church is a major root of social support in African-American communities. Church members are respected and able to excel in the struggle for survival, expression, participation, and fulfillment. The church helps to maintain family solidarity while also allowing for the expression of frustration, distress, and pain. In addition, the church provides a deep sense of spirituality for coping with stress that must be recognized and incorporated into the therapeutic process (Boyd-Franklin, 1989) as one begins counseling.

Without a historical perspective on the African-American family, any model for treatment is likely to fall short of its targets. Wilson and Stith (1991) emphasize that although African Americans share many problems with their European-American counterparts, a racist environment changes and intensifies the meaning and impact of these normative sources of stress. In spite of reluctance by some practitioners to delve into family history, it is essential that counselors study the backgrounds and history of their clients and seek collaborative approaches in conjunction with ethnographic literature to develop a sense of the meaning and impact of environment on clients.

Conceptions of mental health and illness are ultimately derived from a worldview and philosophy of life that prevails in society. Eastern societies (Muslim, Chinese, Korean, etc.), for example, despite modernization, scientific revolution, and technology, remain conditioned by respect for elders, respect for beliefs, and a tendency to appreciate group activities and norms rather than individualistic ideas. Das (1987) suggests that religious traditions define the ideal of the good life and prescribe the rules by which people must live their daily lives if they wish to attain the good life. Psychological distress and disorders are explained within a religious framework in terms of either spiritual possession or violation of religious or moral principles. Healing may take the form of invoking supernatural power or restoring the sufferer to a state of well-being by prescribing right conduct and beliefs.

15

A plethora of literature on counselor education and supervision indicates that mutual influence of personality and culture is often inferred post hoc in the interpretation of findings rather than in the prediction of results obtained. Identifying particular component variables of culture and personality can enhance the design and implementation of counseling in specific cultural situations (Mwaba & Pedersen, 1990). Scholars across disciplinary spectra have directed their studies and teaching toward non-Western and minority cultures (Perry, 1992). Lately, counseling practitioners have experienced shifts in their personal worldviews in response to the recognition of complex ways that exist. The concept of culture, as an example, which is the basis for multiculturalism, has been central to anthropological studies with which the emerging multiculturalists and transculturalists are grappling to understand culture these days.

According to Perry (1992), anthropologists might help transculturalists marry their perspectives with other cultures. Because anthropologists spend years living within other cultures and studying people, listening and grappling with the local vernacular, they possess a respected understanding and interpretation of cultural variations. Such involvement is ideal for multicultural or transcultural counselors to broaden their understanding of those they serve. Attempts to promote this insight could be made by blending some anthropological literature with multicultural and cross-cultural findings, in the process developing a stronger transcultural counseling model for understanding cultural diversity. Perry (1992) senses an exclusion of anthropology from multiculturalism that minimizes transcultural understanding. One explanation Perry gives is that exclusion might be due to a reluctance to acknowledge old or alien cultures because recognizing anthropology would mean that non-anthropologists need to read more anthropological works, and this could be daunting.

Anthropologists believe that multiculturalists are not doing enough. Despite their genuflection to the validity of other cultures (Perry, 1992), multiculturalists do not fully comprehend the complexity of cultures. Multiculturalism tends to assume that other cultural experiences can be sampled through brief encounters. For example, multicultural programs at many institutions include brief faculty and student trips to a foreign institution. Such visceral approaches are rather inadequate because they lack depth sufficient to internalize validity. They may miss or blur important distinctions that can be identified by taking time to study a cultural environment comprehensively. Transculturalism encourages an anthropological approach to understanding cultural diversity because clients come to counselors with different expectations and attitudes about the content of sessions, process, and, most of all, counseling relationships, which reflect their earlier experiences and relationships across cultures (d'Ardenne & Mahatani, 1989). Hispanic or Black clients are frequently offered access to counselors from their own culture, and at the same time, they opt for counselors who are capable, competent, and culturally sensitized to deal with individuals of diverse experiences.

Cultural isolation that has existed over time between social groups continues to perpetuate itself in the United States. For example, there is growing concern among educators and minorities (Blacks, Hispanics, Samoans, Native Americans, etc.) that students from these groups who attend predominantly White colleges and universities are experiencing more and more cultural isolation. The consequences of such phenomena are certainly interfering with stable social existence. The 1992 Los Angeles rebellion reflected the underlying tension brought about by cultural isolation and indifference exhibited toward African Americans and others in American society. Minorities feel that they are frequently pressured to conform to the expectations of the dominant culture. Naturally, such expectations are strongly resented by minorities who want to maintain and promote self-identity. This clash creates serious challenges during the counseling process for all ages and social strata. Cultural isolation in any form leads to feelings of alienation pervasive throughout society.

To combat this phenomenon, transcultural counseling provides guidance and understanding on how to deal with mental and social crises because its work focuses on counseling rather than on a particular school or model (d'Ardenne & Mahatani, 1989). Pearson (1985) describes counseling across culture in terms of using cultural knowledge and skills creatively to help people live satisfactorily in a pluralistic world. Transcultural counselors should draw on family, social networks, religious experiences, political beliefs, and institutional training. The argument is that one needs to exhaust immediate resources before one advocates a given school of thought to pursue as a model.

There is a need for professional counselors to deal with growing multiethnic problems. Although most schools provide counseling programs, they do not prepare their students to interface effectively with most international counseling paradigms. Counselors emerging from such an environment often tend to be "sympathetic" in approaching problems pertaining to minorities. Thus, minorities usually get sympathetic responses instead of objective help. Therefore, to provide relevant counseling, counselors need to deal adequately with the dynamics of cultural variables and related stereotypes. To create constructive counseling processes, an objective approach must be developed to help minimally with partial understanding of cultural, psychological, and social needs and concerns of all clients.

McFadden's (1986) psychosocial dimension of counseling minorities addresses the fundamental elements of effective counseling skills that are paramount in meeting needs of diverse cultural groups. It also deals with cultural, psychological, and social dynamics of a society to respond to unique cultural backgrounds of clients. McFadden states that counselors with global perspectives exercise the responsibility to learn the values particular to each culture to help clients understand their strengths and weaknesses. He emphasizes that counseling must analyze social, political, and economic development from a multicultural context. Because the ultimate goal of counseling is to enable clients to become the persons they need to be to accomplish their goals, clients need to be aware of the strategies they can use as they confront future problems. The counselor's responsibility is to help clients learn to identify and analyze problems, define goals, and generate alternative courses of action that might lead to desired goals. In effect, clients should learn to be their own counselors. To empower clients and provide guidance, counselors must employ transcultural approaches involving listening accurately to inform clients of what different cultures offer and to help clients manage difficulties that occur within clients' cultural context by focusing on feelings expressed in unfamiliar ways.

Transcultural counselors should be in a position to decide and introduce issues without prejudice and be skillful enough to deal with them openly with their clients. Counselors in a transcultural setting must possess skills with which they are comfortable about racial and cultural matters (d'Ardenne & Mahatani, 1989). The issue of prejudice is crucial in a transcultural counseling process, as it comes to us in varying forms, ranging from the usual overt and hostile reactions to more subtle patronizing responses (p. 40). Transcultural counselors are cautious enough to monitor reactions, languages, and signs that may indicate culturally unique differences. These counselors are fully aware of compliments and taboo subjects when they interact with clients in various ways. It is understandably impossible for counselors to absorb and differentiate all the knowledge regarding their clients in a cultural context. Nevertheless, skilled, committed, and open-minded counselors should exercise flexibility to be able to interpret even signs and symbols as they pertain to communication, recognizing and acknowledging when there is something they do not know or understand. Knowledgeable and effective counselors are in a position to sense prejudices and confront them at the earliest stage.

d'Ardenne and Mahatani (1989) hold that all counselors enjoy a position of power; the power position is quite complicated because of the discrepancy of status that exists between cultures in a transcultural setting. They conclude that clients' judgment of the counselors' status is likely to be influenced by a number of factors. So, practitioners bear the responsibility to apply equal status. Only when counselors recognize the difference between individuals and cultures involved in the interactional process can they tackle the problems of their clients and produce some applicable outcome. The differences introduced here need not be based solely on race and color. A range of issues pertain to differences between people. For example, gender, ethnicity, family, age, socioeconomic circumstances, disability, sexual orientation, and varying degrees of talents should be factored into decisions in transcultural counseling.

The status of the counseling profession is vehemently contested today by minorities and feminist practitioners (Katz, 1985). Counseling professionals acknowledge that clients are directly affected by their culture and environment. Such an influence cannot be brushed aside, although many counselors continue to manifest indifference and unawareness and impose their own views. As Katz (1985) states, to make the multicultural approach of counseling responsive and different, we must be willing to engage in a thorough self-examination in reference to underlying cultural values that constitute the basis for the counseling profession. Counselors can proceed to create relationships between cultures by opening themselves up not only to help but also to learn and realize the relative character of their own culture compared to the stature of other cultures. Transcultural counseling is not limited to unique situations, but applies equally to a variety of cultural, social, and ethnic identities. Pedersen (1988) provides a most comprehensive description of personality development in a multicultural environment, one that can be applied in transcultural counseling situations. He notes that as we become more aware of how ethnographic, demographic, status, and affiliation variables systematically influence every one of us, we become more aware of our own identity. In like manner, transcultural counselors are expected to be more culturally skilled so as not to allow a wide gulf to develop between clients or between counselors and clients. Transcultural counselors can see through a window of opportunity the challenge to master principles of understanding, acceptance, and celebration that apply to a multiplicity of cultures for building effective counseling relationships at home and abroad.

CONCLUSION

Counseling professionals have the duty to prepare individuals to live and work cross-culturally. This is a complex task because of the diversity of cultural groups with which a counselor could conceivably interact. The world continues to witness growing numbers of people interacting with increasing frequency and regularity. To these interactions people bring certain values, norms, and beliefs. As people from different backgrounds come together to perform tasks and fulfill common goals in schools, in communities, or in business transactions, diverging views are certain to clash. Adjusting to new ways of life can be quite overwhelming to those ill-prepared for the experience. It is incumbent upon transcultural counselors to bridge the gaps between cultures (Brislin, Cushner, Cherrie, & Yong, 1986) by preparing individuals, families, and communities to meet new challenges and develop by identifying factors that should contribute to mutual acceptance and respect and result in peaceful coexistence.

Therefore, the transcultural counseling notion is an attempt to help individuals or groups achieve the goals of their cross-cultural assignment to improve communication among peoples of the world (Brislin, Cushner, Cherrie, & Yong, 1986). In recent years, counselors have recognized the value of others' cultural traditions. Efforts to counsel the culturally different have attempted to focus on cultural issues in terms of cross-cultural and multicultural practices. Such endeavors are expected to broaden professional understanding in transcultural counseling, which is coming into its own, one hopes. Counseling professionals need to realize the importance of considering clients' cultural backgrounds and traditions. During the rest of the 1990s and the early 21st century, counselors must address the needs and problems of the culturally diverse global society through the transcultural counseling model.

REFERENCES

Atkinson, D. R., Morten, G., & Sue, D. W. (1989). A minority identity development model. In D.R. Atkinson, G. Morten, & D. W. Sue (Eds.), *Counseling American minorities* (3rd ed.) (pp. 35–45). Dubuque, IA: Brown.

Axelson, J. A. (1992). *Counseling and development in a multicultural society.* Monterey, CA: Brooks/Cole.

Boyd-Franklin, N. (1989). *Black families in therapy: A multisystems approach.* New York: Guilford.

Brislin, R., Cushner, K., Cherrie, C., & Yong, M. (1986). *Intercultural interaction: A practical guide.* Beverly Hills, CA: Sage.

Brodin, E. S. (1988). *Psychological counseling.* New York: Meredith.

Burns, R. B. (1983). *Counseling and therapy: An introductory survey.* Boston: MTP.

d'Ardenne, P., & Mahatani, A. (1989). *Transcultural counseling in action.* Newbury Park, CA: Sage.

Das, A. K. (1987). Indigenous models of therapy in traditional Asian societies. *Journal of Multicultural Counseling and Development, 14*(1), 25–36.

Gunnings, T. S., & Stewart, C. S. (1989). *A clinical theory for systematic counseling: The development of a perspective.* Paper presented at the meeting of Meridian Professional Psychological Consultants, Michigan State University, East Lansing, MI.

Hall, E. T. (1976). *Beyond culture.* Garden City, NY: Anchor.

Ibrahim, F. A. (1991). Contribution of cultural worldview to generic counseling and development. *Journal of Counseling and Development, 70,* 13–19.

Katz, J. H. (1985). The sociopolitical nature of counseling. *The Counseling Psychologist, 13,* 616–620.

Locke, D. C. (1992). Beyond US borders. *American Counselor, 1*(2), 11–13.

McFadden, J. (1986). Stylistic dimensions of counseling minorities. *International Journal for the Advancement of Counseling, 9*(3), 209–220.

Mwaba, K., & Pedersen, P. (1990). Relative importance of intercultural, interpersonal, and psychopathological attributions in judging critical incident by multicultural counselors. *Journal of Multicultural Counseling and Development, 18*(3), 106–110.

Odom, G. R. (1989). *Mothers, leadership and success.* Houston: Polybius.

Parham, T. A. (1989). Cycles of psychological nigrescence. *The Counseling Psychologist, 17,* 187–220.

Pearson, R. E. (1985). The recognition and use of natural support systems in crosscultural counseling. In P. Pedersen (Ed.), *Handbook of cross cultural counseling and therapy* (pp. 299–305). Westport, CT: Greenwood Press.

Pedersen, P. (1982). The intercultural concept of counseling and therapy. In A. Marsella & G. White (Eds.), *Cultural conceptions of mental health and therapy* (pp. 333–358). Dordrecht, Holland: D. Reidel.

Pedersen, P. B. (1988). *A handbook for developing multicultural awareness.* Alexandria, VA: American Association for Counseling and Development.

Perry, R. J. (1992, March). Why do multiculturalists ignore anthropologists? *The Chronicle of Higher Education,* p. A52.

Ponterotto, J. G., & Casas, J. M. (1987). In search of multicultural competence within counselor education programs. *Journal of Multicultural Counseling and Development, 64,* 432–434.

Sue, D., & Sue, D. W. (1990). *Counseling the culturally different: Theory and practice* (2nd ed.). New York: Wiley.

Vontress, C. (1981). Racial and ethnic barriers in counseling. In P. Pedersen, J. G. Draguns, W. J. Lonner, & J. Trimble (Eds.), *Counseling across cultures: Revised edition* (pp. 87–107). Honolulu: University of Hawaii Press.

Wilson, L. L., & Stith, S. M. (1991). Culturally sensitive therapy with Black clients. *Journal of Multicultural Counseling and Development, 19*(1), 33–43.

World Health Organization. (1979). *Schizophrenia: An international follow-up study.* New York: Wiley.

CHAPTER 2

EXISTENTIAL WORLDVIEW THEORY: TRANSCULTURAL COUNSELING

FARAH A. IBRAHIM*

The *existential worldview theory* bridges cultural gaps in the counseling literature. Further, it can prepare the helping professional for a shrinking world, where telecommunications and satellite connections enable individuals to communicate with each other from one side of the globe to another within seconds (Ibrahim, 1985b). We live in an extremely pluralistic world, nationally and internationally. As noted in the Introduction, everyone adopts the *mainstream* or First World perspectives and meshes into an ongoing socioeconomic world. The result is cultural oppression for people with varied cultures, worldviews, and perspectives (Ibrahim & Arredondo, 1986, 1990).

The perspectives presented here broaden conceptions regarding the transcultural approach as identified by McFadden in the Introduction, an approach that demands "mutual understanding between counselors and clients." Further, Draguns (1991) notes that training procedures in the past and present provide opportunities for mainstream consumption—that is, middle-class counselors have

---

* The author expresses special thanks for the technical support and assistance provided by Naeem A. Khan in the preparation of this manuscript.

been equipped to deal with middle-class clients. This perspective reduces chances of racial and cultural oppression by emphasizing consideration of issues related to human existence that are pancultural and individual-specific (identify individual worldview and cultural identity), before analyzing how clients are reacting to their crises, social contexts, sociopolitical histories, and race. The tendency to focus on the client, without understanding the person of the counselor, violates the client in many known and unknown ways. In a transcultural encounter, such an act qualifies as *cultural oppression*.

NEED FOR TRANSCULTURAL COUNSELING

For over two decades, counseling literature has expressed concerns regarding the viability of the available models of counseling, specifically because they rest on the values and belief systems of the majority. The United States as the leader in counseling could carry mainstream American philosophies regarding helping to Africa, Asia, Eastern Europe, South America, and the Pacific Rim countries. These models systematically deny the realities of non-Western systems of thinking. Further, in the United States these models violate immigrants, ethnic minorities, women, and people with disabilities or different life-styles (American Association for Counseling and Development, 1987; Ibrahim, 1986, 1991; Ibrahim & Arredondo, 1986, 1990; Pedersen, 1986). Demographic projections show that a century from now, the population of the United States will be closer to the world balance: 57% Asian, 26% White, 7% Black, and 10% people of Hispanic origin (this group may include any of the following races: White, Black, and Native indigenous populations) (Edmunds, Martinson, & Goldberg, 1990; Ibrahim, 1991, 1992a).

The charge for professionals in counseling is to respond to national concerns. Further, we need to consider how theories for relationship building and therapeutic interventions can be expanded to address people internationally (Ibrahim, 1989). Although progress has occurred in clarifying the needs of the underserved in counseling, it has mainly been limited to theoretical formulations and research applications to minority segments of the population (Ibrahim, 1991). The assumption is that these points of view add nothing to the majority assumptions regarding counseling (Ibrahim

& Arredondo, 1990). Ibrahim (1991) proposes a radical shift in perspective—that the literature and research in multicultural counseling make a significant contribution in terms of perspectives and applications to generic models of counseling.

Originally, literature on transcultural encounters focused on effectiveness in these encounters (Arredondo-Dowd & Gonsalves, 1980). The definition of transcultural counseling subscribed to in this chapter is very broad: Any encounter that involves individuals from two different races, cultures, genders, generations, life stages, lifestyles, religions, or other groupings is a transcultural encounter (Ibrahim, 1985a). These variables influence how the counselor or therapist approaches a specific problem or issue. In the narrower definition of transcultural counseling, only race, culture, and nationality are considered. Earlier research in the United States focused on understanding how the counselor's race or culture affects the client (Abramowitz & Murray, 1983; Atkinson, 1985; Banks, 1972; Carkhuff & Pierce, 1967; Griffith, 1977).

Theorists and researchers have offered three major recommendations to ease the process of multicultural encounters in counseling. These include an understanding of worldview (values, beliefs, and assumptions) and its impact on identity; philosophy; modes of interaction with the world, including, but not limited to, problem solving, conflict resolution, and decision making (Ibrahim, 1984a, 1984b, 1985a, 1991; Ibrahim & Schroeder, 1987, 1990; D. W. Sue, 1978; D. W. Sue & D. Sue, 1991); knowledge of specific cultures; and knowledge of culture-specific verbal and nonverbal skills to facilitate encounters (S. Sue & Zane, 1987). Additionally, research has addressed many process and outcome variables (mostly limited to counseling and psychotherapy). These include racial similarity or dissimilarity, client expectations, match between therapist and client, therapist credibility, and attractiveness.

Pedersen, Fukuyama, and Heath (1989) note that research on client, counselor, and contextual variables yielded mixed results. Recommendations that encourage therapists to be culturally sensitive and to know the culture of the client have not proven very effective either (S. Sue & Zane, 1987). Further, culture-specific techniques applied to clients across cultures, without attention to appropriateness for a specific client, pose a threat of cultural oppression.

S. Sue (1988) notes that cultural factors in the treatment of ethnic minority clients have received the greatest attention among therapists. Yet services to minority or culturally different clients remain inadequate because of a lack of bilingual and bicultural counselors, stereotypes and biases that counselors hold, and inability of counselors to provide culturally responsive forms of treatment. This inadequacy is attributed to training models developed for Anglo or mainstream Americans (Ibrahim, Stadler, Arredondo, & McFadden, 1986; Ponterotto & Casas, 1987).

The helping professions are still seeking viable theories and models of training that would prepare counselors to provide valid, effective, reliable, and ethical professional services in transcultural encounters (Corey, Corey, and Callanan, 1988). The models must be theory based to provide counselors with a base from which to operate. It is critical that in this pluralistic and technologically shrinking world, and especially in this multicultural nation, the focus shift to transcultural models of helping and training. It is imperative that counselors acquire specialized skills and be sensitive to culturally different clients (Brown & Srebalus, 1988).

TRANSCULTURAL CONTEXTS AND SELF-DEFINITION

Anthropological research suggests that the cultures of the world, and the cultures of the United States, can be categorized into two polar opposites in terms of how the self is defined, conceptualized, and articulated (Bateson & Mead, 1942; Gaines, 1982; Geertz, 1973; Shweder & Miller, 1985). These two types of cultures are (a) *relational* (Cohen, 1969) and (b) *analytical* or *contextual* (Geertz, 1973; Schweder & Miller, 1985). These two cultures differ in their definitions of the idea of the self, and each forms the individual self according to its cultural template. These cultures, relational and analytical, have different assumptions about the idea of self, autonomy, concept of time, construction of personal control, understanding of mind and body, and construction of morality (Landrine, 1991). In a relational cultural system, the self is indexical, autonomy is defined by the familial or group context, time is polychronic, personal control is secondary, mind and body are seen holistically, and morality is defined by duty. In an analytical cultural system, the self is referential, autonomy is exemplified by individualistic assumptions, time is monochronic, personal control is primary, mind and body are perceived as dualistic, and morality is defined by a rights orientation (Landrine, 1991).

Page and Berkow (1991) note that the self is seen in a variety of ways by different societies: as a basis for prosocial interaction (Adler, 1925), an unconscious archetype (Jung, 1958), a personal construct (Kelly, 1963), a basis for the organization of perceptions (Coombs & Snygg, 1959). Social relationships and expression of psychological distress are influenced by our definition of our self, or identity, as an object or a subject. Marsella and White (1982) note that the meaning, experience, and manifestation of psychological distress vary according to the culturally conditioned epistemological orientation of a given group. They contend that groups toward the subjective pole in self-definition would display more somatic symptoms in response to psychological distress; those toward the objective pole would display more existential or cognitive symptoms. To understand cultural conditioning, we need to move beyond race and ethnicity conceptualizations. We need to understand aspects that clarify the human condition in general, and the specific way people consider their universe, the world, and the people and objects within it. Such an analysis also will help clarify the constraints an individual may experience. Existential Worldview theory can help in identifying these variables, and especially help in clarifying an individual's perspectives with the worldview construct.

ROLE OF VALUES, BELIEFS, AND ASSUMPTIONS IN COUNSELING AND PSYCHOTHERAPY

Counseling and psychotherapy are value-laden professions (Bergin, 1991; Beutler & Bergan, 1991; Strupp, 1978). Controversies regarding the role of counselor values and their impact on process and outcome in counseling have raged for decades (Patterson, 1989). Some argue that there is a distinction between the theory to which counselors subscribe and the personal values they hold (Beck, Rush, Shaw, & Emery, 1979). Others consider this perspective impractical and confusing (Cirillo & Wapner, 1986). Most agree that counselors cannot advocate a value position free of their personal assumptions or interpretations (Frank, 1973; Strong, 1968). Beutler and Bergan (1991) report that research in the last two decades on value similarity and counseling efficacy suggests that two conclusions can be drawn: (a) Value convergence between counselor and client beliefs and attitudes is directly related to positive outcome; and (b) a "complex pattern of similarity and dissimilarity between client and counselor values is conducive to enhancing the strength of this convergence" (p. 18).

Jensen and Bergin (1988) conducted research to define the value positions most relevant to the therapeutic enterprise. They identified 10 value dimensions that encompass most of the concepts used to define mental health: emphasis placed on expressions of feelings, autonomy, coping and work, personal knowledge and growth, interpersonal commitment, self-maintenance, maturity, forgiveness, regulated sexual fulfillment, and spirituality. Among individual practitioners with different theoretical orientations, distinctive patterns existed regarding the relative values placed on specific value dimensions. Reid (1989) extended C. Kluckhohn's (1951, 1956) framework and Speigel's (1982) value domains to clinical practice. He suggests that the dominant culture is characterized by an orientation toward the future, rather than the past or the present. Further, he notes that majority culture has a male, middle-class orientation that emphasizes the importance of doing over feelings, and competition over collaboration. Beutler and Bergan (1991) suggest that people with this profile seek to conquer frontiers, control the weather, constrain natural forces, and domesticate animals. In contrast, both Reid (1989) and Speigel (1982) argue that value orientations of the inner-city poor focus on the present, on group identity instead of autonomy, and on mistrust of people outside the group.

Transcultural counseling, literature, and research become meaningless unless worldview is a mediating variable used to understand the cultural identity of the client (Ibrahim, 1991). Worldview is a significant contribution of the multicultural counseling literature to the generic fields of counseling, education, training, and development (Ibrahim, 1984b, 1985a, 1985b, 1991; D. W. Sue, 1978; D. W. Sue & D. Sue, 1991). This is the mediating variable that makes knowledge of a specific cultural group and knowledge of culture-consistent and culture-specific techniques meaningful (Ibrahim, 1991). Without worldview as a mediating variable, both knowledge of specific cultures and culture-specific techniques can be misapplied, leading to charges of ethical violation and cultural oppression. After clarification of the worldview, appropriate applications of theory and research can take place, despite the specific area these assumptions belong to (i.e., psychodynamic, cognitive-behavioral, or humanistic-existential). An understanding of individual worldview also helps in focusing on within-group variation, a much neglected construct in multicultural psychology and counseling (Ibrahim & Kahn, 1987; Ibrahim & Owen, 1992; Sue, 1988; Sundberg, 1981; Triandis & Brislin, 1984).

The acknowledgment and acceptance that individual worldviews may vary within a group makes the intervention client-specific—that is, useful and meaningful for the particular person, not only as a representative of a certain racial, cultural, religious, age, or regional group, but as an individual. Without knowledge or skills to assess and fully understand worldview, a counselor, educator, or trainer has no alternative but to apply the information regarding a specific culture to a client from that culture, at best, or simply to impose the counselor's worldview on the client. This general application of cultural information, or an assumption that the client is similar to the counselor, can lead to cultural oppression by forcing an idiosyncratic client into a perceived model. Treating persons as stereotypes of their cultural group violates their individuality and may lead to premature termination, with minimal therapeutic effectiveness, and may give clients negative impressions of counselors and counseling (Ibrahim, 1991).

Proposals and models exist for counselors to increase their competence in transcultural encounters by expanding their awareness, knowledge, and skills (Ibrahim & Schroeder, 1989; Pedersen, 1988; Sue & Sue, 1991). Empirical evidence is still being gathered regarding the efficacy of these proposals. Counselors need a strategy to understand their own cultural identity and worldview and their philosophy of life. The strategy must take into account their culture, socioeconomic level, race, age, life stage, ethnicity, gender, and sociopolitical history. The worldview of the counselor is especially critical because the client's welfare depends on the counselor's ability to provide appropriate assistance. If counselors cannot confront their cultural identity and worldview and do not reflect on the multiplicity of factors that have shaped their lives, they will be unable to provide effective transcultural counseling, because their cultural assumptions will systematically operate in the counseling encounter.

TRANSCULTURAL COUNSELING AND THE EXISTENTIAL WORLDVIEW THEORY

Cross-cultural encounters can be greatly enhanced if they are approached from an understanding of the counselor's and the client's worldviews and cultural identities from the perspectives provided by the existential worldview theory (Ibrahim, 1984a). This statement is based on two assumptions: (a) Counseling and psychotherapy are rooted in philosophical views of human nature and people's place in the universe (Wachtel, 1977); and (b) cross-cultural communication breakdowns occur because people from different cultures use different logics that emerge from their philosophical assumptions, and these are not explicitly known to the communicating parties, leading to conflicts and misunderstandings (Maruyama, 1978). The existential worldview theory's central theme and focus is human existence in a pancultural sense, as in existential philosophy. In existential philosophy, the main focus is on understanding what it means to an individual to be in this world (Heidegger, 1961). The themes that emerge from this analysis include, but are not limited to, what it means to be human and how people perceive their sociopolitical history, gender, ethnicity, race, culture, religion, age, life stage, values, and beliefs.

Human beings are philosophical, and whether they reflect on their philosophy or not, it affects every aspect of their lives (Ibrahim, 1984a). Not using this major force that directs a human being's whole experience in the world would be a major loss in counseling and psychotherapy. The existential worldview theory can provide insights into the client's philosophy. The theory uses C. Kluckhohn's (1951, 1956) existential or universal categories to understand human experience and how values may be shaped by experience. These categories are presented with validations from existential philosophy to enhance our understanding of the client's values and the meanings clients ascribe to their experiences.

HUMAN NATURE

The first existential category addresses the age-old need to understand human nature. Binswanger (1962, 1963) discussed a version of this category in defining the idea of *Eigenwelt*, the personal or private world. Probing this domain provides us with an understanding of how people view themselves and others. F. R. Kluckhohn and Strodtbeck (1961) explored the following ways of viewing human nature: (a) Human nature is good; (b) human nature is a combination of good and bad parts; and (c) human nature is bad. Our apprehension of the world and our perceptions of others form our worldview, which influences our relationships with others (Ibrahim, 1984a, 1985a). An understanding of how the self and others are perceived also provides insight into how much alienation an individual is experiencing from self and others. Alienation can be a factor in creating a negative attitude toward self and others. An understanding of how we see ourselves and others can be of tremendous value in understanding the quality of our lives and the meaningfulness of our relationships.

SOCIAL RELATIONSHIPS

The second existential category pertains to people's relationship with other people. This translates to Binswanger's (1962, 1963) idea of the *Mitwelt*, the interpersonal world (Ibrahim, 1984a, 1985a). F. R. Kluckhohn and Strodtbeck (1961) studied social relationships from three perspectives: *lineal-hierarchical*, based on ordered positional succession within the group, continuity through time, and primacy given to group goals; *collateral-mutual*, in which primacy is given to the goals and welfare of lateral extended groups, and the self is enhanced through mutual relationships; and *individualistic*, in which primacy is given to the individual's own goals first, and the family, group, and society are considered secondarily.

Vontress (1979) posits that the need of human beings to be with each other is both a boon and a bane when we consider the global harmony or lack of it. Buber (1970) considers relationships one of the most important issues in human existence. He considers the longing for relationships among people as a given, and he defines people as creatures of the in-between. Further, Buber notes that relationships can be of two types, either "I-Thou" (i.e., mutual, equal, caring) or

"I-It" (i.e., a functional relationship, with no trace of mutuality). Fromm (1963) and Yalom (1980) both believe that the greatest concern for people is existential isolation, an "unbridgeable gap between oneself and any other being" (Yalom, 1980, p. 355). This isolation, according to Fromm, is the source of all anxiety, and a major psychological task facing people is to overcome this anxiety.

NATURE

The third existential category addresses a person's relationship to nature. Binswanger (1962, 1963), in his discussion of the *Umwelt* (natural world), highlights it as survival in the environment. F. R. Kluckhohn and Strodtbeck (1961) note that the perception of people's relationship to nature varies in every cultural context. Some cultures emphasize living in harmony with nature; others emphasize subjugating and controlling nature. Other cultures recognize the power of nature and the frailty of humans. Binswanger underscores that when the relation between people and their natural world is ignored, we fall prey to oversimplification. Each person's apprehension of his or her physical world is critical to an understanding of that person. Simply studying the client's physical world is not enough. Kemp (1971) notes that the challenge for helpers is to understand the meaning of the environment for the client.

TIME

The fourth existential category addresses the concept of time. This overlaps to a certain extent the fifth existential category, activity, in terms of existential philosophical issues. Time is discussed in terms of the basic anxiety people experience about death and the finiteness of life (Frankl, 1978; Yalom, 1980). F. R. Kluckhohn and Strodtbeck (1961) posit that time is an important variable in all cultures around the world. Different cultures focus on the past, the present, or the future. The capacity to relate to time is a uniquely human characteristic (Ibrahim, 1984a). Existentialists emphasize that the profound human experiences of life (e.g., joy, tragedy, and anxiety) occur in a dimension of time rather than space (Kemp, 1971). The temporal focus also addresses the finiteness of life, the basic anxiety regarding death (Frankl, 1978), and our denial of death (Becker, 1973). Yalom

(1980) notes that a recognition of the finiteness of life generally results in a major shift of perspective and can lead to growth.

ACTIVITY

The fifth existential category pertains to human activity. F. R. Kluckhohn and Strodtbeck (1961) defined the range of activity to vary between *Being*, a preference for activities that provide a spontaneous expression of the self; *Being-in-Becoming*, an emphasis on activities that have as a goal the development of all aspects of the self, as an integrated being, including the spiritual dimension; and *Doing*, a preference for activities that result in measurable accomplishments by external standards. This category addresses the idea of people's search for meaning in their lives (Frankl, 1978). According to Frankl, midlife crisis is a crisis of meaning. Yalom (1980) contends that since most clients are suffering from a lack of meaning in their lives, the counselor must catalyze the client's will to act. Existential philosophy has traditionally addressed the issue of meaning of life within the context of the finiteness of life (Ibrahim, 1984a; Sartre, 1953).

Understanding individuals from this theoretical perspective assists in comprehending the universal issues that all humans encounter. This approach takes universal human concerns into account before moving into the specifics of understanding a unique client as a cultural entity. To understand a specific client's world, we need first to grasp the universal human concerns and second to understand the specific individual's reality by clarifying his or her worldview and cultural identity.

WORLDVIEW AND CULTURAL IDENTITY

To provide ethical and appropriate counseling and psychotherapy to clients from different cultural backgrounds, nationalities, ethnicities, races, genders, ages, life stages, educational levels, and social classes, the counselor must understand his or her own worldview and cultural identity and philosophical and psychological assumptions. The counselor must also have knowledge of both the primary and secondary cultural environments he or she comes from (Ibrahim & Arredondo, 1986, 1990).

Sire (1976) states that our worldview consists of the presuppositions and assumptions we hold about our world. Horner and

Vandersluis (1981) maintain that because worldviews are culturally based variables, they influence the relationship between a helper and a client. Our worldview directly acts on and mediates our belief systems, assumptions, and modes of problem solving, decision making, and conflict resolution (Ibrahim, 1991).

The importance of worldviews in multicultural encounters was first highlighted by D. W. Sue (1978). He defined it as an individual's perception of his or her relationship with the world (i.e., nature, institutions, people, things, etc.). Sarason (1984) notes that each of us possesses and is possessed by a worldview as a result of the socialization process. One's worldview influences individual goals and behavior. Worldviews are identified as a critical variable that can enhance or obstruct the process of counseling or communication (Abramovitz & Dokecki, 1977; Ibrahim, 1984b, 1985a; Ibrahim & Kahn, 1987; Strupp, 1978; Sundberg, 1981). Ibrahim (1991) contends that the worldview of the counselor is a critical variable in helping a client because it affects the solutions that clients seek to achieve psychological balance and better adjustment.

D. W. Sue (1978) originally proposed the idea of worldview based on two psychological theories: locus of control (Rotter, 1966) and locus of responsibility (Jones, Kanouse, Kelly, Nisbett, Valins, & Weiner, 1972). This theoretical perspective provided an important tool in cross-cultural encounters. Yet no integrated instrument was developed to assess worldview. Ibrahim (1984b, 1985a) proposed a broader formulation of the construct of worldview based on C. Kluckhohn's (1951, 1956) work on value orientations and value emphasis in various cultures. The Kluckhohn framework accounts for both philosophical and psychological dimensions, including beliefs, values, assumptions, attitudes, and behavior of individuals and groups. Kluckhohn (1951) proposed five universal or existential categories that pertain to a general, organized conception of human nature, social relationships, nature, time, and activity. These conceptions, he postulated, influence human behavior, motivations, decisions, and life-styles.

Ibrahim's (1984a; 1985a) theory has an existential philosophical bent in clarifying human concerns that are pancultural. It has a cognitive-values perspective that uses worldview and cultural identity as mediational forces in an individual life. The theory proposes that each individual in the therapeutic dyad be viewed as a unique "cultural entity" (Ibrahim, 1984b), with an emphasis on the individual's "subjective reality" (Triandis, 1972) or worldview (Ibrahim, 1984b). Such a process of self-examination for the counselor and focused attention to the client's worldview will ease the development and establishment of a positive therapeutic relationship. Further, Ibrahim (1991) contends that it can lead to counselor-client cultural matching based on cultural assumptions and philosophical similarity, instead of race and gender similarity.

COUNSELOR-CLIENT CULTURAL MATCH

Beutler & Bergan (1991) suggest that average middle-class counselors have values significantly different from the values of their average clients. Further, cognitive and information processing theories propose that it is the attitudes of the counselors, not their demographic background in isolation, that determine how clients perceive and respond to interpersonal events (Lazaurs, 1988; Tataryn, Nadel, & Jacobs, 1988). Tyler, Sussewell, and Williams-McCoy (1985) recommend cultural matching to overcome the problems and issues inherent in transcultural encounters.

S. Sue (1988) underscores the importance of cultural matching. According to him, cultural matching is more relevant than ethnic matching. Sue bases his idea on the premise that ethnic similarity does not necessarily imply cultural similarity, because of the multiplicity of factors that can influence counseling. He also notes that although ethnicity is important, what is more important is the meaning of that ethnicity for the client. Further, he states that research in the treatment of ethnic clients has focused on ethnic factors, whereas cultural factors have demanded the greatest attention among multicultural counselors. Sue proposes that a cultural match can be studied in terms of three variables: (a) diagnosis of the client's problems, (b) modes of problem solving and decision making, and (c) goals for treatment. Cultural matching requires that the client's worldview be understood, because there is vast variability within ethnic and cultural groups (Ibrahim & Kahn, 1987; S. Sue, 1988; Sundberg, 1981). This information will allow both the helper and the client to assess whether they are culturally compatible. Further, it encourages conditions that will enable an effective formulation of both process and goals.

In its application, Ibrahim's (1984a, 1985a, 1991) theory includes the following perspectives:

- Both the helper's and the client's worldviews must be clarified. Clarification must include an analysis of both the cultural and gender identity (Ibrahim, 1992b) of the parties involved, and implies ethnicity, culture, age, life stage, socioeconomic level, education, religion, philosophy of life, beliefs, values, and assumptions.

- These worldviews, once clarified, must be placed within a sociopolitical context that includes history of migration, acculturation level, languages spoken, and comfort with mainstream assumptions and values (Ibrahim, 1985a, 1991; Ibrahim & Schroeder, 1990).

The Scale to Assess Worldviews (SAWV) (Ibrahim & Kahn, 1984, 1987) and the SAWV II (Ibrahim, 1993), based on Kluckhohn's (1951, 1956) value orientations and value emphases, cover the following existential categories, with the given range of assumptions:

- Human nature: Good, bad, or a combination of good and bad
- Social relationships: Lineal-hierarchical, collateral-mutual, or individualistic
- Nature: Subjugation and control of nature, living in harmony with nature, or accepting the power and control of nature over people
- Time orientation: Past, present, and future
- Activity orientation: Being, Being-in-Becoming, or Doing (Ibrahim, 1991, p. 15)

The SAWV has adequate reliability and validity (Ibrahim & Kahn, 1987; Ibrahim & Owen, 1992; Sadowsky, Maguire, Johnson, Ngumba, & Kohles, in press). The use of the SAWV helps the counselor in (a) understanding the client's specific worldview, beliefs, values, and assumptions, and how these affect their cognitive, emotional, and social perceptions and interactions with the world; (b) providing an understanding of the expression and experience of the issues and problems that bring the client to the helper; and (c) clarifying the client's worldview as compared to his or her primary cultural group—that is, differentiating the client from family, primary group, and larger society (Lonner & Ibrahim, 1989). The use of the SAWV as a mediational force eliminates the risk of cultural oppression when applying culture-specific information, knowledge, and skills to counseling, psychotherapy, or training (Ibrahim, 1991).

The worldview of the client must be understood within the context of the client's cultural and gender identity. This context incorporates the following variables (Ibrahim, 1992b):

- How gender is conceptualized in the client's primary group and how gender affects the client in the familial and primary cultural context
- Sociopolitical history
- Generation in the United States (group history)
- Social conditions experienced by the client's group, and status of the group
- History of migration to the United States (how the client's group was received and integrated in the United States; the client's own migration history, if an immigrant or refugee)
- Religion (status of client's faith in the United States)
- Age and its meaning in the client's primary cultural group and in mainstream culture
- Life stage and its meaning in the client's primary cultural group, and in mainstream culture
- Languages spoken (impact of the philosophies underlying the languages spoken, bilingually or trilingually, status or lack of status associated with language)
- Ability or disability status and how this is viewed in the client's own culture and among mainstream cultures

The client's cultural identity can be assessed by first administering the SAWV or the SAWV II (Ibrahim, 1993; Ibrahim & Kahn, 1984, 1987). This will provide basic information on how clients view the world in terms of their values, beliefs, and assumptions. The information provided will yield a primary worldview and a secondary worldview (Ibrahim & Owen, 1992). The four possible worldviews that can be assessed using the SAWV or the SAWV II are Optimistic, Traditional, Here and Now, and Ecological. After deriving the worldview, the counselor or therapist needs to administer the

Cultural Identity Checklist (CICL) (Ibrahim, 1990b) at the end of this chapter. The information gained from the client's own statements on the CICL can be used to explore further the variables listed above to understand the client's cultural and gender identity and cultural context. These variables provide information that helps clarify client values and assumptions within the context of their lives and the history of their cultural groups.

After clarifying the client's cultural identity, the counselor can work to develop a relationship with the client in which both parties feel that they understand each other enough to develop trust. Open sharing of similarities and differences in worldviews between the counselor and client needs to take place, on the premise that in transcultural encounters the issues of trust and relationship development become very complicated (Beutler & Bergan, 1991). This sharing will enhance the client's trust. Further, it will help the client understand the counselor as a person and increase the client's self-knowledge, a critically important goal in therapeutic encounters. Eventually, this knowledge can lead to the development of a shared worldview (a composite of the helper's and the client's overlapping belief systems). This shared worldview, according to Torrey (1986), is the basis of highly effective therapeutic relationships in cross-cultural and within-culture encounters. Kelly (1990) also holds that convergence of client and counselor values results in improved feelings or functioning for the client. The second step is to develop a process and goals for counseling that would be consistent with the client's beliefs, values, and cultural identity. Last, the information gained can help the counselor use culture-specific techniques to create the conditions necessary for therapy. According to Rogers (1957), this will lead to positive outcomes in counseling and psychotherapy.

APPLICATIONS IN COUNSELING AND PSYCHOTHERAPY

Transcultural counseling and psychotherapy can be plagued with greater difficulties. These include identifying the client's problem or issues, communicating with persons who have different structures of reasoning and logics, and developing viable outcome goals. Existential worldview theory can help clarify the basic human concerns people confront, regardless of culture, at some time in their lives. Further, using the SAWV and the CICL (Ibrahim, 1990a, 1990b) will help clearly identify what issues the client is specifically confronting and what these mean. The theory and the instrument can help in the following domains.

INITIAL CLIENT ASSESSMENT

The SAWV can be used in counseling and psychotherapy to conduct the initial client assessment (Ibrahim, 1984b; Lonner & Ibrahim, 1989). These instruments help clarify the beliefs, values, assumptions, and cultural identity of the client by making them tangible and explicit. The information provides a reasonable starting point in a culturally diverse world, because there are very few assessment measures that can help clarify cultural identity and worldview, and it is an ethical approach in a culturally pluralistic world (Ibrahim, 1991).

The assessments provide information regarding how well the client fits or does not fit the values, beliefs, and assumptions of his or her primary group. They also assist in developing an understanding of how the client assimilates the worldview of the larger society, providing a measure of acculturation (Ibrahim, 1991). Worldview assessment also assists in clarifying whether the client defines the self objectively or subjectively. The communal perspectives that emerge in lineal-hierarchical and collateral-mutual social relationships signify a perception of the self as a subject, in a relational context. The individualistic perspective on social relationships exemplifies the self as an object, standing at the horizon of the world, ready to make things happen, or choosing otherwise.

DIAGNOSIS

Identifying the client's worldview and cultural identity also helps in the diagnosis of the therapeutic problem (Lonner & Ibrahim, 1989). Diagnosis is an extremely complex process in most therapeutic encounters, but the many factors to be considered in transcultural encounters make it especially difficult. Lonner and Ibrahim recommend three steps to arrive at an accurate diagnosis: (a) understanding worldview; (b) identifying the client's true "norm" group based on an evaluation of the assumptions and cultural outlook of the client and the cultural group or groups the client comes from and identifies with; and (c) using a combination of approaches to clarify the problem—i.e., clinical judgments and standardized and nonstandardized assessments are required to arrive at an accurate diagnosis. The key variables again are the worldview and cultural identity, and understanding them accurately can simplify the diagnostic process and increase the probability of a culturally appropriate intervention.

IMPLICATIONS FOR PROCESS AND OUTCOME

Success in counseling is highly dependent on the process the client experiences. To establish an effective process, one must acknowledge that counseling is a process of interpersonal influence (Strong, 1968). Strong contends that the client's acceptance of the counselor's influence depends on the client's perception of the counselor as an expert, trustworthy, and attractive. Research in counseling and psychotherapy supports this contention (Atkinson & Carskaddon, 1975; Barak & La Crosse, 1975; Merluzzi, Merluzzi, & Kaul, 1977; Schmidt & Strong, 1971).

Torrey (1986) supports the view that the client has to experience the counselor as someone who understands and will be effective in helping provide relief. Basic to this process of interpersonal influence is a shared worldview (Ibrahim, 1984b, 1985a, 1991; Ibrahim & Schroeder, 1990; Torrey, 1986). The most critical task facing the counselor in transcultural encounters is the establishment of a shared worldview or a common culture with the client (Ibrahim & Schroeder, 1990). This can be accomplished by using the SAWV to discuss the client's beliefs, values, assumptions, cultural identity, and ways of problem solving and decision making. During this process counselors may share whatever parts of their personal worldview (beliefs, values, assumptions, etc.) overlap with the client's in an attempt to create a common cultural world to enhance communication, the relationship, and the therapeutic process (Ibrahim & Schroeder, 1990). The goal here is not to minimize or overlook the differences. The process makes the differences explicit and clarifies the outcomes and solutions that may be meaningful for the counselor, but antithetical to the client's beliefs. This discussion gives the client permission to identify and articulate his or her personal perspective and find solutions within it. This process will positively influence the outcomes in counseling.

USING SAWV PROFILES IN COUNSELING AND THERAPY

The SAWV and SAWV II (Ibrahim, 1993; Ibrahim & Kahn, 1984, 1987; Ibrahim & Owen, 1992) provide four worldview profiles that can not only help the counselor or therapist understand the client's worldview, but also provide information that helps outline the appropriate process in therapy and establish appropriate goals in therapy. As suggested earlier, the profiles must be placed within the context of the client's cultural and gender identity to select the appropriate process and goals. Each individual will have a primary set of beliefs and values and a secondary set. If the primary worldview does not help in decision making and problem solving, the client will use the secondary worldview to solve the problem. The four possible worldviews that can be derived from the SAWV are Traditional/Modern, Nature/Human Nature, Human Nature, and Here and Now (Ibrahim & Owen, 1992). These will be discussed below with implications for counseling and therapy process and goals.

TRADITIONAL/MODERN PERSPECTIVE

This worldview emphasizes that relationships are lineal-hierarchical, collateral-mutual, and individualistic, that time has a past and future emphasis, that activity is defined by the Being orientation (i.e., spontaneous), and that nature can be subjugated and controlled by human will. The main characteristics of this perspective are that relationships are primarily lineal-hierarchical, implying that lines of authority are clearly defined, power comes from the top, and traditional gender roles are accepted. However, this profile also supports mutuality in relationships and supports some individualistic values. The time focus is primarily on the past, implying a focus on historical issues, pride in history, and a concern for traditions. There is also a strong future orientation, which implies long-range planning and an emphasis on delayed gratification. In terms of activity, there is an emphasis on spontaneity and doing what feels right at the moment. There is also weak support for the traditional perspective that humankind can control and overpower the elements of nature.

Clients with this worldview require both relationship-oriented and task-oriented approaches. It would be imperative to focus on developing a genuine, empathic, and warm relationship with the client. Counselors must recognize that the client has come to them because they are seen as experts. Source credibility is very important for clients with this worldview. Further, the clients value the opinions of the counselor as an expert. The process that would be most beneficial would involve mutual respect and the client's involvement in generating goals and making decisions. The client will value long-term goals and accept short-term interim goals. Further, the client will be influenced by traditional, historical assumptions, and would value attention to these assumptions. The activity domain, with a focus on spontaneity, would demand that the counselor be prepared to deal with issues that emerge in each session and respect the client's need to focus on these issues.

The communication process that clients who hold this worldview value is both task-oriented and relationship-oriented. They respect authority, and they have sought out the counselor as an expert who can help them with their problem. They prefer a task-oriented approach and have greater respect for the helper if the focus is on the problem and the solutions, rather than the person of the client. The processes to which they respond best are directive and action-oriented. To establish a relationship with such a client, the counselor must recognize and convey respect for the status and achievements of the client. Clients will value a confrontation of the discrepancies in their presentations; otherwise they will lose respect for the counselor.

Long-term goals are beneficial. These must be influenced by family history, individual history, and behaviors. The decision-making model again must be directive; clients value the input of the expert. Further, there is a preference for action-oriented, task-focused therapeutic approaches. The final decisions must rest with the client. The outcomes that this client will prefer emphasize needs of the larger system, family, or group. Too much focus on the client creates discomfort. Further, because there is high group identification and a concern for the larger good, all goals must reflect that dimension.

NATURE/HUMAN NATURE

This worldview emphasizes harmony with nature. It also focuses on human nature and sees it as basically good, but there is also a perception that human nature can be a combination of good and bad qualities. In terms of activity, this worldview values both inner and outer development of the person. There is a concern for spiritual growth, and success by external standards, in terms of measurable rewards. Time emphasis is on the past.

The communication process most beneficial to clients with this worldview is relationship-oriented. Because clients with this worldview are concerned about human nature, they need to be sure that the counselor is a good person, who is morally upright and ethical. A relationship orientation helps the client become comfortable with the person of the helper. A priority is to establish trust and open communication with the client to allay concerns about the trustworthiness of the helper. Once trust is established, the focus can shift to developing goals. Goals for this client must reflect both inner development (moral and ethical concerns) and success as measured by external standards (community, society, workplace, etc.). Clients also value therapeutic interventions that clarify the role of their personal, familial, and sociopolitical histories. An investigation of historical events and how they have influenced the client's life, and specifically the issues presented for resolution, is appreciated.

HUMAN NATURE

This worldview primarily views human nature as basically bad. There is also a belief that human nature may be a combination of good and bad elements. The second main characteristic is that this worldview acknowledges the power of nature and accepts the vulnerability of human beings to this powerful force. The relationship orientations that characterize this worldview are both individualistic and collateral-mutual. In terms of activity, both spontaneity, as characterized by Being, and success by external standards, as exemplified by Doing, are valued.

People with this worldview pose a real challenge to a counselor, primarily in the process domain. Trust development is significantly difficult with this population. It is important not to focus too much on relationship issues. Considering the client's low evaluation of human beings, it may be critical to focus on the task or problem presented by the client. This eases trust development. Because clients with this perspective have an individualistic and collateral-mutual orientation, they need to be respected for their beliefs and will reciprocate with respect for the counselor. The client's feelings of vulnerability also result from the elements of nature and from low trust of human nature. Both these premises must be acceptable to the counselor. The understanding that these are important concerns for the client must be communicated. Goal development needs to be a mutual process. The client may also tend to be spontaneous and may not have an interest in long-term goals. Goal development may occur at the beginning of each session. This demands much flexibility by the counselor who has been trained in traditional counseling and psychotherapy approaches.

HERE AND NOW

The focus here is on only one element, time, with a largely present orientation, and to a lesser extent future orientation. The main characteristic of this worldview is that the client requires a focus on the presenting problem, which may shift from session to session. There may be no possibility of long-term goals. The client comes to each session with specific concerns that require immediate attention. The counselor must respect the client's urgency. The Being orientation means that the client's need to be in the present and the spontaneity and the energy for the issue at hand must be respected. These perspectives could be a challenge for a counselor trained in traditional counseling or psychotherapy programs.

The communication process needs to focus on the client, with an emphasis on relationship building in the present. The process must be nondirective, with the therapist following the client's lead. The decision-making model must be mutual, with a client focus. The outcomes clients seek will be focused on the presenting problem.

This theory, following C. Kluckhohn's (1951, 1956) suggestions, proposes that each client will have a primary worldview, which they will use to solve their problems and deal with life, and a secondary worldview, to deal with issues they cannot resolve using their primary set of assumptions. The outcome for a given individual can be any combination of the four worldviews. Each individual, in essence, will have a primary and a secondary worldview. To highlight how this process will work in counseling and psychotherapy, a case example is provided, with recommendations for developing a relationship.

CASE STUDY

A White middle-class male psychologist in his mid-40s may subscribe to the following worldviews: Traditional/Modern (primary) and Nature/Human Nature (secondary). The main characteristics of this therapist's worldview are that he believes that relationships are lineal-hierarchical, collateral-mutual, and somewhat individualistic. He can be relationship-oriented and can easily establish therapeutic relationships. He also has a primarily past and future time orientation. He tends to value spontaneity in the activity domain and believes that nature can be controlled and subjugated. His secondary worldview emphasizes that we need to live in harmony with nature and that human nature is good but can be a combination of good and bad qualities.

The client is a White middle-class female in her 20s, who may subscribe to the following worldviews: Here and Now (primary), and Nature/Human Nature (secondary). The main characteristics of the client's worldview follow: She is primarily present-oriented in terms of time. There is some emphasis on the future, and this implies that although the client is mostly focused on the present, she may be amenable to long-range goals. She also values an understanding of how the past affects her current life circumstances. She believes in living in harmony with nature. Her understanding of human nature is that it is basically good, but may be a combination of good and bad elements. Her activity orientation focuses on both inner and outer development (both moral/ethical development and success by external standards).

How can a positive counselor-client match be created here? How can the counseling process be enhanced with the above information? Can a positive counselor-client match be achieved by considering the worldview profiles of the counselor and the client? The counselor and the client face the following challenges: The primary issues are age, life stage, gender, and major differences in primary worldview. The counselor will have a conflict with the primary present time orientation of the client. Although both on the surface come from a similar cultural background, on closer inspection we find they face some major challenges.

1. The counselor must help the client find their shared characteristics from the worldview profiles. In this case, their overlapping worldviews are their secondary worldview profiles, the Nature/Human Nature worldviews. If this information is appropriately applied, client engagement will be enhanced as they both develop a common ground, from which they can relate with each other.

2. The counselor must help the client clarify her worldview and respond with empathy and sensitivity to her values and perspectives.

3. The counselor needs to share personal perspectives to reduce mistrust and must confront counselor-client differences and similarities with honesty and courage.

4. The counselor must apply information gained from the profiles in developing appropriate process and goals to enhance the therapeutic relationship. The Here and Now worldview dimensions require that the counselor and client stay focused on the primary issues that the client brings to therapy in a specific session, rather than focusing on the long-term goals that the counselor may believe they must work on given his future orientation and his education that focuses on long-term goals.

5. The counselor must confront and accept his own and the client's limits.

TRAINING AND EDUCATION MODEL FOR TRANSCULTURAL COUNSELING AND PSYCHOTHERAPY

Recognition of the need to incorporate transcultural perspectives in counseling and applied psychology is a recent phenomenon (Bales, 1985; D'Andrea, Daniels, & Heck, 1991; Ibrahim, 1991; Ibrahim, Stadler, Arredondo, & McFadden, 1986; Ponterotto & Casas, 1987). The existential worldview theory has significant implications for the training and education of counselors, psychologists, and other applied mental health professionals. A major difference between this approach and other models is that it is anchored in a theoretical model, with assessment tools available to operationalize the model, and it has been tested and proven to be effective in increasing client-perceived empathy and cross-cultural sensitivity of the therapist (Cunningham-Warburton, 1988; Sadlak & Ibrahim, 1986).

In two studies involving counselor trainees and therapists, the clients reported feeling understood and appropriately responded to by the helpers and reported greater satisfaction in the therapeutic encounter with helpers trained in using the SAWV and cultural information. Additionally, research supported the contention that helpers trained in using the existential worldview theory and the SAWV could develop a shared frame of reference with their clients (Cunningham-Warburton, 1988; Sadlak & Ibrahim, 1986). Further, this model incorporates gender differentiation and does not treat clients as simply cultural beings. It also considers how gender and cultural identity may interact in the problems that clients face and the resolutions they will require (Furn, 1986, 1988; Furn & Ibrahim, 1987; Ibrahim, 1991).

This model uses a cognitive, affective, and skills approach (Ibrahim & Schroeder, 1989). The three approaches used are not discretely separated; they occur as overlapping stages. The training model ensures that the process and goals established to help a client are culturally consistent for the client (Axelson, 1985; Brown & Srebalus, 1988; Corey, Corey, & Callanan, 1988). The approach ensures that helpers are clearly aware of their assumptions, and of the client's, which simplifies interventions at both the process and outcome levels. The specifics of the training model follow.

AWARENESS AND SENSITIVITY

Before the actual training, a need for the training is created among the participants by heightening their awareness of their cultural selves. Further, the cultural pluralism of the world and the relativity of human values are explored. A group-dynamics, experiential approach is taken. This is a critically important stage in creating a readiness among the participants to explore themselves and others in the group. The focus of the exploration is on members as cultural entities, and on hypothesizing about the experience of people who are culturally different from a society or system. Simple exercises are used that help the participants identify their values and the agencies (family, school, church, and society) that may have influenced them. During this stage, the SAWV and the CICL are administered. The participants are encouraged to share information with others in the group. The sharing is voluntary.

AFFECTIVE

This component overlaps to a large extent with the Awareness and Sensitivity and the Cognitive stages. It is highly experiential. Group exercises are used to explore issues of race, gender, culture, socio-economic level, educational level, age, life stage, life-style, and ability or disability status. The goal is to help the participants identify their feelings about their cultural identity, gender, age, and other characteristics. Further, the focus is to develop an understanding of what it means to be different and the many ways that we are similar to and different from each other. A major goal at this stage is to help the participants identify feelings about themselves and others in the group. The participants practice empathic responding skills regarding the differences experienced by the group and others in a specific society.

COGNITIVE

This component provides information about the history and theories of cross-cultural counseling. The existential worldview theory, with the SAWV and the CICL, is presented. The participants learn to administer these instruments and learn about using the information in counseling and psychotherapy (client engagement, counselor-client matching, diagnosis, and process and goal development). Other theories of cross-cultural counseling with information on counseling specific cultural groups are also explored.

SKILLS

Here the participants are exposed to specific counseling and communication skills that would be useful in transcultural encounters. Training tapes that explore cross-cultural counseling issues are used to enhance the participants' ability in transcultural encounters. In the final sessions, the participants identify case vignettes representing different cultures and role-play the vignettes. The participants give each other feedback, and the instructor also provides feedback.

The model has been tested and is effective as noted earlier. However, further research is needed to identify how the varied information on transcultural training models can be merged to prepare highly effective transcultural counselors.

CULTURAL IDENTITY CHECKLIST (CICL)
© 1990 Farah A. Ibrahim

Name: _____ Age: _____ Gender: _____
Race: _____ Religion: _____

Please answer the following questions in the most direct manner. This checklist is designed to help you and the counselor understand your cultural identity. Please respond to the questions as *you really see yourself*, rather than as others define you. If any of the questions make you uncomfortable, you need not answer them. This information will be held in strictest confidence.

1. What is your ethnic background? Please list ethnicities of both your parents and their parents.
2. Which ethnic group do you think has influenced your values and beliefs the most? Which ethnic group do you identify with personally?
3. In which generation did your family migrate to this country?
4. Was migration a free choice or was it forced?
5. How was your ethnic group received?
6. How has your primary group established itself in this country?
7. What do you know about the sociopolitical history of your primary group in this country?
8. How do you feel about the sociopolitical history of your primary group?
9. What was the socioeconomic status of your family of origin?
10. What is your socioeconomic level?
11. What was the educational level of your father? mother?
12. What is your educational level?
13. Is your family monolingual? If your family is bilingual or trilingual, please list the languages they speak, read, and write.

14. Are you monolingual? If you are bilingual or trilingual, please list the languages you speak, read, and write.
15. Do you actively practice your faith and believe in it?
16. What is your birth order in your family of origin—oldest, middle, or youngest child? (please circle)
17. What is your sexual preference? How does your family relate to your sexual preference? How does your cultural or ethnic group relate to your sexual preference?
18. Do you have any disabilities?

Please feel free to add other information that you consider relevant to this checklist.

REFERENCES

Abramovitz, C. V., & Dokecki, P. R. (1977). The politics of clinical judgements: Early empirical returns. *Psychological Bulletin, 84,* 460–474.

Abramovitz, S. I., & Murray, J. (1983). Race effects in psychotherapy. In J. Murray & P. Abramson (Eds.), *Bias in psychotherapy* (pp. 215–225). New York: Praeger.

Adler, A. (1925). *The practice and theory of individual psychology.* New York: Harcourt, Brace.

American Association for Counseling and Development. (1987). *Human rights position paper.* Alexandria, VA: Author.

Arredondo-Dowd, P. M., & Gonsalves, J. (1980). Preparing culturally effective counselors. *Personnel and Guidance Journal, 58,* 657–661.

Atkinson, D. R. (1985). A meta-review of research on cross cultural counseling and psychotherapy. *Journal of Multicultural Counseling, 1,* 138–153.

Atkinson, D. R., & Carskaddon, G. A. (1975). A prestigious introduction, psychological jargon, and perceived counselor credibility. *Journal of Counseling Psychology, 22,* 180–186.

Axelson, J. A. (1985). *Counseling and development in a multicultural society.* Monterey, CA: Brooks/Cole.

Bales, J. (1985). Minority testing falls short. *APA Monitor, 16,* 7.

Banks, W. M. (1972). The differential effects of race and social class in helping. *Journal of Clinical Psychology, 28,* 90–92.

Barak, A., & La Crosse, M. B. (1975). Multidimensional perception of counsellor behavior. *Journal of Counseling Psychology, 22,* 471–476.

Bateson, G., & Mead, M. (1942). *Balinese character: A photographic analysis.* New York: New York Academy of Sciences.

Beck, A. T., Rush, A. J., Shaw, B. F., & Emery, G. (1979). *Cognitive therapy of depression.* New York: Guilford.

Becker, E. (1973). *The denial of death.* New York: Free Press.

Bergin, A. (1991). Values and religious issues in psychotherapy and mental health. *American Psychologist, 46,* 394–403.

Beutler, L. E., & Bergan, J. (1991). Value change in counseling and psychotherapy: A search for scientific credibility. *Journal of Counseling Psychology, 38,* 16–24.

Binswanger, L. (1962). *Existential analysis and psychotherapy.* New York: Dutton.

Binswanger, L. (1963). *Being-in-the-world: Selected papers.* New York: Basic Books.

Brown, D., & Srebalus, D. J. (1988). *An introduction to the counseling profession.* Englewood Cliffs, NJ: Prentice Hall.

Buber, M. (1970). *I and Thou.* New York: Scribner's.

Carkhuff, R. R., & Pierce, R. (1967). Differential effects of therapist race and social class upon patient depth of self-exploration in the initial interview. *Journal of Consulting Psychology, 31,* 632–634.

Cirillo, L., & Wapner, S. (Eds.) (1986). *Value suppositions in theories of human development.* Hillsdale, NJ: Erlbaum.

Cohen, R. (1969). Conceptual styles, culture conflict and nonverbal tests of intelligence. *American Anthropologist, 71,* 825–856.

Coombs, A., & Snygg, D. (1959). *Individual behavior.* New York: Harper & Row.

Corey, G., Corey, M. S., & Callanan, P. (1988). *Issues and ethics in the helping professions* (3rd ed.). Monterey, CA: Brooks/Cole.

Cunningham-Warburton, P. (1988). *A study of the relationship between cross-cultural training, the Scale to Assess World Views, and the quality of care given by nurses in a psychiatric setting.* Unpublished doctoral dissertation, University of Connecticut.

D'Andrea, M., Daniels, J., & Heck, R. (1991). Evaluating the impact of multicultural counseling training. *Journal of Counseling and Development, 70,* 143–150.

Draguns, J. (1991, April). Keynote address, Cross-cultural psychology in 1991, at the national meeting of the American Counseling and Development Association, Reno, NV. *Journal of Cross-Cultural Psychology, 22,* 6–7.

Edmunds, P., Martinson, S. A., & Goldberg, P. F. (1990). *Demographics and cultural diversity in the 1990's: Implications for services to young children with special needs.* Washington, DC: Office of Special Education Programs, U.S. Department of Education.

Frank, J. O. (1973). *Persuasion and healing* (rev. ed.). Baltimore: Johns Hopkins University Press.

Frankl, V. E. (1978). *The unheard cry for meaning.* New York: Simon & Schuster.

Fromm, E. (1963). *The art of loving.* New York: Bantam.

Furn, B. G. (1986). *The psychology of women as a cross-cultural issue: Perceived dimensions of worldviews.* Unpublished doctoral dissertation, University of Connecticut.

Furn, B. G. (1988, August). *Worldviews and gender: Implications for counseling and psychotherapy.* Paper presented at the annual meeting of the American Psychological Association, Atlanta, GA.

Furn, B. G., & Ibrahim, F. A. (1987, August). *The psychology of women: Perceived dimensions of world views.* Paper presented at the annual meeting of the American Psychological Association, New York, NY.

Gaines, A. (1982). Cultural definitions, behavior, and the person in American psychiatry. In A. J. Marsella & G. M. White (Eds.), *Cultural conceptions of mental health and therapy.* Higham, MA: Reidel.

Geertz, C. (1973). Person, time, and conduct in Bali. In C. Geertz (Ed.), *The interpretation of culture.* New York: Basic Books.

Griffith, M. S. (1977). The influence of race on the psychotherapeutic relationship. *Psychiatry, 40,* 27–40.

Heidegger, M. (1961). *An introduction to metaphysics.* New York: Doubleday.

Horner, D., & Vandersluis, P. (1981). Cross-cultural counseling. In G. Althen (Ed.), *Learning across cultures.* Washington, DC: National Association for Foreign Students Affairs.

Ibrahim, F. A. (1984a). Cross-cultural counseling and psychotherapy: An existential-psychological perspective. *International Journal for the Advancement of Counseling, 7,* 559–569.

Ibrahim, F. A. (1984b, March). *Cross-cultural counseling and psychotherapy: Initial assessment.* Paper presented at the annual meeting of the American Association for Counseling and Development, Houston, TX.

Ibrahim, F. A. (1985a, April). *Cross-cultural counseling training.* Paper presented at the annual meeting of the Association for Counseling and Development, New York, NY.

Ibrahim, F. A. (1985b). Human rights and ethical issues in the use of advanced technology. *Journal of Counseling and Development, 64,* 134–145.

Ibrahim, F. A. (1986, August). *Reflections on the cultural encapsulation of the APA's ethical principles.* Paper presented at the annual meeting of the American Psychological Association, Washington, DC.

Ibrahim, F. A. (1989). Response to psychology in the public forum on socially sensitive research. *American Psychologist, 44,* 847–848.

Ibrahim, F. A. (1990a). *Cultural Identity Checklist (CICL).* Unpublished checklist. University of Connecticut, Storrs.

Ibrahim, F. A. (1990b, August). *Workshop on clinical applications of the Scale to Assess World Views.* Workshop presented at the annual meeting of the American Psychological Association, Boston, MA.

Ibrahim, F. A. (1991). Contribution of cultural worldview to generic counseling and development. *Journal of Counseling and Development, 70,* 13–19.

Ibrahim, F. A. (1992a). Children's rights in a pluralistic society. *Journal for Humanistic Education and Development, 31,* 64–72.

Ibrahim, F. A. (1992b, March). *Identity development from a culture and gender perspective.* Paper presented at the annual meeting of the American Association for Counseling and Development, Baltimore, MD.

Ibrahim, F. A. (1993). *Scale to Assess World Views II.* Unpublished scale. University of Connecticut.

Ibrahim, F. A., & Arredondo, P. M. (1986). Ethical standards for cross-cultural counseling: Preparation, practice, assessment, and research. *Journal of Counseling and Development, 64,* 349–351.

Ibrahim, F. A., & Arredondo, P. M. (1990). Essay on law and ethics: Multicultural counseling. In B. Herlihy & L. Golden (Eds.), *American Association for Counseling and Development: Ethics casebook* (4th ed.). Alexandria, VA: American Association for Counseling and Development Press.

Ibrahim, F. A., & Kahn, H. (1984). *Scale to assess world views.* Unpublished scale, University of Connecticut.

Ibrahim, F. A., & Kahn, H. (1987). Assessment of world views. *Psychological Reports, 60,* 163–176.

Ibrahim, F. A., & Owen, S. V. (1992, August). *Factor analytic structure of the Scale to Assess World Views.* Paper presented at the annual meeting of the American Psychological Association, Washington, DC.

Ibrahim, F. A., & Schroeder, D. G. (1987, October). *Effective communication with multicultural families.* Paper presented at the annual meeting of the Connecticut Association for the Education of Young Children, Storrs, CT.

Ibrahim, F. A., & Schroeder, D. G. (1989, March). Americans can learn to be free of racism and sexism. *Hartford Courant*, p. B11.

Ibrahim, F. A., & Schroeder, D. G. (1990). Cross-cultural couple counseling: A developmental psychoeducational intervention. *Journal of Comparative Family Studies, 21*, 193–207.

Ibrahim, F. A., Stadler, H. A., Arredondo, P. M., & McFadden, J. (1986, April). *Status of human rights issues in counselor preparation: A national survey*. Paper presented at the annual meeting of the American Association for Counseling and Development, Los Angeles, CA.

Jensen, J. P., & Bergin, A. E. (1988). Mental health values of professional therapists: A national interdisciplinary survey. *Professional Psychology: Research and Practice, 19*, 290–297.

Jones, E. E., Kanouse, D., Kelly, H. H., Nisbett, R. E., Valins, S., & Weiner, B. (Eds.). (1972). *Attribution: Perceiving the causes of behavior*. Morristown, NJ: General Learning Press.

Jung, C. G. (1958). Aion. In V. S. de Laslo (Ed.), *Psyche and symbol* (pp. 1–60) (S. C. R. Hull, Trans.). New York: Doubleday/Bollingen Foundation. (Original work published 1958.)

Kelly, G. (1963). *A theory of personality: The psychology of personal constructs*. New York: Norton.

Kelly, T. A. (1990). The role of values in psychotherapy: Review and methodological critique. *Clinical Psychology Review, 10*, 171–186.

Kemp, C. G (1971). Existential counseling. *The Counseling Psychologist, 2*, 2–30.

Kluckhohn, C. (1951). Values and value orientations in the theory of action. In T. Parsons & E. A. Shields (Eds.), *Toward a general theory of action* (pp. 388–433). Cambridge, MA: Harvard University Press.

Kluckhohn, C. (1956). Towards a comparison of value-emphasis in different cultures. In L. D. White (Ed.), *The state of social sciences* (pp. 116–132). Chicago: University of Chicago Press.

Kluckhohn, F. R., & Strodtbeck, F. L. (1961). *Variations in value orientations*. Evanston, IL: Row, Petersen.

Landrine, H. (1991). Culture in psychology: A constructivist approach. Book under review.

Lazaurs, R. S. (1988). Constructs of the mind in mental health and psychotherapy. In A. Freeman, K. M. Simon, L. E. Beutler, & H. Arkowitz (Eds.), *Comprehensive handbook of cognitive therapy* (pp. 99–122). New York: Plenum.

Lonner, W. J., & Ibrahim, F. A. (1989). Assessment in cross-cultural counseling. In P. B. Pedersen, J. G. Draguns, W. J. Lonner, & J. E. Trimble (Eds.), *Counseling across cultures* (3rd ed., pp. 229–334). Honolulu: University of Hawaii Press.

Marsella, A. J., & White, G. M. (Eds.). (1982). *Cultural conceptions of mental health.* Higham, MA: Reidel.

Maruyama, M. (1978). Psychotopology and its applications to cross-disciplinary, cross-professional, and cross-cultural communication. In R. E. Holloman & S. A. Arutiunov (Eds.), *Perspectives on ethnicity.* The Hague: Mouton.

Merluzzi, T. V., Merluzzi, B. H., & Kaul, T. H. (1977). Counselor race and power base: Effects on attitudes and behavior. *Journal of Counseling Psychology, 24,* 430–436.

Page, R. C., & Berkow, D. N. (1991). Concepts of the self: Western and Eastern perspectives. *Journal of Multicultural Counseling and Development, 19,* 83–93.

Patterson, C. H. (1989). Values in counseling and psychotherapy. *Counseling and Values, 33,* 164–176.

Pedersen, P. B. (1986, August). *Cultural encapsulation of the APA's ethical principles.* Paper presented at the annual meeting of the American Psychological Association, Washington, DC.

Pedersen, P. B. (1988). *A handbook for developing multicultural awareness.* Alexandria, VA: American Association for Counseling and Development.

Pedersen, P. B., Fukuyama, M., & Heath, A. (1989). Client, counselor, and contextual variables in multicultural counseling. In P. B. Pedersen, J. G. Draguns, W. J. Lonner, & J. E. Trimble (Eds.). *Counseling across cultures* (3rd ed., pp. 23–52). Honolulu: University of Hawaii Press.

Ponterotto, J. G., & Casas, J. M. (1987). In search of multicultural competence within counselor education programs. *Journal of Counseling and Development, 64,* 430–434.

Reid, T. (1989, May). *Cultural differences.* Paper presented at the annual meeting of the Society for the Exploration of Psychotherapy Integration. Berkeley, CA.

Rogers, C. R. (1957). The necessary and sufficient conditions of therapeutic personality change. *Journal of Consulting Psychology, 21,* 95–103.

Rotter, J. (1966). Generalized expectancies for internal versus external control of reinforcement. *Psychological Monographs, 80,* (1, whole number 609).

Sadlak, M. J., & Ibrahim, F. A. (1986, August). *Cross-cultural counselor training: Impact on counselor effectiveness and sensitivity.* Paper presented at the annual meeting of the American Psychological Association, Washington, DC.

Sadowsky, G. R., Maguire, K., Johnson, P., Ngumba, E., & Kohles, R. (in press). Worldviews of White Americans, Mainland Chinese, Taiwanese, and African students: An investigation into between group differences. *Journal of Cross-cultural Psychology.*

Sarason, S. B. (1984). If it can be studied or developed, should it be? *American Psychologist, 39,* 477–485.

Sartre, J. P. (1953), *Being and nothingness.* New York: Philosophical Library.

Schmidt, L. D., & Strong, S. R. (1971). Attractiveness and influence in counseling. *Journal of Counseling Psychology, 18,* 348–351.

Shweder, R., & Miller, J. (1985). The social construction of the person: How is it possible? In K. Gergen & K. Davis (Eds.), *The social construction of the person* (pp. 41–69). New York: Springer-Verlag.

Sire, J. W. (1976). *The universe next door.* Downers Grove, IL: Intervarsity.

Speigel, J. P. (1982). An ecological model of ethnic families. In M. McGoldrick, J. K. Pearce, & J. Giordano (Eds.), *Ethnicity and family therapy* (pp. 31–54). New York: Guilford.

Strong, S. R. (1968). Counseling: An interpersonal influence process. *Journal of Counseling Psychology, 15,* 215–244.

Strupp, H. H. (1978). Psychotherapy research and practice: An overview. In S. L. Garfield & A. E. Bergin (Eds.), *Handbook of psychotherapy and behavior change: An empirical analysis* (pp. 3–22). New York: Wiley.

Sue, D. W. (1978). World views and counseling. *Personnel and Guidance Journal, 56,* 458–462.

Sue, D. W., & Sue, D. (1991). *Counseling the culturally different.* New York: Wiley.

Sue, S. (1988). Psychotherapeutic services for ethnic minorities. *American Psychologist, 43,* 301–308.

Sue, S., & Zane, N. (1987). The role of cultural techniques in psychotherapy: A critique and reformulation. *American Psychologist, 42,* 37–45.

Sundberg, N. D. (1981). Cross-cultural counseling and psychotherapy: A research overview. In A. J. Marsella & P. B. Pedersen (Eds.). *Cross cultural counseling and psychotherapy* (pp. 28–62). New York: Pergamon.

Tataryn, D. J., Nadel, L., & Jacobs, W. J. (1988). Cognitive therapy and cognitive science. In A. Freeman, K. M. Simon, L. E. Beutler, & H. Arkowitz (Eds.), *Comprehensive handbook of cognitive therapy* (pp. 83–98). New York: Plenum.

Torrey, E. F. (1986). *Witchdoctors and psychiatrists.* New York: Harper & Row.

Triandis, H. C. (1972). *The analysis of subjective cultural.* New York: Wiley.

Triandis, H. C., & Brislin, R. W. (1984). Cross-cultural psychology. *American Psychologist, 39,* 1006–1016.

Tyler, F. B., Sussewell, D. R., & Williams-McCoy, J. (1985). Ethnic validity in psychotherapy. *Psychotherapy, 22,* 311–320.

Vontress, C. E. (1979). Cross-cultural counseling: An existential approach. *Personnel and Guidance Journal, 58,* 117–121.

Wachtel, P. L. (1977). *Psychoanalysis and behavior therapy: Toward an integration.* New York: Basic Books.

Yalom, I. D. (1980). *Existential psychotherapy.* New York: Basic Books.

CHAPTER 3

STYLISTIC MODEL FOR TRANSCULTURAL COUNSELING

JOHN McFADDEN

INTRODUCTION

In a world charged by enormous social changes and by challenges of rapid technological innovations, counselors and other helping professionals are called upon to respond to an array of emotional and psychological needs of clients living in a pluralistic society. The complexities of the modern age often confound persons seeking order or purpose in life. Thus, the realization of wholesome development in individuals toward the attainment of their fullest potential is a fundamental goal of the counseling profession. Helping individuals respond to their social and technological environments is the focus of many professional counselors. The emotional and psychological needs of individuals do not necessarily transcend their cultural, racial, or ethnic identity and environment. In a pluralistic society such identities are inextricably connected to an individual's perception of self and the surrounding world. Transcultural counselors, therefore, play an important societal role, especially with individuals whose ethnicity or cultural background may differ from their own.

Counselor educators recognize, too, that greater efforts must be made to further improve curricular and instructional methods used to educate those seeking careers as helping professionals. Counseling knowledge and skills must include a global perspective and the recognition of cultural influences, which will enable counselors to respond more effectively to a diverse client population. These changes in counseling and counselor training approaches are essential to enhancing counselor effectiveness. Recognition of the efficacy of responding to a continually changing social and cultural environment is necessary for effective counseling. It is essential that transcultural consciousness be maintained among counselors and related professionals to ensure relevance for ethical and efficient service for the public sector.

The stylistic model for transcultural counseling is introduced, therefore, as one approach to improving cultural understanding and contributing to our quest for focus and efficiency in meeting contemporary challenges. The model represents a reflective process, for it epitomizes what we really are, what we believe, and what we experience. It establishes a basis for cultural transcendency on behalf of transcultural counselors who adopt a belief system or philosophy of political change for the historically oppressed. In transcending differences, a call for basic education and training that represents cultural values in their own right with ethical dimensions is made vis-à-vis transcultural counseling. The final goal of this counseling imperative then is education without frontiers and limitations to yield relevant services for clients.

Breaking away from a historically culture-confined environment allows transcultural counselors to realign themselves toward building a strong sense of community, to know the impact of global dynamics, and to promote a worldview of humanity through counselor-client interaction. Transcultural counselors play a primary role in sharing insight through professional practice. They recognize that cultural introspection and the sociocultural milieu with which they relate and participate supplement their experience with transculturalism. Cultural introspection is paramount in working through the stylistic counseling model.

SCOPE OF MODEL

The stylistic counseling model focuses on fundamental elements of effective counseling techniques, specifically on those crucial in meeting the needs of ethnic minority clients—persons who have been historically underrepresented as traditional counseling theories and techniques have been developed. As opposed to techniques that address mainly surface problems of clients, stylistic counseling has greater concern for the deep-rooted core of counseling issues of minority clients. Understanding the client within total perspectives—cultural, historical, psychological, social, scientific, and ideological—is a basic premise that the stylistic counseling approach embraces as a prerequisite to any counseling encounter. The focus is long-range and provides for substantive solutions to human problems, rather than solely extinguishing fires of an immediate nature.

Techniques suggested or implied in the stylistic counseling model thus revolve around one central springboard factor, namely, understanding the distinct composition of the client's background. To know the unique origin of racial and ethnic minorities is to assure oneself of the initial step to success in transcultural counseling. The model focuses on the requirement common to all minority counseling: to master a knowledge of and feeling for the culture and history of the client whose life has been marked by separation, disregard, and oppression.

The stylistic counseling model

- Provides foundation for hierarchical movement—vertically, horizontally, and diagonally
- Is composed of a series of cubical descriptors
- Is universal in its approach as it permeates various segments of society, encompassing all clusters of cultural, ethnic, and racial groups, and immigrants
- Proclaims the need to engage minority clients relative to their specific cultural orientation and social perspectives
- Has implications for use across gender, sexuality, disability, and economic categories
- Recognizes multiple dynamics relative to culture that operate between counselor and client

The basic premises for the stylistic model are as follows:
1. The counselor should, via reading and research, become fully cognizant of the parallels and diversities between minority and nonminority history and culture.

61

2. The counselor should know the following about clients when counseling people of color: the structure of their thinking, the incentives for their aspirations, and the diverse problems they confront.
3. The counselor should maximize the use of "I can" and "I will."
4. The counselor should build self-images by consistently providing successful cultural and ethnic experiences.
5. Family (biological, adoptive, or extended) is a survival mechanism for clients in the stylistic model.

THE MODEL

The stylistic model allows persons who already have initial training in counseling or those who are receiving training to develop their own mode or style so that they can be effective in helping others who have experienced oppression. It encourages eclecticism as an approach in achieving transculturalism.

Stylistic counseling incorporates within its design a structure that supports prerequisites for effective transcultural counseling. It is a model geared toward the development of a framework for counselors to apply their knowledge and skills in counseling across cultures. Individuals historically excluded from and underrepresented within the social system, frequently known as *minorities*, can be well served by helping professionals using this model.

The model originally emerged out of a need for assistance, training, programming, and outreach on behalf of African Americans in the United States (McFadden, 1983, 1987, 1988a, 1988b). However, stylistic counseling has proven subsequently to be applicable to a number of oppressed groups on an international level regardless of race, ethnicity, gender, disability, geography, sexual orientation, culture, and the like. To effect change through transcultural counseling, this approach holds that counselors should demonstrate knowledge of and sensitivity to the history, psychology, sociology, and ideology of their clients. Failure to gain an in-depth knowledge in these areas would obviously damage the process of interpersonal interaction and communication, for, as Sue (1981) emphasizes, effective counseling can only occur when the counselor and the client are able to appropriately and accurately send and receive both verbal and nonverbal messages.

ANATOMY OF STYLISTIC COUNSELING

The design of stylistic counseling is thematically constructed around three dimensions (Figure 2): cultural-historical, psychosocial, and scientific-ideological. The dimensions, being hierarchical in nature, suggest by their cubical arrangement that transcultural counselors progress through the model in an ascending manner—that is, cultural-historical to psychosocial to scientific-ideological.

The basic and fundamental dimension is cultural-historical, relating specifically to the culture of a people and how their history evolved over time. The author assumes a theoretical position that one cannot counsel effectively in terms of developing a style or

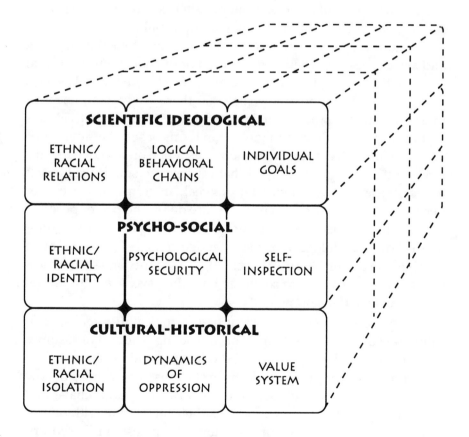

SCIENTIFIC IDEOLOGICAL

| ETHNIC/ RACIAL RELATIONS | LOGICAL BEHAVIORAL CHAINS | INDIVIDUAL GOALS |

PSYCHO-SOCIAL

| ETHNIC/ RACIAL IDENTITY | PSYCHOLOGICAL SECURITY | SELF-INSPECTION |

CULTURAL-HISTORICAL

| ETHNIC/ RACIAL ISOLATION | DYNAMICS OF OPPRESSION | VALUE SYSTEM |

FIGURE 2. Stylistic counseling

communicating with clients unless one has an intuitive, rather accurate perspective and identification with the culture of the particular ethnicity or race one is counseling (i.e., knowing something about the history and evolution of people, germane to the subject, over a period of time). This dimension as related to transcultural counseling, therefore, focuses primarily on how people themselves relate to their own heritage, how they perceive themselves in a broader social context, and how they envision their cultural norms perpetuating themselves over time in the larger context of a societal framework.

The second dimension, psychosocial, relates specifically to the psychological framework, the formation of a mind-set of how a person's psychic influence affects his or her scope and development, such as in the case of a person's interaction based on how the person sees his or her own cultural heritage. The social component of this dimension relates primarily to the dynamics of interaction between and among people, whether it is within or outside of one's cultural constellation. When we examine ethnic, racial, and cultural aspects of a person's development, we see that there are varying forms of pressure that affect the psychological framework of the individual's identity, how each begins to interact in terms of social influences or various stimuli. What is it that motivates a person to move toward a relevant sociological group? What causes a person to see himself or herself as strong, moderate, or weak in terms of his or her heritage? What value does a person place on self-help as opposed to dependency? Does a person derive sustaining humanistic confidence from the biological or the extended family? We relate much of this to the person's form of psychological security and sociological competence, the ability to converge both the psychic and the social components of development.

The third dimension is scientific-ideological. It refers specifically to an action-oriented aspect of counseling. The author assumes that, if a counselor is going to be effective while examining the science and ideology of a people, he or she must have a grasp of how various ethnic, racial, and social groups perform, speak, behave, and interact among themselves as well as their interaction with others. Another phase of the scientific-ideological dimension is based primarily on the cultural-historical component, that is, on the roots of one's existence—the origin of how an individual is able to perform in neocultural environs and how that individual is able to find ways of interplaying in relationship with a diverse sociological mentality with other individuals and simultaneously maintain a sense of oneness.

The scientific-ideological dimension of counseling is effective to the extent that it has ascended from the cultural-historical and psychosocial dimensions. The transcultural counselor must have tools to put into a broader context a strategic plan applicable for individuals who need, seek, or aspire to a transcultural counseling relationship. The scientific-ideological dimension of counseling evolves over time. It is geared more toward making things happen— in other words, a developmental process of empowering an individual to function—given that there is a support system whereby the client becomes optimally productive.

CUBICAL DESCRIPTORS

Each of the three dimensions (cultural-historical, psychosocial, scientific-ideological) encompasses nine cubical descriptors that are graphically depicted in Figure 3 and concisely described below:

1. *Ethnic/Racial Discrimination:* An emphasis on historical and cultural effects of discrimination on ethnic/racial groups. This component is important because one cannot counsel another person transculturally unless one is extremely knowledgeable and very sensitive to discrimination the client may have experienced.
2. *Ethnic/Racial Identity:* A study of the psychological and social aspects of ethnic/racial identity of underrepresented persons. This component includes factors that involve the sociological and psychological impact of discrimination affecting the self-concept and identity of ethnic/racial groups. This component is designed to address ingredients essential in the formation of individual identity.
3. *Ethnic/Racial Relations:* An analysis of the science of race relations and ethnic interactions and the ideology of these relations as they influence a particular nationality. This is a cubical descriptor for an action-oriented dimension of the model.
4. *Dynamics of Oppression:* A history of the major aspects of oppression as they impact on the formation of various ethnic/racial cultures.

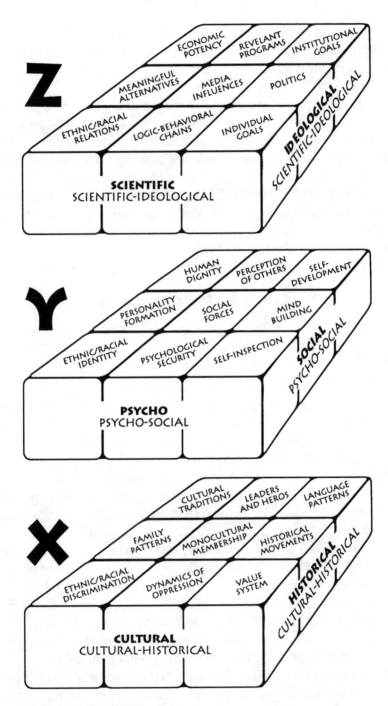

FIGURE 3. Cubical Descriptors

5. *Psychological Security:* A study of the psychology of the oppressed as it pertains to an internal and external sense of security. The psychosocial dimension of counseling individuals allows them to build their own sense of psychological security relative to coping skills required in managing the dynamics of oppression.

6. *Logic-Behavioral Chains:* An investigation of the scientific logic that undergirds one's thoughts and behaviors. This component allows a client to be directed or helped behaviorally, based on a logical pattern that emerges from a sense of psychological security reflected in the form of survival skills.

7. *Value System:* An exploration of the history of values embraced by a given culture and how these values influence the lives of an ethnic or racial group. The evolution of the value structure and the value orientation of a group of people from infancy to adulthood becomes crucial in this component.

8. *Self-Inspection:* A psychological and social study of an individual's self-concept formation. This entails the definition of self-concept and its development toward a mentality of how one feels or perceives oneself.

9. *Individual Goals:* A scientific exploration of the identification of goals of historically underrepresented ethnic/racial groups and their aspirations toward the development of a clear ideology for goal attainment.

10. *Family Patterns:* An examination of the various family patterns to which particular ethnic/racial persons belong. The family patterns are based on the history of the oppressed groups.

11. *Personality Formation:* Identification of the ways personalities are formed among ethnic groups and races—how they develop varying personalities to build a system for survival.

12. *Meaningful Alternatives:* Selecting a variety of situations and alternatives that govern efficient and productive lives; scientifically examining choices for effective decision making and successful career development.

13. *Monocultural Membership:* A description of the advantages and limitations of monocultural membership. The advantages of belonging to a particular cultural group and ways to optimize this fundamental membership are assessed.

14. *Social Forces:* A discussion of social forces that affect the lives of persons outside the mainstream of society, such as unemployment, underemployment, alcoholism, substance abuse, and homelessness.

15. *Media Influences:* An examination of the positive and negative ways by which the media influence ethnic/racial perceptions in society, and the controlling force of print and audiovisual media.

16. *Historical Movements:* An indication of the impact of certain historical and legislative movements and the alteration of government and community programs as related to ethnic/racial groups.

17. *Mind Building:* Conditioning of one's mental capacity to become productive and useful to oneself and others through transcultural methods.

18. *Politics:* An indication of the influences of ethnic/racial groups in politics; the variation in ways that politics embraces and establishes parameters within which the public is expected to function.

19. *Cultural Traditions:* A reflection of the culture that, by virtue of its beginning and tradition, manages to be transferred from one generation to another; how cultural traditions develop to affect others through continuity.

20. *Human Dignity:* Maintenance of identity so that individuals can have feelings of self-satisfaction, self-enhancement, empowerment, dignity, and ethnic or cultural pride.

21. *Economic Potency:* Ability of ethnic/racial groups to unify and solidify their power (i.e., influence, ability, and impact on the economics of a particular system).

22. *Leaders and Heroes:* Individuals who, by virtue of their function in society, have attained a level of respect as leaders or heroes. They serve as role models and mentors for ethnic/racial groups.

23. *Perception of Others:* Ideas and visions of people based on certain experiences that may have emerged as a result of interaction within a societal context toward a level of transcendency.

24. *Relevant Programs:* Formation of a programmatic thrust within a particular group. Such programs are perceived to have true

meaning and significance as they bond with values that ethnicities and races may hold to be special.

25. *Language Patterns:* The development of languages and linguistic orientation that prove themselves to be optimally communicative between or among individuals, allowing for and respecting dialects and language differences.

26. *Self-Development:* The enhancement or improvement of oneself so that one can provide for oneself and others within an ethnic/racial context. It is self-improvement aimed at reaching a level of productivity or orientation for accomplishment.

27. *Institutional Goals:* Aspirations of an institution, organization, community, or society that may have some utility to an ethnic/racial group. These goals are geared to serve a large group of people and can be linked to a cultural or sociological context that could have significance.

To understand the model, one should observe a correlation among the three primary dimensions and the various cubical cells within each group. Within the cultural-historical dimension, it is critical for transcultural counselors to understand the covert and overt forms of discrimination historically practiced toward ethnic and racial minority people and the oppression to which these individuals have been systematically subjected. Combining such awareness with ethnic/racial identity under the psychosocial dimension, transcultural counselors possess basic knowledge of how, why, and when clients feel the need to become integrally and ethnically/racially identified with their own cultural group. This identity is based on what counselors, having inflicted or having been victimized by discrimination throughout their lives, perceive and believe.

In applying the stylistic model to transcultural counseling, there are sociocultural-political implications for helping professionals. The following initiatives are recommended particularly for the counselors in pursuit of this model:

- Sponsoring through local institutions cultural centers or think tanks to provide a forum for learning, research, and social debate

- Promoting understanding across cultures to advance the concept of a citizen's world in developing young minds

- Researching distinctions and similarities between a *nation* and a *culture*

- Interrelating research and development programs and their cultural action dimension in education and training

- Providing diversity training and transcultural awareness for local leaders

- Stimulating intercultural mobility for the expansion of human capital within the community

Although ingredients for effective counseling, such as empathy, trust, and openness, are essential in stylistic counseling, transcultural counselors are perceptive enough to recognize that mere possession of these qualities does not ensure the elimination of historically ingrained barriers between counselors and clients. Oppression permeates slowly through the culture of the oppressed; similarly, this phenomenon cannot be removed or replaced instantly by cultural, ethnic/racial worth and pride. It requires counselors to shape their consciousness and concurrently to demonstrate a capacity to analyze, digest, and assimilate pertinent information to ensure their ability to function efficiently in this technological world on behalf of their clients.

The following principles capture primary themes that sustain stylistic counseling as a model for effecting change through transculturalism. They provide the basis for rendering evidence through counseling encounters that transcend cultural differences as a basic mode toward the implementation of transcultural counseling. Standards for successful counseling practice are as functional and useful as the individuals trained and experienced in applying these standards. To this extent, the principles of stylistic counseling are advocated as fundamental guidelines to understanding the proposed model in meeting the challenges of transcultural counseling.

PRINCIPLES OF STYLISTIC COUNSELING

1. Stylistic counseling proposes a model for formulating an individual counseling program compatible with the counselor's orientation and conducive to effectively meeting the needs of clients.

2. Stylistic counseling suggests that cubical descriptors of a person's behavior are hierarchical in nature.
3. Stylistic counseling is an approach to helping others that integrates the cultural-historical, psychosocial, and scientific-ideological dimensions of human behavior.
4. Stylistic counseling advocates the establishment of a cultural-historical base as the foundation for effective helping relationships.
5. Stylistic counseling states that one's psychological-social experiences are inherent factors that affect one's perception of self and others.
6. Stylistic counseling encourages implementation of an active dimension to the helping professions through clear articulation at the scientific-ideological level.
7. Stylistic counseling requires that the counselor develop a genuine concern and commitment to the client's best interest regardless of cultural differences.
8. Stylistic counseling requires that the counselor develop an ability to open and maintain effective cross-cultural channels of communication.
9. Stylistic counseling requires that the counselor develop the attitude that each client in a counseling situation has a cultural experience unique to the client.
10. Stylistic counseling requires that the counselor develop an active awareness of his or her own attitudes and feelings toward minority individuals and groups.
11. Stylistic counseling requires that the counselor's role become that of an agent and helper within the scope of the client's frame of reference.
12. Stylistic counseling requires that the problem be redefined with emphasis placed on societal responsibility for human dignity and enhancement.

CASE STUDIES

Several counseling situations have been developed to challenge readers to apply their understanding of the stylistic model to a variety of problems that confront clients. Issues related to race, culture, nationality, and gender are introduced, thus offering a spectrum of questions for resolution. The author recommends, if the opportunity permits, that you participate in extensive dialogue with a small group of colleagues to generate broad knowledge about the situations that are of interest to you but also pertinent to transcultural counseling.

SITUATION 1: MARKETING AND COUNSELING FOR WHOM?

Michael Tirada, age 22, was the fourth of eight children born to a Panamanian immigrant family. Very early in life, Michael discovered that both of his parents, now fairly old and never having spoken English, were alcoholics. Despite limited childhood love, care, and attention, Michael appears to be a fine young man, attractive, active, intelligent, and admirable at what he does as manager of marketing for a local grocery store. He describes the life of his parents as simply appalling and dismal.

Michael's personality and career began to gather momentum over time. He sought interpersonal relationships outside the family and tended to attract friends who mirrored his accomplishments and life-style. After joining a local group-counseling session, Michael began to use these same interpersonal dynamics in trying to control others in order that they reflect a positive image of his definition of success to him. Initially, he was worried that the group would ask him to leave when they began to see his self-centeredness. Instead, the group was able to help him become aware of his dysfunctional family background, which needed mending. The group encouraged Michael to explore the source of his problem and to be himself. In fact, the group enjoyed the person who was not always pretending and saw this aspect of Michael's personality as more relaxed, fun-loving, vulnerable, and appealing to know.

Questions

1. How would you as a transcultural counselor facilitate the process and momentum of this growth group?
2. List 10 do's and 10 don'ts in working with Michael and this group, using the stylistic model as a frame of reference.
3. What are some approaches a transcultural counselor could use in providing support for this dysfunctional family?

4. Indicate local agencies that might serve as a referral source for Michael if he wishes to pursue a career change. Document through the stylistic counseling model.

SITUATION 2: CORPORATE INTERVENTION OF THE DIFFERENT

Peter Malimba, an African scholar residing in the United States with his German wife and their three children—Batu, 11, Genemie, 9, and Ursala, 5—is an aspiring executive in a plastic engineering company. Peter has been alleged to have problems with his supervisor, who decided to contact an interventionist and requested that Peter seek counseling. The vice-president of the company indicated that Mr. Malimba has had substance abuse problems. Although Peter's family knew that he enjoyed casual drinking on some occasions, they never saw him intoxicated, nor was the supervisor sure that Peter had a serious problem related to substance abuse. The supervisor could not identify any specific behaviors that impaired job performance. Despite almost nonexistent evidence and perhaps undocumented generalizations, the company chose to proceed with intervention and counseling for Peter. The result was disastrous. Peter, who knew he did not suffer from a substance abuse problem, quickly identified the move as sabotage by his colleagues who desired to see him removed because he was different. Needless to say, Peter was justified in proceeding with a protest against the intervention without a proper background assessment being conducted.

This vignette illustrates the pivotal importance of an accurate assessment of the person's background by a relevant professional before proceeding with any intervention.

Questions

1. Describe generally some cultural-historical, work-oriented values unique to Peter.

2. How might the fact that Peter and his wife have an intercultural marriage affect the psychosocial dynamics of Peter's functioning at the plastic engineering company?

3. What approach would you as the employee counselor at the plastic engineering company use in helping Peter?

4. Trace insights and behaviors influencing the outcome of this case through several cubical columns of the stylistic model.

SITUATION 3: CULTURE OUTSIDE THE MAINSTREAM

Tonka Klugan is a member of one of the small groups of Native Americans in the western part of the United States. Because of the rapid changes that have inundated Tonka's people and the profound and substantive effects these changes have wrought on the fabric of his society, the odds of Tonka's committing suicide before his 25th birthday are higher than average.

Tonka's birthplace in the Southwest, a small reservation, consists mainly of volcanic rocks, shrubs, cacti, and trees. Life is rather mundane in this warm climate. There are very few known natural resources. In response to this dearth of resources, however, Tonka's people developed a culture that was materialistically simple, eminently ecological, and in harmony with its environment. Their main source of protein was animal meat from hunting. They cultivated maize, or corn, which provided their staple diet.

In contrast to their simple material life, Tonka's people developed an intricate system of social relationships suited for living in an otherwise inhospitable environment, with dry, hot summers and cold winters, surrounding a small, neglected rural community. This system was based on an extended family concept and depended largely on a feeling of oneness with others and a sense of cooperation on the part of each family member. Everything belonged to the family in common and was doled out to members of the family by the elected elder or, for matters involving more than one family, by a council of elders. Each person's labor contributed to the welfare of the entire family, not to the accumulation of wealth by an individual or a family.

Disputes were settled within the family. Punishment was normally given in the form of restitution. There was no need for police, courts, or prisons. Children were considered a gift from a higher power and loved by the entire extended family and the whole community. If both parents passed away, children would be welcomed into the home of relatives or even neighbors who would love them and care for them as if they were their own. Obviously, there was no need for orphanages, social workers, or social welfare. Theirs was a hierarchical society with orders flowing downward from the elders to the young while respect flowed upward toward the old and the wise. Older children took on the task of educating and socializing the younger children, and each took on more responsibility as his or her abilities matured. It was a culture that respected age, wisdom, and obedience. Individuality was not encouraged; the welfare of the group was paramount.

Then entered the White man, with his ideals of Christianity, style of clothing, and numerous other life-styles. This Indian group fell under immense outside pressure, resulting in heretofore unheard-of social problems. Unfortunately, this is not a problem unique to Tonka's people. Other minorities in mainstream America find themselves confronted with similar dilemmas, perhaps differing only in degree rather than in kind. Faced with a majority culture that has been historically intolerant of divergent ethnic group values, America's minority groups have had to wage a constant struggle to obtain a fair share of the bounty the country has to offer. Over the years, we have seen American minorities adopt two conflicting attitudes toward a resolution of this problem: assimilation and separation, neither of which has proven to be a satisfactory strategy.

Questions

1. Describe fundamental issues that may be paramount with Tonka and his family on the scientific-ideological dimension of stylistic counseling as they explore problems to be resolved with the help of a transcultural counselor.
2. What are the psychosocial implications for Tonka within the context of his family as he engages in counseling interviews?
3. Discuss ways by which a counselor may ascertain in-depth knowledge of Tonka and his heritage in order to enhance his or her transcultural encounter with this cultural group.
4. What critical role might a transcultural counselor play in this case?

SITUATION 4: YOUNG AT UTOPIA

Nicholas Young is a freshman at Utopia University and is experiencing academic difficulty in four of his six courses. Nicholas does not socialize with either Black or White students at Utopia. Nicholas lives off campus with his maternal grandmother in the inner city, in a housing development area of the city of Utopia.

Nicholas's mother and father died in an auto accident when he was 12 years old. He has lived with his grandmother since then. Nicholas's grandmother works two jobs because she wants him to graduate from college. He works 30 hours a week at the local service station to help with his college expenses. His parents were hard workers, but neither attended college and their savings were meager. The family work ethic has always been strong.

Nicholas's parents wanted him to graduate from college. His grandmother believes college is the key to a bright future. Nicholas is extremely loyal to his grandmother and the memory of his parents. He fears that he will fail in college, for this would be a disappointment to his grandmother, to himself, and to the memory of his parents. Nicholas decides to seek assistance from the counseling center and is assigned to a counselor who is a 53-year-old White male. Nicholas is somewhat hesitant about meeting with Dr. Phillips, the counselor, but decides that he needs to try to get some help.

When using the stylistic model to intervene in Nicholas's crisis, Dr. Phillips needs first to become familiar with aspects of Nicholas's cultural-historical development. This information will allow the counselor to see where Nicholas came from, what his racial/ethnic identity is, and how this identity may influence his interactions with other students and faculty. Because of Nicholas's limited exposure outside of his community and to persons other than his grandmother, he may not feel self-assured enough to reach out to other students or to family for support. Because he returns to the same environment each day after class, he may not have the time or opportunity to develop the social skills that would enhance his adjustment in the university setting. Yet his love for his grandmother and his desire to go to college for his parents' sake may continue to force him into a strange environment regardless of his apprehension and discomfort.

If Dr. Phillips can effectively extract essential information from Nicholas, he may be able to help Nicholas enhance his self-esteem and adjustment. Directing Nicholas toward financial assistance would decrease his hours of working. Additional hours would allow for more study time, perhaps with a tutor. This approach could increase Nicholas's involvement in the campus environment. And, perhaps, feeling some success with academic work would free Nicholas to begin to expand his social skills.

Questions

1. What stylistic knowledge and skills would Dr. Phillips have to demonstrate in working with Nicholas to be considered a transcultural counselor?
2. With which cubical descriptors does financial assistance correlate? How?
3. Discuss the loss of Nicholas's parents relative to family patterns, personality formation, and meaningful alternatives.
4. If you were a colleague of Dr. Phillips at Utopia University, what form of encouragement could you provide for the transcultural counselor?

SITUATION 5: NO PROSECUTION BY MR. YANG

A Chinese doctoral student, Mr. Lee Yang, was struck on the head and seriously injured on his way back to his apartment on campus at the beginning of the spring semester. He remained in the hospital for 1 month, spending approximately $1,200 of his own money in medical care fees. Since his release from the hospital, he has frequent headaches and experiences a great deal of dizziness. Nobody claims that he is responsible for this physical condition. Lee does not want to prosecute his attacker, but he has become depressed emotionally and is inactive in pursuing legal alternatives. Many people aware of his situation have asked why he chose not to prosecute to receive some type of compensation. Though Lee does not consult anyone, you, as a transcultural counselor, should be prepared to analyze this case. Why did he keep silent?

Questions

1. What are the legal and ethical implications for the transcultural counselor?
2. How might stylistic counseling be applied to Lee Yang's case?
3. How can a transcultural counselor use the stylistic counseling model in identifying referral sources for him?
4. What are the limitations of working with Lee solely on the scientific-ideological dimension?

SITUATION 6: THE PRICE OF A HIGHER EDUCATION

Ida Atanes, an African-American female, is a freshman at the University of the State. She is extremely bright and is doing very well in her classes. Before college, she never had been out of Miami, Florida. Now, Ida is exposed to a different culture; she is challenged to think and speak openly about concerns as well as to interact with fellow students. She has hopes of becoming a lawyer. Ida's grandmother feels that she should forget about school and return home to help out. Ida comes seeking counseling.

Begin by exploring the cultural-historical dimension and the values cubical descriptor: Ida needs to explore her values, those developed at an early age and the new outlook and values she now has adopted. Are they congruent? How are these new values incorporated? How have her values molded her? Much has to be explored in this area—Ida needs to explore how her culture affects her goals.

Now explore the psychosocial dimension and the self-exploration cubical descriptor: Ida, with assistance from the counselor, must now explore herself and who she is. This stage is crucial because she must feel secure with herself before she can make decisions concerning her dilemma. Is she comfortable with herself? Does she trust herself to make meaningful choices?

Finally, explore the scientific-ideological dimension and the individual goals cubical descriptor: Ida must establish goals for herself. In this case, it may be difficult to disengage from her grandmother, setting significant goals for herself. Her first goal could be to finish a semester and agree to visit home one weekend per month to help out. Her advisor also helped her to obtain a part-time job at a law office (answering the telephone, filing, etc.) to make extra money. Ida is hoping to convince her grandmother to allow her to remain in college. If her grandmother objects, Ida feels secure enough with herself to continue her education.

This approach allowed Ida to lay the foundation upon which to build her goals. The stylistic counseling model could be effective in that it allows the client to explore areas that are of concern but have also aided in her development—to appreciate her culture and values and to understand the impact of these areas on her life.

Questions

1. Develop your approach as a transcultural counselor to helping Ida enhance her academic performance and cultural orientation at the University of the State.
2. Identify experiences that you have had which enhance your understanding of Ida's dilemma.
3. Cite cubical columns in the stylistic counseling model that relate most to Ida's being female and African American.
4. What actions could you implement in pursuing family counseling on behalf of Ida?

SITUATION 7: SHOULD RON JUSTICE BE GRANTED PROMOTION?

Ron Justice, a Black male, was denied a promotion at his job of 10 years. David Johnson, a young White male, was given the promotion after being at the company for only 2 years. Ron perceives the incident as being racist, and he is very angry, resentful, and frustrated. He knows that he has been on the job longer and has more experience, but David has more education.

First, the employee counselor handling this case examines the cultural-historical level, beginning with oppression. Ron's experience, like that of other Blacks, has been one of oppression. The counselor wants to acknowledge this and help Ron move from the cultural-historical level to the psychosocial one of understanding his being in more depth, his psychological identity, and how to concentrate on his own feelings. The counselor wishes to help Ron feel better about himself and to advise him of ways of building an inner strength to cope with similar incidents in the future. A subsequent step is to examine the logical behavior chain on the scientific-ideological dimension, where he decides to re-enroll in school and further his education in order that in his present job, or a future job, he will be able to use his experience and expand his education for a position at a more satisfying level. He could feel better about himself as he achieves his personal goals and works within the system.

Questions

1. As Ron seeks insight into his case, on which dimension should the employee counselor concentrate—cultural-historical, psychosocial, or scientific-ideological?

2. In applying the stylistic counseling model to this case, would you involve David? If so, how?

3. Describe the interrelationship between politics and transcultural counseling with the stylistic counseling model as a frame of reference.

4. What specific steps would you recommend that the employee counselor follow in moving Ron from an affective mode to one of action?

SITUATION 8: CARLOS LOPEZ TRIES TO FIT IN

Carlos Lopez, a Hispanic male, is starting a new job at a predominantly White company. Despite his efforts to fit in and be liked by his co-workers, he is unsuccessful. He seeks counseling after experiencing feelings of inadequacy. The counselor begins at an early stage by examining the cultural-historical dimension, specifically the cubical descriptor of ethnic discrimination. It is important to understand the history as well as the social and economic factors that may be playing a role in Carlos's problems. Ethnic discrimination leads to ethnic identity at the psychosocial level. Helping Carlos decide who he is enhances positive ethnic relations, which interfaces at the scientific-ideological level. Another dimension is dynamics of oppression at the cultural-historical level. This may or may not have an effect on Carlos's psychological security at the psychosocial level. Security leads to logic-behavioral chains at the scientific-ideological level for Carlos.

Carlos finds it necessary to separate his cultural values from those of his White co-workers as he strives for an opportunity to fit in at the company. Carlos has to decide who he is and what he really wants.

Questions

1. How can you as a transcultural counselor help Carlos?

2. Identify three cubical columns from the stylistic counseling model and discuss their application to Carlos.

3. What probable dilemmas might Carlos encounter as he seeks to fit in?

4. Describe the social, political, and economic assets Carlos might bring to this company from his cultural background.

REFERENCES

McFadden, J. (1983). Stylistic counseling of the Black family. *Black marriage and family therapy.* Westport, CT: Greenwood.

McFadden, J. (1987). The essence of communicating values to children in a multi-ethnic climate. *The many faces of teaching* (pp. 373–375). Washington, DC: University Press of America.

McFadden, J. (1988a). Cross-cultural counseling: The international context. *Journal of Multicultural Counseling and Development, 16*(1), 36–40.

McFadden, J. (1988b) (Guest Ed.). From awareness to action. *Journal of Multicultural Counseling and Development, 16*(1), 2.

Sue, D. W. (1981). *Counseling the culturally different.* New York: Wiley.

CHAPTER 4

TRANSCENDENT COUNSELING: A TRANSCULTURAL THEORY

FREDERICK D. HARPER AND WINIFRED O. STONE

Transcendent counseling first appeared in the literature during the mid-1970s as a theory for counseling African Americans (Harper & Stone, 1974). Since its origin, transcendent counseling has been transformed, with the changing times, into a transcultural or multi-cultural theory of counseling—having universal applications and value for many different cultural groups (Harper & Stone, 1986).

During the early development of transcendent counseling, we were repeatedly confronted by questions from practitioners concerning typology or classification of the theory: "Is it more of a behavioral or humanistic model, or something else?" Although we have not sought nor do we seek to classify transcendent counseling under one of the traditional theoretical schools of counseling or within a taxonomy or typology of traditionalism, we would, in helping persons get a handle on its applications, now like to believe that transcendent counseling is more closely related to concepts and themes of both existential psychotherapy and cognitive-behavioral approaches—that is, existential in terms of its concept of transcending one's culture and one's life-style, and cognitive-behavioral with regard to thought-altering verbal techniques and action-oriented training modalities for life-style modification.

Transcendent counseling maintains that it is the person's life-style or how the person lives that influences and maintains behavior;

that is, behavior that can be (a) ineffective, negative, destructive, or unhappy, on the one hand, or (b) effective, positive, constructive, and happy, on the other. For example, it is a life-style of frequent, heavy drinking of alcohol that leads to alcoholism and its consequences. Only when the alcoholic changes his or her life-style will that person cease to suffer from the numerous psychophysiological symptoms of alcoholism as a disease, as well as alcoholism's social and economic consequences. Therefore, the goal of transcendent counseling would be to change the life-style of frequent, heavy drinking to help the person transcend the alcoholic life-style and culture of drinking.

As a caveat, transcendent counseling does not ignore that genetic predisposition can sometimes influence or contribute to life-style, as with some alcoholics. Along the same line, another example is a person with a neurochemical predisposition for heightened appetite that can contribute to a life-style centered around frequent or heavy meals, a life-style that can lead to behaviors of obesity, low self-esteem, and guilt. Although this type of person may find more difficulty in weight control than the average person, such a problem of counseling is not beyond the realistic goal of transcendence because modifiable cultural and cognitive factors also contribute to obesity.

In other words, we often adopt a life-style over time that results primarily from genetic predisposition, perceptions of cultural experiences, or the interaction of both. With this presupposition, the goal of transcendent counseling becomes to change the client's life-style or way of living.

The purpose of this chapter is to discuss transcendent counseling with regard to its (a) assumptions and major concepts, (b) goals, (c) steps and techniques, and (d) applications and implications. The chapter also presents vignettes of therapeutic cases that may help the reader understand how transcendent counseling can be used in the actual counseling milieu.

ASSUMPTIONS AND CONCEPTS

Any theoretical model sets forth a peculiar set of concepts and interrelated assumptions that are conceptualized into a whole framework of thought. Transcendent counseling posits the following assumptions about the nature of humankind and the dynamics of the counseling relationship:

1. Counseling is a learning experience wherein clients learn to change the way they live and the way they see the world.

2. Lasting change in the client's behavior comes with a change in life-style. The life-style of the client is influenced mainly by genetic predisposition and perceptions of cultural experiences. One's culture is one's way of life as it evolves over time, place, experiences, and social class. A person's basic cultural set or orientation is developed during the formative years of youth; however, it continues to evolve with cross-cultural and cross-social-class experiences. Fromm (1941) speaks of this common cultural orientation as one's "social character," defined as attributes and behaviors common to a given culture. It is not just cultural experiences that influence one's life-style or behavior, but also one's perceptions of those experiences.

3. Cultural socialization creates a common social character for people of a particular culture, while simultaneously creating differences from people of other cultures. Cultural differences are often represented by life-style differences in terms of daily activities, customs, habits, language patterns, and ritualistic ways. These life-style activities are influenced by learned thought and, in turn, can serve to reinforce ways of thinking in terms of a person's attitudes, beliefs, values, and perceptions.

4. Although human beings differ across cultures by life-style and worldview, we have the same basic needs, drives, emotions, and capacity for thought (Maslow, 1970).

5. As biological and social organisms, we are limited by our inherent human frailty and vulnerability; nonetheless, we are capable of transcendence and self-improvement.

6. As human beings, we are relatively fixed in a daily life-style. However, we are capable of changing that life-style toward a direction of self-improvement and ultimate transcendence of a socialized and often ineffective way of living. This assumption is further explained by the seven subordinate "we" assumptions that follow:

   - WE tend to do today what we did yesterday, and we likely will do tomorrow what we do today.

- *WE* do what we do until we perceive the need to do differently, a need often precipitated by a crisis or insight through cognitive reorganization.

- *WE* do what we do until we acquire the willpower to do what we must do.

- *WE* and only we can change our lives; nobody can do it for us, for we and only we are the masters of our own energy, our own vessels of life.

- Unless *WE* change, we are destined to live our miseries over and over in our minds and in our experiences. If we change, we will discover the fulfillment, happiness, and peace that come with existential choice and action.

- *WE* cannot know what true happiness is until we experience it. We experience happiness by seeking it; we experience pain by letting it capture us.

- *WE* are nobody until we feel like somebody. Life remains an empty shell until we fill it with meaningful experiences worthy of our memories and our living.

7. Regardless of one's cultural background or ethnic identity, the "good life" can be universally defined as a life-style characterized by (a) holistic health, (b) meaningful activity or work, (c) positive self-management of one's energy, and (d) a healthy, respectful, and homeostatic relationship with life and life's spiritual source.

8. Presenting behaviors that come to counseling are often interrelated in a mosaic pattern that has developed over time. The route to changing patterns of behavior is through a sustainable change in one's life-style (i.e., one's daily or weekly habits, activities, and orientations). This road to positive change of life-style takes time, patience, and consistency and is not free from human frustration and resignation.

9. Behaviors to a great degree are need-driven and mood-driven and even programmed over time as automatic responses. Nevertheless, the human being is capable of self-control (stopping and pacing behavior) and self-initiation (starting and maintaining behavior). This possibility for change comes with new ways

of perceiving and relating to one's world from day to day and, thus, new ways of acting and living.

10. Insight, cognitive reorganization, willpower, and action make up the orderly sequence of human change. However, the most frightening phase of the chain is action, because action connotes the unknown or escape from the known.

11. A person's most powerful resource is the existential choice to change, the will to change, and the capacity to act—that is, to transcend social forces and human imperfections to a higher level of fulfillment, health, and human functioning.

GOALS OF COUNSELING

The goals of transcendent counseling are governed by the nature of the presenting concerns of the client coupled with assessment and diagnostic information from the intake interview concerning the client's life-style. The categories of transcendent goals are as follows.

NEED FULFILLMENT

The goal of need fulfillment refers to the basic needs common to all human beings regardless of culture or ethnic origin. They include the need for physical maintenance and survival, safety and security, affiliation and sense of belonging, love, self-adequacy or esteem, and development of one's common and peculiar potential or talent. In great part, this grouping of needs is based on Maslow's (1970) theory of personality and human motivation. It is our belief that the ease or difficulty of fulfilling basic needs by the client is influenced by that client's ethnic, social-class, political, or religious status within a given culture or country.

LIFE-STYLE CHANGE

The goal of life-style change involves assessing the client's present life-style and subsequently substituting positive or more effective activities or ways of living for negative or destructive ones. The judgment of what is the good or effective life-style is based on universal knowledge of health, happiness, and peace. Examples of frequent activities (day-to-day or week-to-week) and habits attributable to ineffective and effective life-styles follow.

Activities of Ineffective Life-Styles	Activities of Effective Life-Styles
Sedentary orientation/living	Physical work, sport/recreation, exercise
High-stress orientation (hurrying, overreacting, excessive talking vs. thinking, limited rest/relaxation)	Low-stress orientation (pacing activities, organizing activities, self-control, thinking vs. reacting, sufficient rest)
Poor eating habits	Healthy eating habits
Use or inappropriate use of alcohol and other drugs	Nonuse of tobacco and illicit drugs, appropriate and limited use of other drugs (e.g., alcohol and medicinal drugs)

MEANINGFUL WORK OR ACTIVITY

This goal includes a meaningful job that yields self-fulfillment as well as a useful service or product for other human beings or the enhancement of the world ecology. This goal also includes (a) any meaningful leisure activity for one's own happiness or self-fulfillment, (b) volunteer work as service to the community or the environment, and (c) training, education, travel, or any learning experience for personal growth and development.

HOLISTIC HEALTH

In transcendent counseling, holistic health is defined as a state of physical, psychological, and spiritual health developed primarily from a life-style of wellness, disease prevention, and a respect for life and Earth's resources. Transcendent holistic health is further characterized by a sense of peace, well-being, intermittent states of euphoria, meaning, fulfillment, and maximal all-around health. It is a welding together of the mind, the body, and the spirit into one synergistic balance characterized by a constant state of well-being of the organism as a whole.

THE TRANSCENDENT BEING OF THE COUNSELOR

The transcendent counselor comes to counseling with a healthy attitude about self and clients.

1. The transcendent counselor believes that all clients, regardless of culture, ethnicity, social class, or gender, are equally worthy of help, growth, and holistic health to the greatest extent possible. Therefore, the transcendent counselor attempts to understand and help while avoiding bias against and invalid judgment about the client as a member of any predefined group.

2. The transcendent counselor attempts to understand the client as a unique person and not as a stereotypical cultural image—although culture may play a part in helping the counselor understand and address the client's problem.

3. The transcendent counselor perceives the counseling relationship as an opportunity for professional self-growth in cultural and human understanding. Therefore, the counseling relationship becomes an experience from which both the client and the counselor grow.

4. The transcendent counselor pursues the overall goal of helping the client change his or her life-style with relative permanence.

5. The transcendent counselor possesses the same ideals for himself or herself as for the client—that is, ideals of holistic health and transcendence. Having these ideals, the transcendent counselor is more qualified to present himself or herself as a positive social model for imitation and inspiration.

6. The transcendent counselor serves as information giver, facilitator, motivator, social model, and group trainer.

7. The transcendent counselor believes in the capacity of all human beings, regardless of culture, to develop to the highest level of their potential and capabilities.

8. The transcendent counselor views healthy ethnic identity as approximating or attaining a panethnic view of the world or an acceptance of oneself as a member of a world culture of humanity. The counselor values the positive ways, customs, habits, and achievements of his or her culture of origin and rejects or transcends those that are nonproductive and destructive. The transcendent counselor also encourages clients to use this same type of cultural analysis for themselves and their growth.

STEPS OF TRANSCENDENT COUNSELING

The five steps of transcendent counseling are represented by the acronym APART, which corresponds to assessment, prescription, action, review, and transcendence. Also, the APART acronym emphasizes the need to grow *apart* from the old self or old life-style to a new self identity and a new way of living.

STEP 1: ASSESSMENT

In this initial step of the counseling relationship, the transcendent counselor establishes rapport with the client and assesses the client's problem or concern. The counselor focuses on the life-style and the daily habits of the client. Moreover, the counselor enlists the client to express concerns about things the client would like to change.

Along with a focused or structured interview, the counselor might use other assessment instruments or techniques such as (a) a *dual listing and sorting* of life-style activities that would include a listing and prioritizing of daily activities and habits the client would like to stop or minimize (on the left side of a sheet) and things the client would like to start or maximize (on the right side) or (b) *standardized instruments* for assessing life-style or life-style activities.

After an assessment of the client's concerns and perceived needs for life-style change, the counselor attempts to categorize these concerns and needs into one or more modules. A *module* represents an area of living. For each module, there are related modalities for life-style change. The six modules of transcendent counseling are described later in this chapter.

STEP 2: PRESCRIPTION

After the counselor assesses the client's current life-style, goals of counseling and a prescription of intervention activities are derived for life-style modification. The prescription usually results in additional scheduled individual counseling sessions for the primary purpose of information giving as well as facilitating, motivating, and monitoring action by the client. The prescription may also provide for activities such as homework, training modalities (e.g., relaxation training, meditation, and biofeedback), and group counseling activities (e.g., role-playing, nonverbal exercises, and psychodrama). In prescribing activities for life-style modification, the counselor involves the client in the development of the program and its activities and solicits a sense of commitment for action and follow-through.

STEP 3: ACTION

Carkhuff & Berenson (1977) note that the client moves from exploration to understanding to action in effecting change. Nicholson and Golsan (1983) also emphasize the importance of client action in finalizing change in behavior or life.

Whereas traditional counseling theories have tended to focus on change of behavior, transcendent counseling emphasizes the client's change in life-style through action. The client's action is based on the prescribed program or activities of Step 2, and involves motivation, support, and necessary information giving from the counselor to enhance the client's progress. If appropriate, the counselor attempts to serve as a model or to expose the client to successful models of life-style change. Moreover, the counselor anticipates barriers, pitfalls, and problems of life-style change, follows the client's actions and activities closely, and encourages a record of daily and weekly changes in life-style activities. (A complete record of activities and successes is kept by both the client and the counselor.)

STEP 4: REVIEW

Step 4 entails an evaluation or review of the client's progress based on preestablished goals of Step 1. The evaluation is summative as well as ongoing. If there is insufficient success by preestablished criteria of progress, the counselor and client may have to recycle to a previous stage in order to reassess a prescribed activity chosen or a goal (Step 2). This recycling and reassessment is for the purpose of possibly revising goal statements or modalities and techniques for change.

STEP 5: TRANSCENDENCE

Transcendence is evidenced by a significant change in a specific area or module of the client's life to a point at which it seems that the change will be maintained and sustained over time. Follow-up, after termination of counseling, is required to minimize the chance of relapse to a previous life-style.

THE COUNSELING PROCESS:
RELATIONSHIP AND TECHNIQUES

Transcendent counseling takes the position that thoughts drive not only behavior but life-style or daily activities. Therefore, the counseling process aims to persuade the client to change ways of thinking and thus ways of living. The counselor goes about changing the client's ways of thinking and living by (a) teaching the client to say "I won't" and not "I can't," (b) initially persuading the client to make an expressed commitment to change one significant thing in his or her daily living and intermittently soliciting an expression of recommitment if necessary (the counselor emphasizes incremental changes), (c) motivating the client to act on that expression of commitment, and (d) guiding the client to focus on the two W's—*what* and *when,*—that is, "*What* are you going to do about your life, and *when* are you going to do it?"

In reference to *won't* and *can't,* these counseling concepts force the client to confront the reality that he or she is using *can't* as an excuse or defense for inaction, when the client really should be saying "I won't change" and not "I can't change my life." This dichotomy of terminology (*won't* versus *can't*) further suggests that people often know what they need to do but are not willing to do it. As an example, thousands, if not millions, of persons often end up yearly making New Year's resolutions that are broken from the start. We tend to tell ourselves that changing our lives is much too hard, and eventually we resign to the cognition of "I can't."

The counselor's modus operandi is to orient the client to think about initiating something new and constructive in daily living and eliminating something old and destructive. Constructive habits in life are based on activities that are valued for health, interpersonal effectiveness and fulfillment, personal growth and development, achievement based on one's talent and ability, and harmonious living with Earth's life and ecology. While holding important these universal values of the human culture, the counselor also takes into consideration the client's cultural perceptions about what is the good and constructive life-style. In working with the client, the counselor maintains a respect for the client as a human being and not a physical image that represents preconceived and predefined attributes of personality, gender, culture, social class, or educational level. Moreover, the counselor believes in the client as a person who is capable of changing his or her way of living and, therefore, holds high expectations for the client's possibilities while being patient and recognizing that relatively permanent change takes time.

The counselor's rapport and effective helping relationship is facilitated by his or her orientation to continually (a) grow as a person; (b) maintain a state of peace and balance as much as possible; (c) strive toward a healthy self in mind, body, and spirit; and (d) maintain a constant orientation of helping and giving.

The transcendent counselor primarily employs verbal counseling techniques that can be divided into three categories: supportive techniques, teaching techniques, and action-provoking and action-sustaining techniques.

SUPPORTIVE TECHNIQUES

- *Approval:* Verbal reward, agreement, or observation for a positive expression of commitment or a positive act completed.

- *Reassurance:* A verbal expression of comfort or support during a difficult or painful moment in counseling or a difficult period in life.

- *Encouragement:* A verbal expression of support during an ongoing pursuit of a difficult goal or challenge.

TEACHING TECHNIQUES

- *Information giving:* Providing the client with basic verbal information about living; also providing any helpful information related to the client's concerns or life-style goals.

- *Modeling:* Using various techniques of social modeling as learning tools, including covert modeling, vicarious modeling, bibliocounseling (or bibliotherapy), personal illustration, impersonal illustration, and modeling through imagery. The purpose is to use positive or successful social models to inspire the client to imitate the behavior of the model, whether the model is real or vicarious. Although appropriate models are not always available, the counselor considers the use of models that reflect a client's ethnic or cultural image or a client's gender. Again, the purpose is to get the client to change toward improving his or her life-style or way of living.

- *Advice giving:* Providing options, courses of action, or solutions for the client's consideration. The counselor solicits the client's feedback and opinions, especially as related to that client's cultural and experiential viewpoint. This exchange becomes a learning experience for the client's decision making rather than a telling experience of a tunnel-visioned counselor with limited answers for multicultural situations.

ACTION-PROVOKING AND ACTION-SUSTAINING TECHNIQUES

- *Motivating:* Providing verbal motivation as a means of persuading the client to start or stop an activity or habit or to maintain an activity or habit once started.
- *Confrontation:* Confronting a client who is consistently resistant or in denial, in a nonthreatening manner, to free anxiety that blocks awareness and action. The client will often provide illogical reasons for procrastinating or avoiding action necessary for growth and change.

MODULES AND MODALITIES OF CHANGE

MODULES OF LIVING

Transcendent counseling theorizes that there are six major areas of living, referred to as *modules* of living. These six modules represent rubrics under which the client's problems or concerns may fall: (a) eating orientation, (b) exercise versus sedentary living, (c) human/ethnic relations, (d) knowledge of living, (e) meaningful and productive work or activity, and (f) self-regulation. These modules of living are described below:

- *Eating orientation* represents concerns related to proper nutrition, optimal caloric management, and individualized diets. The client's presented concerns may relate to eating disorders, obesity, lack of money for proper nutrition, and moods or psychophysiological reactions related to different foods and chemicals within foods.
- *Exercise versus sedentary living* is related to concerns about a life-style of either physical activity or sedentary living. Transcendent counseling values a life-style of regular, vigorous

exercise over one of inactivity, which can result in health problems and mood problems. As an alternative to sedentary living, transcendent counseling advocates regular, sustained physical efforts, such as walking, jogging, swimming, dancing, aerobics, and weight exercises. At least one nonstop, nonspasmodic, or aerobic exercise is recommended in one's life to improve and maintain cardiovascular and respiratory health and provide the psychological benefits of relaxation and resistance to stress.

- *Human/ethnic relations* focuses on areas of human living related to interpersonal effectiveness, human relations, and ethnic relations (including race relations). Problems and concerns of counseling represented within this module would include family conflict, job-related interpersonal conflict, romantic-relations conflict, intergroup conflict (racial, ethnic, age, etc.), and teacher-student conflict.

- *Knowledge of living* represents problems and potential problems in life related to a lack of information or a lack of valid and effective knowledge. This knowledge or know-how can include information, attitudes, values, and skills acquired via the counselor, training, reading, and other media. Knowledge about quality and effective living is for both resolving problems or indecision and maximizing the client's potential and growth.

- *Meaningful and productive work or activity* suggests that the holistically healthy person must have some work that is productive and/or meaningful. Lack of such activity creates a void in one's life-style that can result in a sense of emptiness, lowered self-esteem, and unworthiness. This work or activity should provide fulfillment for the person in some way, a product for or service to society, or preparation for a future occupation or endeavor. Examples of productive work or meaningful activity include higher education, occupational training, volunteer work, career work, and avocations or hobbies.

- *Self-regulation* involves an area of living that affects all human beings, regardless of culture or ethnicity. It relates to the person's ongoing effort to regulate or manage his or her energy in terms of (a) achieving or maintaining organismic balance, peace, or equilibrium, (b) energizing the self for work or activity, and (c) relaxing or slowing down body energy because of stress or extreme anxiety.

MODALITIES OF COUNSELING

Along with facilitative verbal techniques of interpersonal counseling, modalities are additional methods or adjuncts to counseling, mainly treatment-training adjuncts, employed to facilitate life-style changes. The modalities discussed in this section are those recommended for given modules or areas of concern in counseling. Nonetheless, the counselor should not limit his or her creativity in using or developing other modalities that could be effective in changing the client's life-style.

For example, client problems of extreme reactions to stress and wasted time in daily living would fall under the module of self-regulation and would incorporate modalities of stress reduction such as relaxation training or meditation. One or both of these modalities can be incorporated into the client's life-style through a formal group (meditation or relaxation group) or via individualized homework between counseling sessions after the client learns relaxation techniques or meditation techniques. The counselor may also suggest daily techniques for learning new habits of time management to address the problem of wasted time.

The following outline lists the six modules of transcendent counseling and suggested modalities for each module:

- *Eating orientation:* Self-help groups, bibliocounseling, information groups.
- *Exercise versus sedentary living:* Activity groups or individualized exercise programs (e.g., jogging, dancing, swimming, walking, aerobic exercises, biking).
- *Human/ethnic relations:* Psychodrama, sociodrama, role-playing, rehearsal, bibliocounseling, interpersonal effectiveness training, group counseling, ethnic relations training, academic courses in multicultural education and ethnic studies, and homework assignments for cross-ethnic experiences.
- *Knowledge of living:* Bibliocounseling, information groups, orientation programs, values orientation groups, attitudinal exploration groups, health education workshops, various seminars and groups related to living.

- *Meaningful and productive work/activity:* Career information groups, career practicum experience, volunteer experiences, occupational or avocational training, career planning.
- *Self-regulation:* Biofeedback, meditation, relaxation training, hypnosis or self-hypnosis, other energy-management training exercises.

ETHNIC AND CULTURAL IDENTITY

In an increasingly multiethnic and multicultural world, there is a developing concern in counseling for topics of effective ethnic relations and ethnic identity development (Carter & Helms, 1992; Cross, 1971, 1980; Helms, 1989; Smith, 1991). Most of the identity models of these authors suggest that as the client or counselor moves from accepting his or her own ethnicity of origin to accepting other cultures or ethnicities, that person moves toward cultural maturity or transculturalism (i.e., going beyond one's own culture).

Transcendent counseling accounts for problems and concerns of ethnic identity, ethnic identity development, and ethnic relations within its modules of human/ethnic relations and knowledge of living, described earlier. These two modules provide for cultural and ethnic growth through therapeutic-skills training and information giving.

Figure 4 explains the major identity phases applicable to all ethnic groups. For earlier presentations and discussions of this ethnic model of development, see Stone (1975, 1984) and Harper and Stone (1986).

For the effective counselor or practitioner, understanding the five phases of ethnic development can significantly affect the outcome and quality of counseling service provided. To aid in understanding the paradigm, Spielberger, Gorsuch, and Luschene's (1969) state-trait anxiety theory is helpful as an explanation. It is proposed that ethnic identity, like anxiety, has state and trait qualities. For example, the state quality reveals how we feel about our ethnic identity from moment to moment. This quality is volatile and may change frequently. Accordingly, it may also influence the client's perception of self as well as the environment. The trait quality reveals how we generally feel about our ethnic identity. This quality is more stable and less affected by individual incidents in the

> ### PHASE 5: PANETHNICITY

The person demonstrates a transcendent world view. There is an inclination to view himself or herself as a member of ethnic groups of the world; there is a sense of sharing a common world culture as well as that of his or her unique culture. ↑↓

> ### PHASE 4: TRANSETHNICITY

The person exhibits a tendency to move across or beyond his or her ethnic group or culture to significantly experience others. ↑↓

> ### PHASE 3: ETHNOSYNCRETISM

The person accepts new ideas about his or her ethnicity and culture, and at the same time accepts new ideas and practices from other cultures, without sacrificing his or her own cultural identity. ↑↓

> ### PHASE 2: ETHNOCENTRISM

The person believes in the inherent superiority of his or her ethnic group. There is a tendency to view various or other ethnic groups as inferior. ↑↓

> ### PHASE 1: ETHNOENTROPY

The person tends to be alienated from his or her own ethnic identity or ethnic group of origin. There is a tendency to avoid other ethnic groups or other cultures when possible.

FIGURE 4. A paradigm of multiethnic phases of development

environment. The state-trait principle of ethnic development is represented by the up and down arrows between levels of the five phases of development in Figure 1. These pairs of arrows indicate that identity has dynamic or static qualities that change depending on environmental conditions and circumstances.

The paradigm of ethnic identity development that employs state and trait identity may help the counselor and client understand the appropriateness or inappropriateness of ethnic identity qualities and responses.

Subsequently, the counselor, upon identifying the trait and state phases of ethnic identity, can select appropriate counseling techniques and strategies to enhance the probability of achieving desired outcomes.

Within the paradigm, some additional observations and cautions are warranted for optimal use of the model, especially if the assessment involves the trait quality of ethnic identity in Phases 1 and 2. Counseling implications for each phase of the paradigm follow:

1. *Phase 1: Ethnoentropy.* The prognosis for progress within the framework of individual counseling is minimal. However, if the client continues with counseling over a significant period of time, cross-cultural group sessions may offer the greatest promise. If the client is terminated early in the individual counseling relationship, he or she may be referred to a group on the theme of ethnic relations.

2. *Phase 2: Ethnocentrism.* The prognosis for progress is improved. Individual and group counseling techniques may be effective in achieving desired goals. Also, information groups and ethnic relations training may be considered.

3. *Phase 3: Ethnosyncretism.* This phase appears to be the one selected by most college students as ideal. Clients in this phase are considered healthy; however, they are often interested in feeling more comfortable with their own ethnic identity and ethnic group vis-à-vis seeking experiences with other ethnic groups. They often assume that they are liberal and have learned enough about other ethnicities for now. In this case the counseling encourages ongoing cross-cultural learning via

books (bibliocounseling), academic courses, group experiences, travel, field experiences, and other methods.

4. *Phase 4: Transethnicity.* Problems of rejection by one's own ethnic group may be encountered when significant contact and interface are maintained with another ethnic group. One may be rejected by both ones own ethnic group and the interfacing group. Increased support by the counselor and the development of awareness by the client are realistic areas of focus for counseling.

5. *Phase 5: Panethnicity.* This phase of ethnic identity represents transcendence on the part of the individual. Approximate states of self-actualization and self-realization are observed and readily apparent in the life-style. However, it appears that after individuals have been recognized nationally or internationally, this status is assigned to them by multiethnic groups of the world. At this phase, the client (a) realizes a state of comfort with human beings regardless of ethnicity or culture, (b) is comfortable with knowing and appreciating his or her own ethnic identity of origin, and (c) is not affected by the negative ethnic reactions, rejections, or comments of others. This person has reached the highest level of ethnic maturity and is no longer in need of counseling related to concerns of ethnic identity or development.

The paradigm of multiethnic phases of development is useful as a counseling framework when assessing counseling clients with ethnic identity concerns. Nevertheless, further research regarding the five phases of development is recommended with a variety of cultural and ethnic populations.

CASE STUDIES

The following are two brief summaries of cases as examples of how transcendent counseling works. These summaries represent real cases that have been modified to protect clients' privacy. The summaries do not represent ideals for imitation, but are simply examples for further explaining the principles and techniques of transcendent counseling.

A FAILING COLLEGE STUDENT

Eduardo was a Mexican-American second-semester college fresh-man who presented himself for counseling related to his academic probation. Eduardo was referred by the academic advisement center and had the challenge of pulling his academic grade point average up by the end of the semester to avoid being dismissed from college.

Eduardo's explanations for his poor academic achievement were that two Anglo teachers discriminated against him because he was Mexican American, that he got to his 8:00 a.m. class late each morning because his alarm clock was broken, and that he could not study in the evenings because his male friends in the residence hall persuaded him to play the game machines until late at night.

The transcendent counselor realized that Eduardo was giving illogical reasons for his failure to be academically responsible and thus proceeded with Step 1 (assessment) to further examine and evaluate Eduardo's life-style. The counselor found that Eduardo got up around 7:30 a.m. on mornings when he had an 8:00 a.m. class and ended up rushing to class and arriving late. Moreover, Eduardo was hanging out with friends at the university union during free time between classes, never spending time in the library or study halls. At the end of the day, he usually ate dinner at the university union and returned to his residence hall, where he played games on the machines or just sat around talking and joking with his friends. On nights before an announced quiz, Eduardo reported waiting until the last minute (usually late at night or early in the morning of the day of the quiz) to study or cram.

After inquiring into and assessing the client's daily activities and explaining how these contributed to his academic problem, the counselor commenced to set goals and prescribe (Step 2) ways Eduardo could change his life-style to improve his academic per-formance. With the client's expression of commitment, the plan for action (Step 3) was for the client to make two immediate life-style changes after the first counseling session: (a) to buy an alarm clock and set it for 6:30 a.m. on the mornings of his 8:00 a.m. class, and (b) to go to the library for 1 hour each day before returning to his residence hall in the evening. (The purpose of these two modest goals was to allow for initial successes and gradual changes in life-style.)

During the second and third counseling sessions, Eduardo reported improvements; however, he continued to be late to class on a few occasions. Although he studied more, he continued to waste valuable time that could have contributed to academic progress and quality living. Immediately after the third counseling session, with Eduardo's permission, the counselor arranged for Eduardo to join a study habits and skills group held in the university counseling center. This group, in time, proved very helpful to Eduardo in his academic progress and daily study habits.

Around the sixth counseling session, with the counselor's consistent motivating, persuading, and evaluating (Step 4), Eduardo had gradually changed his daily activities to studying at least 4 hours a day (2 hours between classes in the library and 2 hours in the evening at his residence hall). At the end of the semester, the client received his grades and barely made enough points to pull his overall grade point average up in order to remain in school into his sophomore year.

To survive in college, Eduardo actually had to change daily habits of life or what he did from day to day. This was one of the most difficult things for Eduardo to do, as he reported. The counselor elicited a commitment to action from this client and monitored the daily changes from counseling session to counseling session.

A BORED PROFESSIONAL

Nicole was a 25-year-old African-American marketing professional who complained of a boring and nonproductive life outside her job, which was relatively fulfilling. An assessment of her life-style revealed that she (a) never made up her bed before leaving for work (something about which she felt guilty), (b) ate mainly sandwiches and candy bars and frequently drank soft drinks, and (c) regularly went home to an evening of TV after picking up fast food for dinner. Nicole's weekends were not much better; she reported no weekend dating or time spent with close friends. Having just moved to the city to take her new job, she had left behind her few friends. Nicole's life was highly sedentary, with no exercise program, although a fitness and health club was two blocks from her apartment building. She revealed she was especially despondent about an apparent lack of accessible African-American men in this small town—men who could be acceptable dates or future spouses.

During the prescription stage, both the counselor and Nicole discussed possible changes in life-style that would improve the overall quality of her life, thus decreasing the boredom. Homework between the first and second session was for Nicole to make a commitment and follow through to make up her bed each morning, and she agreed that she had when she returned for the second counseling session. She also reported that making up the bed was very difficult; however, she wanted to keep her word to herself and the counselor. Considering her poor diet, Nicole agreed at the second session to cook nutritious meals that were not difficult to prepare, starting with at least three home-cooked meals a week. Moreover, she suggested cooking enough to have leftovers for additional meals or sandwiches for lunch at work. Nicole followed through with this plan with some intermittent setbacks, and eventually began to eat nutritious meals occasionally at the cafeteria in her office building. Immediately after the sixth counseling session, Nicole joined the fitness and health club near her residence, a life-style change that contributed to her physical health, appearance, and psychological mood, and one that provided an opportunity for her to meet new friends her age.

Nicole's more nutritious eating habits, her regular exercise at the fitness and health club, and the new habit and practice of making up her bed all created a sense of well-being, achievement, and good use of time that diminished her feeling of boredom and emptiness. Moreover, after a few visits to the fitness and health club, Nicole had met several persons with similar interests.

IMPLICATIONS AND APPLICATIONS FOR COUNSELING

Transcendent counseling's primary focus is change—changing the client's life-style, as opposed to the traditional counseling focus of changing the client's behavior. Furthermore, transcendent counseling differs from most traditional counseling theories in the following ways:

- Instead of seeing human beings as good, evil, or neutral, it simple views people as vulnerable (some more vulnerable than others).

- Instead of influencing the client to adjust, in some way, to the norm, it encourages growth and transcendence or going beyond the norm.

- Instead of involving talk therapy only or primarily, the theory strongly encourages homework and treatment-training for life-style modification.

- Instead of focusing on the limited goal of psychological homeostasis or psychological health, transcendent counseling values the goal of holistic health (a healthy mind, body, and spirit).

- Instead of focusing only on growth for the client, the transcendent process values counseling as a helping and learning process whereby both the client and the counselor grow personally and culturally.

Life-style change toward positive growth is the modus operandi and highest good of living. Murphy's (1992) *The Future of the Body* reminds practitioners of the difficulty encountered when attempting to understand the human capacity for change—change that occurs through transformative practice, a practice defined as "a complex and coherent set of activities that produce positive changes in a person or group (p. 589). Additionally, Murphy contends (p. 3):

> We live only part of the life we are given. Growing acquaintance with once-foreign cultures, new discoveries about our subliminal depths, and the dawning recognition that each social group reinforces just some human attributes while neglecting or suppressing others have stimulated a worldwide understanding that all of us have great potential for growth.

Two early advocates of transformative practice in counseling, Jourard and Overlade (1966), described the change or growth process as transcendent behavior, behavior in which the client demonstrates something in the realm of the possible that he or she had once perceived as impossible.

In light of these observations by Murphy (1992) and Jourard and Overlade (1966), transcendent counseling can be viewed as an appropriate multimodal model for multicultural transformative practice through which a relatively permanent change in life-style is achieved by an individual or group (Harper & Stone, 1986).

To a great degree, transcendent counseling is a psychoeducational process as well as a counseling experience. That is, it teaches the client how to live through its training modalities, its homework activities, its verbal teaching techniques, and its six modules that all focus on information, attitudes, and skills related to living. Within this framework, transcendent counseling, implicitly or explicitly, conveys universal values of quality and effective living through its modules of counseling. These values can be construed as healthy living, effective interpersonal and intergroup relations, productive and meaningful activity, self-management of one's organism, and an orientation toward growth rather than stagnation and resignation.

Transcendent counseling is a preventive counseling theory as well as a remediative one. It serves to correct or remedy human problems, and it can be a functional model for preventing problems and educating clients for growth toward an improved quality of living.

As a multimodal and multicultural theory, transcendent counseling encourages the client to identify with his or her culture of origin while striving to transcend that culture as a means toward growth. Through multicultural education, information, and experience, the client learns to accept and respect the good and proud things about his or her own culture of origin while maturing to accept and appreciate other cultures or ways of life.

Transcendent counseling embraces the recent movements in multiethnic and multicultural education and encourages clients and counselors to take advantage of sound opportunities for cross-cultural academic learning and real-life field experience (Banks, 1979, 1991; Boyer, 1983; Farley, 1988; Marger, 1991; National Council for Accreditation of Teacher Education, 1982). By the same token, transcendent counseling encourages counselors to read and remain up-to-date on the current changes in the literature of multiculturalism and transculturalism to acquire and maintain an understanding of cross-cultural effectiveness and sensitivity (Baruth & Manning, 1991; d'Ardenne & Mahatani, 1989; Pedersen, 1988, 1991; Ponterotto & Casas, 1991).

From a life-style perspective, transcendent counseling has applications for all areas of counseling (career, educational, and personal-social), all ethnic or cultural groups, different age groups, males and females, and other special client populations. Most human problems certainly are maintained by a habitual life-style acquired over time and maintained by habit. Life-style problems of drug addiction (including tobacco and alcohol), spousal abuse, family conflict, interpersonal conflict, poor study habits, ineffective work styles, marital discord, some health problems, overeating, loneliness, and financial management and sufficiency are examples of relatively universal concerns related to how a person lives from day to day. Ineffective life-styles can be minimized or reversed with life-style modification training and techniques such as those used in transcendent counseling.

In today's increasingly stressful and shrinking world, social, political, economic, and ethnic strife repeatedly captures worldwide headlines. The world has changed significantly over the last decade or two with regard to social, geographic, and political relationships and boundaries. Effective multicultural and transcultural practices must be examined if pluralistic efficacious solutions to these personal and universal problems are to be realized. Transcendent counseling appears to be a logical beginning that merits utmost consideration by practitioners.

REFERENCES

Banks, J. A. (1979). *Teaching strategies for ethnic studies.* Needham Heights, MA: Allyn & Bacon.

Banks, J. A. (1991). *Teaching strategies for ethnic studies* (5th ed.). Needham Heights, MA: Allyn & Bacon.

Baruth, L. G., & Manning, M. L. (1991). *Multicultural counseling and psychotherapy: A lifespan perspective.* New York: Merrill.

Boyer, J. (Winter, 1983). *Multicultural education: From product to process.* New York: Educational Resources Information Center/Clearinghouse on Urban Education. (ERIC Document Reproduction Service No. ED 240 224).

Carkhuff, R. R., & Berenson, B. G. (1977). *Beyond counseling and therapy* (2nd ed.). New York: Holt, Rinehart and Winston.

Carter, R. T., & Helms, J. E. (1992). The counseling process as defined by relationship types: A test of Helms' Interactional Model. *Journal of Multicultural Counseling and Development, 20,* 181–201.

Cross, W. E. (1971). Negro-to-Black conversion experience: Toward a psychology of Black liberation. *Black World, 20,* 13–27.

Cross, W. E. (1980). Models of psychological Nigrescence: A literature review. In R. L. Jones (Ed.), *Black Psychology* (pp. 81–98). New York: Harper & Row.

d'Ardenne, P., & Mahatani, A. (1989). *Transcultural counselling in action.* Newbury Park, CA: Sage.

Farley, J. E. (1988). *Majority-minority relations* (2nd ed.). Englewood Cliffs, NJ: Prentice Hall.

Fromm, E. (1941). *Escape from freedom.* New York: Holt, Rinehart and Winston.

Harper, F. D., & Stone, W. O. (1974). Toward a theory of transcendent counseling with Blacks. *Journal of Multicultural Counseling and Development, 2,* 191–196.

Harper, F. D., & Stone, W. O. (1986). Transcendent counseling: Toward a multicultural approach. *International Journal for the Advancement of Counselling, 9,* 251–263.

Helms, J. E. (1989). Considering some methodological issues in racial identity counseling research. *The Counseling Psychologist, 17,* 227–252.

Jourard, S. M., & Overlade, D. C. (Eds.). (1966). *Reconciliation: A theory of man transcending.* Princeton, NJ: Van Nostrand.

Marger, M. N. (1991). *Race and ethnic relations: American and global perspectives* (2nd ed.). Belmont, CA: Wadsworth.

Maslow, A. (1970). *Motivation and personality* (2nd ed.). New York: Harper & Row.

Murphy, M. (1992). *The future of the body: Exploration into the further evaluation of human nature.* Los Angeles: Tarcher.

National Council for Accreditation of Teacher Education (1982). *Standards for the accreditation of teacher education.* Washington, DC: Author.

Nicholson, J. A., & Golsan, G. (1983). *The creative counselor.* New York: McGraw-Hill.

Pedersen, P. (1988). *A handbook for developing multicultural awareness.* Alexandria, VA: American Counseling Association.

Pedersen, P. (1991). Multiculturalism as a fourth force in counseling [Special issue]. *Journal of Counseling and Development, 70*(1).

Ponterotto, J. G., & Casas, J. M. (1991). *Handbook of racial/ethnic minority counseling research.* Springfield, IL: Charles C. Thomas.

Smith, E. J. (1991). Ethnic identity development: Toward the development of a theory within the context of majority/minority status. *Journal of Counseling and Development, 70,* 181–188.

Spielberger, C. D., Gorsuch, R. L., & Luschene, R. E. (1969). *The State-Trait Anxiety Inventory (STAI): Test manual for Form X.* Palo Alto, CA: Consulting Psychologist.

Stone, W. O. (1975). Career development for ethnic minorities. In R. C. Reardon & H. D. Burck (Eds.), *Facilitating career development: Strategies for counselors* (pp. 248–267). Springfield, IL: Charles C. Thomas.

Stone, W. O. (1984). Serving ethnic minorities. In H. D. Burck & R. C. Reardon (Eds.), *Career development interventions* (pp. 267–291). Springfield, IL: Charles C. Thomas.

CHAPTER 5

TRANSCULTURAL FAMILY COUNSELING: THEORIES AND TECHNIQUES

DAVID A. KAHN

Somewhere in the United States a White middle-class family counselor walks into his office to meet a newly emigrated Vietnamese family. This family has come to him because their 15-year-old son is displaying behavior problems and is performing poorly in school. The identified patient has been suspended from school several times for fighting and showing disrespect to his teachers. Family members present include the father, mother, paternal grandfather and grandmother, a 13-year-old sister, and a 5-year-old brother.

Immediately a special set of questions arises: How should the counselor begin his initial session? Whom does the counselor address first? What is the most important goal of this first session and how is it accomplished? Which therapeutic paradigm will be most effective with this family? Which therapeutic techniques will provide the most effective change mechanisms? These are very difficult questions to answer, and the answers obviously depend upon a wide set of variables.

The most significant factor that determines the success of the counselor is how he adapts his personal worldview and therapeutic skills to the worldview of the family that has come for help—this and the counselor's ability to transcend the cultural differences so that previous family systems training and experience will be used as effectively as possible.

Family counselors have a tremendous responsibility when counseling culturally different families. As in any other counseling field, the counselor's responsibility is to provide clients with the best, most effective therapy possible. All counselors have an ethical responsibility to treat only those clients they are qualified to treat. In this world of cultural diversity and transient life-styles, family counselors are attempting to treat more families who have differing worldviews. To treat these families, family counselors require more training and experience in transcultural counseling if they are to effectively serve the needs of families who face the multitude of issues of modern society.

The extended family, structural, and experiential schools are well-known theories of the family systems approach. These three paradigms use techniques that can help family counselors bridge cultural gaps. Each paradigm has something to offer the transcultural counseling perspective if the techniques described in this chapter are used with wisdom, insight, honesty, and sensitivity to cultural norms and perspective. It is every counselor's responsibility to provide the most effective treatment available, without letting value judgment or personal perspective dictate the change that must occur to help others grow.

Families in need of professional help exhibit similar developmental issues, communication problems, hierarchical imbalances, subsystem issues, and boundary problems. These issues may stem from culture-specific problems, but they exist in all cultures. Celia Falicov (1982) says that "dysfunctional family patterns may be aggravated by cultural adaptation, but they belong to categories of universal or at least, transcultural human problems" (p. 158).

Traditional family therapy theories and interventions are effective in the treatment of families from varying cultural backgrounds. When counselors encounter dysfunctional behavior that transcends cultural patterns, the more traditional family therapy approaches are the therapies of choice (Falicov, 1982). These therapeutic approaches should adjust therapeutic goals according to the cultural differences and values of the families being treated. The strongest of these theories was born in a part of society where cultural differences were the rule, not the exception.

STRUCTURAL SYSTEM PARADIGMS AND TECHNIQUES

The structural family therapy approach was developed by Salvadore Minuchin along with Braulio Montalvo and others. Structural family therapy has been a leading systemic approach since the 1970s and continues to gain in application as its effectiveness continues to be proven.

Structural family therapy was born at the Wiltwyck School for delinquent boys where Minuchin and Montalvo worked with culturally diverse boys of lower socioeconomic status and their families. Minuchin felt that the therapeutic approaches of Nathan Ackerman and Don Jackson were not appropriate for his clients. Therefore he developed a simple and practical theory of family therapy. The theory uses concrete, action-oriented techniques to help family counselors effectively help families.

This family system approach places emphasis on the process of family therapy rather than its content. Structural family therapy provides a theoretical framework that guides counselors' interventions through consistent strategies of treatment that in turn reduce the need to use specific techniques for various occasions. Interaction between family members gives the therapist the information needed to change the system.

Structural family therapy uses three constructs as a basis for understanding and identifying the issues involved in family interaction: structure, subsystems, and boundaries.

Structure refers to the organized pattern in which family members interact. This structure is supported by universal and idiosyncratic constraints, such as the hierarchy in which children and parents maintain different levels of authority. Family structure is highly dependent upon the cultural heritage and traditions of families. The interactions that create structure tend to be repeated and turn into transactions that establish enduring patterns and become resistant to change. Family structure is supported by a set of covert rules that govern the transactions. Counselors need to realize that family structure is not easily recognizable and that only through actual interactions will the structure make itself evident.

Subsystems are the primary building blocks of the family. Each individual is a subsystem of the family, and these individuals combine into dyads or larger groups to form other subsystems. The subsystems often are determined by gender, generation, or interests. Subsystems make themselves known both overtly and covertly, with the covert systems being of prime importance in family therapy. The possible combinations of subgroupings are endless.

Boundaries are the invisible barriers that surround individuals and subsystems within the family system. Boundaries help protect the independence and separateness of the subsystem in the family. Boundaries can be rigid or diffuse and create disengagement or enmeshment between various family members. Disengagement creates isolation and autonomy and can promote independence, growth, and mastery. Enmeshment creates a heightened sense of mutual support, but at the expense of independence and autonomy. The most important boundary in the family system is the generational boundary, which divides the family into two subsystems: the executive subsystem and the sibling subsystem (Shultz, 1984). Realigning boundaries can strengthen the boundaries of subsystems and increase autonomy in enmeshed families. Realignment also creates boundaries in disengaged families that encourage members to discuss their conflicts.

Structural family therapy is effective with families of cultural diversity because it focuses on the process and restructuring of family interactions instead of the content and emotions (Shon & Ja, 1982). Jay Lappin (1983) emphasizes that process is process in any language. Issues such as overinvolvement, enmeshment, disengagement, and diffusion still require working with and realigning family boundaries and subsystems. Families will interact with each other through the established subsystems and within the boundaries they have created. The content often provides an emotional catalyst that can highlight the typical patterns of family interaction, making it easier for the counselor to identify trouble areas. Teaching families to communicate, interact, and relate more effectively can produce better functioning families.

Counselors must be careful not to attempt to change family process in a way that could cause cultural inconsistency. Counselors cannot always assume that the best way to interact is the Western way. Trying to reduce the generational boundary between parents and child in an Asian family could prove disastrous. It would be important to help the parents maintain their executive power as parents while improving their acceptance that children with independent coping skills can be beneficial to the family. Lappin (1983) cautions that "what is distance in one culture may have a very different meaning in another" (p. 129).

Structural family therapy allows the counselor to create a structural map of a family's boundaries and subsystems. This map shows the counselor how family members interact and where issues of enmeshment or diffusion may exist. Structural mapping helps the counselor assess issues and develop treatment strategies and serves as a baseline for determining whether interventions have been useful (Shultz, 1984). Family structures typically do not remain the same; they change within each family as situations change. Highly dysfunctional families tend to display very rigid structures that are not very flexible across situations. Cultural differences may spotlight rigid generational boundaries that differ from those of the Western world, but structural mapping can help assess where these boundaries are detrimental to the functioning of the family and where they are not. From this point, the mapping can be used to develop treatment goals by helping the counselor assess which boundaries require modification and which subsystems may need alterations. Finally, structural maps developed by the counselor may be used as focal points to plan interventions to help the family. For instance, if the original map indicates enmeshment by one parent with a particular child, homework assignments may be given to the peripheral parent and that child.

One of the strongest techniques employed by structural family therapy is the joining technique. *Joining* is the process by which the counselor and family form a partnership to free the identified patient of symptoms, reduce family conflict, and learn new coping skills (Minuchin & Fishman, 1981). Joining and accommodating is the first step in structural family therapy. This initial step should take place during every family session. The counselor should then try to join with each family member present. Joining is the process that binds the therapeutic system together (Minuchin & Fishman, 1981), and it takes more time in transcultural counseling (Lappin, 1983).

Marshall Jung (1984) indicates that joining helps a counselor control the session without alienating any family members. For Chinese families, Jung emphasizes the importance of exhibiting caring, understanding, support, and sympathy for each member while taking into consideration, and being aware of, the cultural values of individual family members. In transcultural counseling, a counselor must understand a family's cultural style of forming trusting relationships, particularly helping relationships, if the joining is to be effective (McGill & Pearce, 1982). Part of the process of understanding how a family learns to trust is being what a family expects of a counselor (McGill & Pearce, 1982). This can be done by researching the cultural background of a family before regular therapy sessions. Information about cultural expectations can come from various literature (sociological, anthropological, psychological, and historical) and from interviews of professionals and acquaintances who come from similar cultures. Be careful not to stereotype families based on this research; within every culture there remain individual and societal differences. Issues of class, caste, income status, and especially roles are critical in transcultural work and should be taken into account when joining with a family (Lappin, 1983).

Joining with families of different cultures can be difficult because of their reluctance to trust outsiders with family information. Many culturally different families have experienced racism, oppression, and discrimination in various institutional settings. These bad experiences understandably influence their ideas about the helping profession. The counselor may avoid risking insult and difficult trust issues by being open and honest about limited exposure to the cultural mores of the family.

Working with interactions is an enactment technique employed by structural family therapy. Enactments occur in three phases: spontaneous transactions of the family, counselor-organized scenarios of family interaction, and alternative ways of interacting suggested by the counselor (Minuchin & Fishman, 1981). Spontaneous enactments provide the counselor with a picture of how the family may normally interact. This step is an essential part in creating structural maps for diagnosis and treatment planning. Spontaneous enactments allow the counselor to highlight particular actions and to help the family gain insight into the ways they interact.

When working with any family, counselors should be aware of families' tendencies to try to appear as healthy as possible. In other words, some spontaneous interactions may not truly reflect how the family typically interacts at home. Braulio Montalvo and Manuel Gutierrez (1983) say that families often offer a "cultural mask" (p. 16) to hide the way they normally operate when trying to solve family problems. The family can use its culture as a defense against accepting help for its issues.

To get behind this mask, the counselor can suggest scenarios for family enactments. If the counselor suggests interactions involving potentially touchy situations, the family could be caught off guard and forced to drop its facade of normality. This gives the counselor an opportunity to view the family at its most real. Structural family therapy is designed to help families correct their flawed boundaries, and this can only be accomplished if the counselor has a real idea of how families interact in their typical environment. This has particular importance for counselors attempting to help families from different cultural backgrounds. Counselors must focus on the fundamental aspects of what it takes to uphold marriages and socialize children if they are to be effective with families of cultural diversity (Montalvo & Gutierrez, 1983). Unless a counselor can understand the typical pattern in which a family interacts, regardless of ethnic background, there is little opportunity for helping members develop appropriate problem-solving skills.

The counselor who suggests new ways of interacting in enactments provides families with an experiential learning tool for using new structural process within the family. This helps the family develop options different from their typical interactions and provides an opportunity to experience new skills for solving problems. It is important for the counselor to take into account the dysfunctional patterns in which the family typically operates and suggest interactions that can improve family functioning.

Diagnosing is another important technique of structural family therapy. This is a process in which the counselor describes the way a particular family works systemically using the concepts of boundaries and subsystems. This process helps the counselor know where to focus therapeutic energies to help the family improve. Diagnoses change over time and become more refined as the counselor is able to understand the familial relationships. Diagnosing helps the counselor to see beyond the various content issues that family members focus on and to remain focused on the structural changes that need to take place.

Highlighting and modifying interactions helps families better understand how they remain stuck or dysfunctional because of particular interactions. This technique must be employed with a great deal of intensity to challenge a family's perceptions of reality. The trick is to get the family to hear the message that highlights the dysfunctional interaction in order to open up the prospect of change (Minuchin & Fishman, 1981). The counselor often has to be very active and may have to highlight the same interaction several times before the family members actually begin to change their interactions. Awareness of cultural diversity is important with this technique, but again it is more important to understand how families universally work in order to determine which interactions are detrimental. Temper every intervention with knowledge about the family's cultural heritage, but apply universal rules around family functioning, especially in terms of structure, boundaries, and subsystems.

EXTENDED FAMILY SYSTEMS PARADIGM AND TECHNIQUES

The extended family therapy paradigm was developed by Murray Bowen, a leading figure in family therapy. *Bowenian, historical,* or *extended family therapy* grew out of Bowen's work with schizophrenic families. Bowen is concerned with the multigenerational family system, but he usually works with individuals or couples. He developed a three-generational hypothesis of schizophrenia that proposes that interlocking triangles connect one generation to the next (Nichols, 1984). Triangulation within families is a major component of Bowen's theory.

Eight interlocking concepts make up Bowen's theory: emotional triangles, differentiation of self, nuclear family emotional system, family projection process, multigenerational projection system, influence of sibling position, emotional cutoff, and societal regression.

116

Bowen's theory emphasizes differentiation of the individual from the family of origin. He felt that families become emotionally fused because of their unhealthy exaggeration of people's instinctual need for others (Nichols, 1984). Man Keung Ho (1987) says, "Differentiation of self is a universal process, varying only in quantity and quality in different cultures" (p. 141). The goal of therapy is to help clients begin a lifelong effort at self-discovery. Bowen gives his clients the tools to make trips back into the family of origin in order to differentiate the self. Differentiation is a process of becoming independent of, but still in contact with, the family of origin, both nuclear and extended. Differentiation is marked by an ability to separate thinking from feelings through rationality and objectivity (Nichols, 1984).

Bowen's idea that the interpersonal system of the family comprises three people gave rise to the concept of emotional triangles. A family begins when two people marry and leave their families of origin. According to Bowen, any two-person relationship is unstable because it is difficult to relate to one other person for long before some emotional crisis or stressor interferes. Couples handle these instances by pulling a third person or object into the situation to relieve anxiety or tension. For instance, if the husband becomes anxious about a marital issue, he may begin to use his job as the tension reducer by working longer hours. Couples typically decrease the anxiety by focusing on the children. Although this reduces tension in the relationship, it does not resolve the original issue. This process is called *triangulation*. The triangle is said to be the smallest stable relationship that can occur among people. Triangulation appears to be a universal occurrence within families, although cultural differences sometimes dictate who or what is used as the third part of the triangle. Triangles also occur within systems and are not limited to three individuals (Nichols, 1984). Cultural differences may dictate how triangles are set up and who plays major roles in them. Grandparents may be at one point with the mother at another and the spouse, children, or identified patient at the third. Effective family therapy with the triangle means the counselor must become involved with the most important part of the triangle, usually the marital couple, to be a catalyst for detriangulation, thus increasing chances for differentiation. To do this, the counselor becomes a third part of the triangle and remains neutral and nonjudgmental, thus not becoming triangulated. In a family with a different cultural perspective it may not be easy to identify the part of the triangle that affects the marital couple the most, the part that triangulates the marital relationship, or to develop strategies for effectively detriangulating the couple without offending their cultural mores or values.

Even though Bowen's family therapy focus relies upon the extended family, he usually works only with the married couple or whoever presents the family for therapy. This technique rests upon the idea that change in one triangle will effect change throughout the family system. Bowen teaches families about triangulation and then uses a technique called *coaching* to help clients return to their family of origin to detriangulate themselves and become more differentiated (Nichols, 1984).

Another technique used by Bowen is to work with the family member who is the most differentiated or respected. This technique can be very useful when working with clients who place emphasis upon resolving problems solely within the family. Formal family therapy may be too threatening for many culturally different families, and this technique provides an effective alternative (Ho, 1987). This technique relies on changing one family member to effect change throughout the family system.

Nuclear family emotional system is the process by which patterns of functioning occur within the family of a single generation. It is presumed that various patterns of previous generations will be repeated in the current family. This occurs because of the levels of differentiation existing in each individual in the marital couple. Little differentiation by spouses from their families of origin can lead to fusion within the marriage. Typically people pick mates who have similar levels of differentiation from their families. The degree of fusion in a marriage can determine the difficulty of future problems within the family.

Parents emotionally transfer their immaturity and lack of differentiation to their children through *family projection process* (Ho, 1987; Nichols, 1984). Bowen believed that the marital conflict often resulted in emotional distance between the spouses. This can lead to one parent's fusion with a child, usually through an overly dependent bond or a struggling conflict. The child who undergoes this fusion often suffers emotional impairment, further encouraging dysfunctional behavior. This process is universal and occurs in all families with children (Jones, 1980).

Multigenerational transmission process is important to transcultural counseling issues. It describes the way families transfer family patterns from one generation to the next. Bowen believed family problems do not originate with the individual or with the nuclear family alone. Identified patient dysfunction is a process of at least a three-generational transmission. The theory is that the identified patient's symptoms result from an ever-decreasing level of differentiation that occurs across generations. The way this happens is that people marry other people with like differentiation and then the children of such marriages who have the least differentiation marry similarly differentiated spouses. This process continues until a child exists with such low differentiation that schizophrenia develops. This concept can be important when working with families who value close relationships with their extended families. A counselor can better understand the dysfunction in a family if the important extended family members are used in the treatment process rather than excluded.

Sibling position is important in that Bowen believed certain children may have personality characteristics based on their position in the family. The many variables involved in determining personality characteristics make prediction complex, but Bowen encouraged counselors to have a working knowledge of the general characteristics to determine how the children are involved in the emotional processes of the family. In many culturally diverse families, sibling position can determine much about the individual childrens' futures or importance in the family. Sibling order and hierarchy often play congruent roles in the family. The values held about birth order can create interesting problems when, for example, an older sibling is taking on the role of the youngest sibling because of the youngest's tendency to be the most triangulated by the parents. When attempting to help families from variant cultures, the counselor should be familiar with the cultural perspectives on birth order.

Emotional cutoff indicates that people are emotionally or physically cut off from their parents to start a new life with their peer generation. Problems occur when an individual abruptly and totally abandons the family of origin, usually creating family problems mirroring those of the family of origin, only with greater intensity. The other extreme is when an individual never emotionally cuts off from parents, therefore hindering differentiation of self. The way to battle dysfunction due to emotional cutoff issues is for the new nuclear family to remain in contact with the family of origin (Jones, 1980).

Emotional cutoff is important when working with culturally different families because of the issue of migration. Culturally different families may have migrated long distances from their families of origin and may be experiencing difficulty keeping contact with them. Emotional cutoff is intensified by distance and may not only be a function of children's attempts to remove themselves emotionally from the family of origin. The family counselor must be prepared to use creative measures to help families who suffer from emotional cutoff because of distance.

EXPERIENTIAL SYSTEMS PARADIGMS AND TECHNIQUES

Experiential family therapy is a direct outgrowth of the humanistic psychotherapies that originated in the 1960s. This therapeutic approach stresses the here-and-now experience of each individual member of a family. The focus of therapy is to help the family grow through genuine, honest expression and experience of feelings. According to Nichols (1984), the aim of experiential therapy is to help "individual family members become sensitive to their needs and feelings, and to share these within the family" (p. 272). Helping individual family members grow is combined with strengthening the family unit.

Carl Whitaker is considered the prime proponent of experiential family therapy. Whitaker supports the idea that the most effective aspect of experiential family therapy is the personality and style of the counselor. He puts little emphasis on the use of theory within the therapy setting and supports strong use of intuition, spontaneity, honesty, and personal disclosure of feelings to help promote growth and honest expression of feelings by the clients. The counselor is the primary change agent in family therapy—the one willing to take educated risks that will be most beneficial to families.

Experiential counseling relies very little on theory or many structured techniques. Most experiential counselors would claim to be eclectic in their theoretical approach to family treatment and to borrow from various counseling theories. The goal of experiential family therapy is to help each family member experience further growth and understanding. Reliance on problem solving is not a major focus (Nichols, 1984).

In transcultural counseling the greatest tool available to the counselor is not a technique but rather the counselor's own personality and style. Families of differing cultures often have difficulty developing trust in a counselor from the majority culture. This difficulty can more easily be overcome if counselors present themselves with an open, honest, dynamic style in which intuition can help guide effective therapeutic interventions. Effective counselors present themselves as individuals who lack motivation for personal gain within the counseling sessions. These skills cannot be easily taught and more often than not are developed through years of experience working with families.

The effectiveness of any technique used in family therapy depends upon the counselor's skill and insight. Choosing the appropriate technique for various situations cannot be reduced to a cookbook mind-set in which counselors can choose a technique by set formula. The techniques of family therapy are useful only if applied in an appropriate setting, with appropriate style, and in the correct time frame. This is especially true when working with culturally different clients. The key to follow is "Know your client."

"Know your client" is a rule any counselor should follow when working in a therapeutic setting. When treating families of different cultures this is often difficult to do because of differing worldviews and experiences brought into therapy by both the clients and the counselor. It is impossible for any counselor to understand and be aware of every cultural aspect presented in the therapy session. Counselors therefore must take responsible measures to afford themselves appropriate training and exposure to transcultural issues. As Derald Wing Sue (1992) states, "counselors must learn about the client's culture and about how the sociopolitical system in the

121

United States operates with respect to its treatment of minorities" (p. 13).

TRANSCULTURAL FAMILY THERAPY TECHNIQUES

Family therapy techniques that could prove very useful in transcultural counseling originate from structural, strategic, extended, and experiential schools of family therapy and from individual, psychodramatic, and Gestalt counseling theories as well. They include link therapy, the fishbowl technique, family sculpting, family drawing, role-playing, auxiliary ego, hug therapy, homework assignments, coaching, family meetings, circular questioning, reframing, and modeling.

Link therapy is a strong transcultural approach for working with families who have migrated from a culture that values extended family input in solving problems so highly that all such problems are kept within the family system. Landau-Stanton (1990) states that in instances of family migration some members acculturate to the new society faster than others, which can cause a transitional conflict. This conflict has to be addressed in such a way as not to alienate the traditional, more rigid, hierarchical structure of the extended family while still including the more acculturated members in an effort to help the family resolve the transitional conflict (Landau-Stanton, 1990).

Link therapy approaches this problem by choosing an important family member to function as the counselor within the family. The link counselor is trained through coaching to provide the therapy for the family. The link counselor must be chosen with care and wisdom. The person seeking therapy is usually an acculturated or entrenched family member and biased toward one side of the conflict. A family member who can work with both aspects of the transitional conflict and who is trusted and respected by the counselor to be available and workable is the ideal choice. Landau-Stanton (1990) suggests choosing a family member whose position in the acculturation process has not been firmly defined and who generally is not the complainant but a peripheral member of the family. The link therapist is responsible for the direction of the solution of the transitional conflict, and the family counselor supports that decision through the coaching and training.

Link therapy is similar to Bowen's coaching but has three major distinctions (Landau-Stanton, 1990): (a) Link therapy is problem focused and does not focus on differentiation of the family member; (b) the family counselor chooses an appropriate change agent from available family members and does not necessarily work with the person presenting with the problem; and (c) link therapy is much briefer and more geared toward rapid resolution of the problem.

Landau-Stanton also says that link therapy is useful when transitional problems are prime issues, as in adolescence. Link therapy has proven useful when the adolescent is chosen as the link counselor because it reduces trust issues of parent-counselor coalitions and helps to balance the adolescent's typically oscillating nature. Other transitional situations can include multigenerational issues, blended families, and nuclear families in which some family members are not available for therapy (Landau-Stanton, 1990).

The *fishbowl technique* is borrowed from group therapy. This technique can be adapted to individual family therapy to allow the therapist to work with important triangles in the system or to help healthier members of the family model appropriate behavior. This technique takes various subsystems within the family and places them inside a circle of other family members. The counselor then works with only those members in the inner circle and asks the family members in the outer circle to remain quiet and focus on personal thoughts and feelings. The counselor then provides a question or starts an enactment with the inner circle to begin the process of highlighting and modifying interactions or developing opportunities to work with triangulation. Fishbowling can be a useful transcultural counseling technique in that it does not really exclude any family members from therapy. The counselor encourages feedback from family members in the outer circle after approximately 20 minutes of therapy. Including extended family members who place an emphasis on the value of kinship roles is a strength of this technique.

Family sculpting, developed by David Kantor and Fred Duhl, gets the family to show itself in the form of a "meaningful tableau" (Nichols, 1984, p. 285). The counselor usually gets each family member present to sculpt the family as that member typically sees them on a normal day when the family would be together. Empty chairs, the counselor, or other objects can take the place of important family members not present. This technique emphasizes the perceptions about family functioning in terms of distance, stance, and attitude. The counselor usually asks each family member questions such as: What do you notice about your family? How do you feel about where each of your family members is in relation to you? Are you comfortable with how the sculptor portrayed you? Is this how you typically see yourself? The counselor can then get individual family members to sculpt the family as they would like it to be. This technique provides the counselor with invaluable information about how each member perceives the rest of the family. The sculpts often project possible changes for the family in terms of boundaries and levels of diffusion or enmeshment.

Showing scenes from the past to help facilitate understanding in families who may be suffering from transitional conflicts associated with migration issues is an appropriate transcultural counseling application. Families guarded about family secrets will often tell the counselor valuable information if the sculpt is approached in such a way that the family is asked, "Remember a time when (an event) happened; now walk into the room and describe, through a sculpt, what typically occurred." Addressing the past will often show patterns of functioning that can be addressed in later therapy sessions.

Sculpting can be modified to help families with transitional conflict or acculturation issues by working specifically with the two parts involved in the conflict. Landau-Stanton (1990) calls this technique *transitional sculpting*; the goals are to provide "a visual and experiential joining of past to present and this continuity allows experimentation with future direction" (p. 270).

In some cultures, sculpting could be sabotaged by starting with the leading patriarch or matriarch in the family because the rest of the family will rarely vary their own sculpts from that of a strict authority figure. It is a good idea to start with younger members of the family in order to tap into playfulness and naive honesty. If the family is approached playfully with this technique they will find it amusing as well as informative. Caution is encouraged for cultures that guard their family secrets tightly. Join well with the family before attempting a sculpt. Telling the family up front that the purpose of the sculpt is to help them understand how they are viewed by other family members or that they will learn what other members expect from them could reduce apprehension.

Family drawing is a projective device and technique for starting discussions or enactments. The counselor may use several methods of family drawing to help loosen up the family, build rapport, gain insight into individual family members' perceptions of the family, and decide what types of enactments may be important to the family therapy. It also is effective in helping the counselor identify important boundaries or subsystems.

The basic instructions in family drawing are to tell the members to draw a picture of the family as they see it, to draw one family picture with the members placing themselves in the picture where they feel comfortable, or to draw a circle and place the family inside the circle and any aspect of people or institutions that are not part of the family, but are important to its functioning, outside the circle (Nichols, 1984). Each of these methods provides the therapist with insight into individual family members' perceptions. The methods also help improve members' understanding of their own perceptions of the family and challenge them to move toward desired changes.

This technique can be a nonthreatening way to convince members to talk about their personal perceptions of their own family. It also shows how the family works together naturally in solving problems or completing tasks. With some families, depending on their cultural orientation or worldview, the purpose of this task should be explained up front to help the family respect the counselor as an individual and expert.

Role-playing is another important family therapy technique that can be adapted to work transculturally. This technique involves having family members place themselves in the shoes of others for short periods to improve understanding and promote insight into others' actions. The counselor asks one family member to play the role of another significant member and act out a specific situation. An alternative to this is to have two family members switch roles and carry on a conversation to promote understanding of diverse perceptions. Yet another option is to have family members role-play a scene from their own childhood to underline the importance of past experience in current behavior.

Rapport should be well established and appropriate topics addressed before starting in-depth role-plays. It is often advisable to start with role-plays that involve children and their parents or to use only one individual acting out a childhood scene. The amount of time spent on role-playing varies and can last from only part of a session to the entire session. When working with families the counselor should constantly be in tune to the attitudes and feelings that surface. Unexplained behavior or strong feelings should be explored to facilitate understanding within the family.

Doubling or the use of *auxiliary ego* is a technique borrowed from group psychodrama that is used in experiential family therapy. This technique uses family members or the counselor to stand beside or behind another family member and tell the group what that person is really thinking or feeling. The counselor can set up an enactment between two or more family members and then, while they are talking, have the auxiliary ego interrupt with his or her own perception of what the client is really trying to convey. The participant in the enactment is always given the opportunity to correct any incorrect interpretations by the auxiliary ego.

The counselor must use wise judgment when deciding who is to be which family member's auxiliary ego. Sometimes it may be wise to use only the counselor to avoid any potential issues of hierarchical boundaries, such as the wife of an Arabic husband telling their son what the husband is really thinking or feeling during an enactment. Even though she may be the best authority on her husband's thoughts, speaking them without his permission could create more family problems than already exist. If the counselor uses his or her own insight into the husband's thoughts or feelings, there is less risk in sharing them with the son. By giving the father an opportunity to refuse or admit the feelings, the counselor allows the father to remain the perceived head of the household.

Hug therapy or *holding therapy* comes from the work of Leon Yorburg, a child psychologist working with schizophrenic families (Wolberg & Aronson, 1980). This technique is geared toward decreasing alienation between family members where breakdowns in communication and in intimate physical contact have occurred. This technique can only be used between the marital couple, between parents and their children, and between siblings and is not meant for use between strangers, with unrelated authority figures, or between differing ethnic groups in a transcultural setting. The goal of reducing alienation between family members is to confront the rage, anger, and hurt that each person feels toward the other by helping them to get to deeper feelings of caring and nurturing. Great care must be taken when using this technique, because family members could experience further rejection if someone refuses to follow through with the technique as requested. Children who have experienced extreme physical or sexual abuse or emotional rejection are not good candidates for this therapy early in treatment. Knowledge of cultural taboos, such as displaying public affection or exhibiting close physical contact with others, should also be incorporated when making a decision to use this technique.

To begin this technique, the counselor asks permission from the two family members who are the most alienated from each other to try an experiment. Once permission is granted, the counselor asks the dominant person in the relationship, or the person whose role it is to be the more nurturing of the two, to hold out his or her arms and offer the other family member a hug. The counselor instructs them to hold each other until they are told to stop. Other instructions include no patting on the back and no talking about issues not related to the hugging. Questions can be asked of the nurturing partner such as: Remember when your child was very young? Hold your partner as you would have then. How long has it been since you have held your child/spouse this way for this long? Similar questions can be asked of the other partner. The hug can last as long as the counselor feels necessary, but 1 to 2 minutes after the initial movement to break apart is sufficient to begin reestablishing a sense of emotional bonding. This is usually enough time to create a topic for discussion or an enactment with the family.

Transcultural issues of importance with hug therapy are those that involve public touch between spouses and values related to touching in front of strangers or children. The counselor can emphasize that this touch is not meant to be sexual and is used only to provide nurturing.

Homework assignments are an important factor in counseling with a transcultural perspective. Various cultures have a preferred mode of activity that lies in their "doing" realm (Ho, 1987). Giving homework assignments often taps into this preferred mode of activity and helps motivate the family to continue therapeutic gains outside the therapy session. Homework assignments can range from having various subsystems spend more time together in an activity of their choice as a way of supporting or diffusing appropriate boundaries, to establishing guidelines for conducting family meetings. Some cultures may view homework assignments as an aspect of the counselor's professional and expert duty to prescribe treatments that will help the family improve.

Teaching families to hold *family meetings* is another technique that works well transculturally. Family meetings are times during the week when the family gets together to talk about problems and make important decisions regarding family functioning or parent-child limits. The meetings last for a preestablished amount of time, dictated by the family, and all business must be conducted during this time. Agendas can be determined by any method agreed upon by the family. Issues such as family outings, household responsibilities, and children's privileges can be discussed. Any topic not addressed because of the time constraint can be tabled until the next family meeting. Emergency family meetings can be called through an agreed-upon method. When teaching the family about family meetings it is a good idea for the counselor to help set up the initial guidelines in order to model compromise and timing and ensure fairness within the meeting. It is suggested that when there are no major issues to be addressed or the issues take only a short time, the family spend their family meeting playing games or doing something else that requires interaction (watching television is not a suggested option).

Family meetings are important in that they support strong family interaction and often improve communication and negotiation skills. They are also a good medium for families to accomplish homework assignments given by the counselor. They tie into many families' wishes to spend more time together and support use of learning after therapy sessions.

Reframing or *relabeling* has been used in many forms of therapy and is said to have its roots in the Adlerian school of therapy and in

Haley's and Minuchin's work. Reframing is the process of redefining perceived negative behaviors into more positive, desired ones. The counselor frames a behavior as being different and more positive, thus changing the family's worldview of the behavior previously perceived as negative (Sherman & Fredman, 1986). An example would be for the counselor to reframe a father's perception that his son is stubborn by suggesting that this behavior indicates that the son is tenacious and loyal to his own beliefs.

Ho (1987) says that reframing is extremely useful when working with minority and ethnic families suffering from cultural conflicts. By viewing behavior once perceived as undesirable in a more favorable light, family members can feel better about each other and move away from blaming a problem directly on a specific individual. Reframing can help families cross cultural boundaries if negative behaviors can be viewed more appropriately as being within the family's cultural heritage.

CONCLUSION

Transcultural family counseling has its roots in traditional family counseling theories. Every family therapy theory may have something to offer counselors working with culturally different families, but this author believes that the structural, extended family, and experiential schools provide excellent frameworks and techniques for working with families with varied cultural backgrounds.

The best use of these theories would be to combine them. The counselor should understand the important role of change and, as Ho (1987) quotes Bowen, the counselor should be a "culture broker." Structural family therapy, with an emphasis on the joining process, should be used as the initial phase of therapy. Extended family therapy would be used as an important adjunct to the structural work, and various techniques from this approach should be incorporated, especially when dealing with issues such as emotional cutoff or migration and acculturation and when emphasis on family history is warranted.

Transcultural family counseling can be viewed as an eclectic form of family therapy that adapts itself to the cultural differences within every family that seeks treatment. If families of different cultures are to receive quality treatment in this country, family counselors must be responsible for developing skills to meet the needs of these families. The information in this chapter is meant only as a starting point from which family counselors can begin to develop awareness and skills for treating culturally different families. The responsibility to provide quality mental health care will ultimately rest upon the individual counselors who attempt to help families of all races, creeds, nationalities, and combinations thereof. Therefore, consider the conclusion of this chapter as a challenge to gather more information and experience in the world of multicultural and transcultural counseling in order to obtain the "ethical-ethnicity" required to treat such families.

REFERENCES

Falicov, C. J. (1982). Mexican families. In M. McGoldrick, J. K. Pearce, & J. Giordano (Eds.), *Ethnicity and family therapy* (pp. 134–163). New York: Guilford.

Ho, M. K. (1987). *Family therapy with ethnic minorities.* Newbury Park, CA: Sage.

Jones, S. C. (1980). *Family therapy: A comparison of approaches.* Bowie, MD: Robert Bradley.

Jung, M. (1984). Structural family therapy: Its application to Chinese families. *Family process, 23*(3), 365–374.

Landau-Stanton, J. (1990). Issues and methods of treatment for families in cultural transition. In M. P. Mirkin (Ed.), *The social political contexts of family therapy* (pp. 251–275). Boston: Allyn & Bacon.

Lappin, J. (1983). On becoming a culturally conscious family therapist. *Family therapy collections, 6,* 122–136.

McGill, D., & Pearce, J. K. (1982). British families. In M. McGoldrick, J. K. Pearce, & J. Giordano (Eds.), *Ethnicity and family therapy* (pp. 457–479). New York: Guilford.

Minuchin, S., & Fishman, H. C. (1981). *Family therapy techniques.* Cambridge: Harvard University Press.

Montalvo, B., & Gutierrez, M. (1983). A perspective for use of the cultural dimension in family therapy. *Family therapy collections, 6,* 15–32.

Nichols, M. P. (1984). *Family therapy: Concepts and methods.* New York: Gardner.

Sherman, R., & Fredman N. (1986). *Handbook of structured techniques in marriage and family therapy.* New York: Brunner/Mazel.

Shon, S. P., & Ja, D. Y. (1982). Asian families. In M. McGoldrick, J. K. Pearce, & J. Giordano (Eds.), *Ethnicity and family therapy* (pp. 208–228). New York: Guilford.

Shultz, S. J. (1984). *Family systems therapy: An integration.* New York: Aronson.

Sue, D. W. (1992). The challenge of multiculturalism: The road less traveled. *American counselor, 1*(1), 6–14.

Wolberg, L. R., & Aronson, M. L. (1980). *Group and family therapy: 1980.* New York: Brunner/Mazel.

CHAPTER 6

RATIONAL BEHAVIOR THERAPY: AN APPROACH TO TRANSCULTURAL COUNSELING

TONY A. GORE AND MAXIE C. MAULTSBY, JR.

INTRODUCTION

Rational behavior therapy (RBT) represents an effective approach to transcultural counseling because of its universal appeal. Countries in the East, West, North, and South embrace various ethnic groups and races with unique mores and folkways. At the same time, each is confronted with experiences and problems that can be resolved from a behavioristic perspective. RBT is presented to offer the reader an alternative method for providing mental health services through transcultural counseling.

RBT is a technique of psychotherapy that bases its therapeutic concepts and techniques on the well-established neuropsychophysiological facts described by Bogen (1969a, 1969b), Gazzaniga (1970), Luria (1966a, 1966b, 1973), and others about the unique specialized functions of the right and left hemispheres of the human brain in emotional and behavioral control.

RBT has the six main characteristics of all ideal psychotherapies. RBT (1) is comprehensive, (2) is short-term, (3) is transcultural, (4) is drug-free, (5) produces long-term results, and (6) enables state schools and community groups to offer effective, yet economical, mass mental health improvement programs (Maultsby, 1984).

What is the evidence that RBT actually has the six features of an ideal psychotherapy?

1. RBT is comprehensive because it deals directly with all three groups of human behaviors: cognitive, emotive, and physical.

2. RBT is short-term psychotherapy because it routinely teaches clients the research-tested, drug-free, emotional self-help technique called *rational self-counseling* (Maultsby, 1975a). This emphasis on scientific emotional self-help enables people to help themselves at will, between therapy sessions. This greatly speeds up therapeutic progress while making it as comprehensive as possible.

3. RBT is a transcultural psychotherapy because it is acceptable to and effective for people whose ages, races, cultural values, and life-styles differ widely from those of their psychotherapists (Brandsma, Maultsby, & Welsh, 1979; J. Fowler, personal communication, 1980; Maultsby, 1975a, 1980; Patton, 1976; G. Ross, 1978; M. Ruhnow, personal communication, 1977; Schwager, 1975; L. Werito, personal communication, 1981). This fact makes RBT ideal for treating the traditionally "good" psychotherapy candidates as well as adolescents, the elderly, the poor, members of racial and ethnic minorities, and other traditionally "poor" psychotherapy candidates.

4. Medical science has not yet been able to improve on nature at its best. That is why RBT therapists believe that healthy, undrugged brains are the safest and most reliable therapeutic aids. Consequently, RBT is drug-free psychotherapy for people with physically healthy brains.

5. RBT produces long-term results because adequately treated people learn proven, effective emotional self-help skills. Such people are better able than ever before to cope successfully with future problems in daily living (Maultsby, 1982).

CONCEPTS OF RATIONAL BEHAVIOR THERAPY

The 10 basic theoretical concepts in RBT theory are listed below:

1. The brain is the main organ of survival, learning, and control of both healthy and unhealthy cognitive, emotive, and physical habits.

2. There are no significant differences between the brains of members of different races (Tobias, 1970).

3. Effective psychotherapy and counseling will accurately reflect the established facts about human right- and left-brain neuropsychophysiology as described by Bogen (1969a, 1969b), Gazzaniga (1970), Luria (1966a, 1966b, 1973), and other modern neuropsychophysiologists.

4. In physically healthy people, words (especially nouns, verbs, and adjectives) are the most common learned stimuli for the neuropsychological activities that produce and maintain healthy and unhealthy emotional and physical habits (Hudgins, 1933; Luria, 1960; Mowrer, 1966; Pavlov as quoted by Volgyesi, 1954; Staats & Staats, 1957, 1958; Watzlawick, 1978).

5. Human emotions are inner urges (i.e., specific motivations) for actions, caused by learned emotive or visceral responses elicited and controlled by semipermanent neuropsychological units called attitudes and beliefs (Adams & Victor, 1977; Grace & Graham, 1952; Maultsby, 1975a, 1978, 1984).

6. The neuropsychophysiological mechanisms of learning are the same for healthy and unhealthy emotional and physical habits (DiCara, 1970; Maultsby, 1984; Miller, 1969; Olds, 1969; Rotter, 1954, 1966, 1971).

7. People react to two worlds: the world of objective reality outside their minds and the world of subjective reality created and recorded by their minds. The world of subjective reality is the only reality people can experience directly. But emotionally healthy living most consistently occurs when a person's world of subjective reality accurately reflects the world of objective reality (Eaton, Peterson, & Davis, 1976; Maultsby, 1984; Watzlawick, 1978).

8. Successful psychotherapy without drugs or electric shock is an experience in therapeutic cognitive and emotive reeducation

135

that requires clients to learn the emotionally healthy use of their brains.

9. For clients to achieve permanent psychotherapeutic change, they must follow a specific therapeutic treatment plan at least as diligently and for as long as they would if they were trying to learn any complex new skill, for example, speaking a foreign language, driving a car, or typing (Maultsby, 1984).

10. There are three major groups of human behavioral problems: learned behavior problems due to unhealthy learning and conditioning of psychoemotional responses; unlearned (or organically caused) behavioral problems (Smythies, 1966); and psychosomatic problems. Learned problems respond best to RBT alone; unlearned problems respond best to medication; and psychosomatic problems respond best to a combination of RBT and medication.

THE ABC MODEL OF LIFE EXPERIENCES

The RBT therapist conceptualizes clients' problems as based on the ABC model of life experiences. This model is a theoretical extension of the research-supported original ABC model of human emotions described by Ellis (1962); Grace and Graham (1952); Graham, Stern, and Winokur (1958); and Graham, Kabler, and Graham (1962).

According to the ABC model, life experiences consist of

A. Perceptions, or what people notice; plus

B. People's sincere evaluative thoughts about their perceptions; plus

C-1. People's "gut" or emotional feelings, triggered and maintained by the evaluative thoughts at B; and

C-2. People's physical behaviors, also triggered and maintained by the evaluative thoughts at B.

The ABC model makes this clear. It is a popular overgeneralization to think that external events alone cause either emotional feelings or physical reactions. The hypothesis of RBT is that people cause their own emotional and physical reactions by the ideas they have come to believe.

At first, many people resist accepting the ABC model of life experiences. It does not seem right to them to think that they cause their own emotions, especially the painful ones they have always angrily blamed on others or on their situation. RBT therapists help clients quickly get past that initial resistance by pointing out that all new ideas initially feel wrong when they conflict with old beliefs. For example, most people laughed when the first person said that the world was round, but the only people who laugh at that fact now are naive children and equally uninformed adults.

After reflecting on this, clients almost always begin to discover that before they (and all other people) have a new emotional feeling three things happen. First, they notice something; they perceive some real event, or they imagine or remember one. Second, they have sincere evaluative thoughts about what their perceptions mean to them and about them. There are three major types of evaluative thoughts: relatively positive, relatively negative, and relatively neutral. That is why the third thing that generally happens when people have a new emotion is that their sincere evaluative thoughts trigger and maintain both emotional feelings (positive, negative, or neutral) and physical reactions they have in response to their perceptions at A.

This psychoemotional hypothesis takes the magical "IT" (which supposedly upsets people) out of human emotional control. We help clients discover the truth of the hypothesis for themselves as follows:

Imagine that there are three people looking at the same bottle of whiskey in a shop window, but each person has different emotional feelings about it. Could they each have different emotions if IT, the bottle of whiskey, controlled their emotional feelings? Obviously the bottle cannot do anything to anyone but is merely an object of each person's awareness; each person chooses his or her emotional reaction with his or her choice of beliefs about the bottle.

One person could have positive thoughts about how nice a cool cocktail would taste. Another person could have negative thoughts about his last drunken-driving conviction. The third person could have neutral thoughts that enabled her to quickly ignore the bottle and admire the sterling silver place setting it occupied.

But what would happen if each of those people took a drink of coffee that was too hot? Each person's mouth would feel the same physical pain, because physical feelings do not work like emotional feelings. IT, a stimulus in the outside world (e.g., hot coffee), can and will cause physical feelings. But only the person who feels emotional feelings can cause them.

After learning their emotional ABCs, people most often ask, "Isn't there more to my emotions than ABC? Are human emotions really that simple?" The hypothesis of RBT is, Yes, before people's emotional reactions become habitual, they are just that simple. But after people with normally functioning brains think the same sincere evaluative thoughts at B, about the same perceptions at A, and get the same emotive and behavioral Cs enough times, the following extremely important thing happens: The left brain converts those repeatedly paired perceptions and sincere thoughts into semipermanent, personally meaningful, conscious, appreciative units, or mental programs, called beliefs (Maultsby, 1975a, pp. 34–40).

From ABC to a-BC: Belief-Controlled Reactions

A	Perceptions		A	No external perceptions
B	Evaluative thoughts	after enough repeated pairings	a-B	Only beliefs (that is, habitual evaluative thoughts)
C	Emotive and physical reactions		C	Emotive and physical reactions

In RBT, the a-B apperceptive unit represents a belief. The capital B in the a-B unit indicates that spoken or conscious self-talk is the controlling cue in the apperceptive unit. Neuropsychologically, the words at B (in the a-B apperceptive unit) trigger in the right brain holistic mental images of real and imagined A events. Therefore, the a-B apperceptive unit triggers the same habitual emotional and physical reactions at C as the real As and Bs triggered in the original ABC pairing.

After people form beliefs, the left brain no longer needs to process old A stimuli as single mental events. At this point, the left brain's words elicit internally stored a-B apperceptive units, which then trigger right-brain-controlled habitual emotional and physical reactions at C. Every repetition of that a-BC sequence is an instance of practicing those habitual C reactions.

THE ROLE OF BELIEFS IN SELF-CONTROL

RBT maintains that beliefs free people from subhuman, animal-like dependence on the external world for appropriate emotional, physical, and behavioral cues.

Neuropsychophysiologically, imagination is all that healthy brains need to trigger the appropriate mental images necessary for both physical and emotional learning. Those same mental mechanisms enable people to practice daily—purposefully or unwittingly—all their emotional habits. Unfortunately, though, people rarely see their daily emotional reactions as emotional practice. Why? Simply because most people don't use the word *practice* when they think about their emotions. Yet, whether or not people realize it or admit it, every time they repeat a specific emotional reaction in specific situations, they are practicing having that emotion in those situations.

In RBT, the A-b perception represents attitude. The small *b* in the A-b unit indicates that attitudes are wordless, and therefore unspoken, superconscious forms of belief. *Superconscious* refers to psychological phenomena that can be operative with little or no conscious thought. Beliefs are the spoken or conscious form of attitudes. That important clinical insight enables a counselor to help clients take the magical ITs out of their emotional understanding.

Neuropsychologically, attitudes index or code every habitual thought, cognitive map, and mental image of the objects, events, and actions we perceive. That is why after people form attitudes, the right brain no longer perceives old external stimuli at A as single mental events. Instead, it perceives those stimuli as conditioned cues, coded with A-b attitudes that trigger holistic brain programs for habitual emotional and physical reactions at C. Therefore, with little or no conscious thought, people can react with instant, seemingly involuntary, but correct emotional and physical reactions to their old attitude-coded perceptions of old external activating events.

Those instant, involuntary, but correct reactions indicate that clients have reached the advanced stage of habit learning called *emotional insight*. Emotional insight indicates that these specific A perceptions and B thoughts have been paired enough times with the same emotive response for the right brain to have taken that emotive response and used it as an "emotive rope" to tie those separate ABC components into a behavioral gestalt. During the practice (Stage 2 of habit learning), the left brain used those separate As and Bs to direct and control the early learning process. But the right brain's behavioral gestalts indicate that behavioral habits have formed. People commonly describe that new behavioral state with ideas like: "Now I've got the feel of it. Now I see it. Now I feel I know how to do it." The "emotive ropes" or "emotive bindings" (commonly described as "feeling right") that hold behavioral gestalts together are probably the main bases of prosody and dysprosody. *Prosody* and *dysprosody* are the nonverbal affective components of vocal and so-called body language. Monrad-Krohn (1947) and E. D. Ross and Mesulam (1979) describe the essential role prosody plays in effective interpersonal communication and the severe emotional problems dysprosody causes. We mention those concepts merely as examples of the essential contribution that the silent right brain makes to effective linguistic communication.

An important therapeutic insight is that people's wordless, superconscious attitudes create the impression that magical, external HEs, SHEs, ITs, and THEYs are in control of their emotions. Fortunately, though, these impressions are often illusions. Otherwise, psychotherapy would be a waste of time and money.

Another way the client's problems are conceptualized in RBT is in terms of how rational or irrational the beliefs and attitudes associated with the problem seem to be. We teach the patient how to make this decision about rationality versus irrationality on the basis of whether or not the thought, emotional feeling, or physical behavior of concern is based on three or more of the five rules for rational behavior used in RBT.

Before we describe those rules, however, we will first discuss what the word *rational*, as used in RBT, does *not* mean. It does not mean what most people mean when they use the word.

Most people (including most traditional psychotherapists) use the word *rational* to describe their carefully thought-out, logically coherent ideas and actions, and use the word *irrational* to describe the illogical, unreasonable, or contrary ideas and actions of other people. There is a universal tendency to consider one's own ideas and actions more rational, or more frequently rational, than other people's.

When you tell people that their ideas or actions are irrational (or they tell you that yours are), are you and they usually in agreement or disagreement? Most probably you and they are in disagreement almost every time. That fact applies to most people who have healthy, undrugged brains.

People with healthy, undrugged brains rarely feel that their most sincere, deeply held beliefs are wrong or irrational. So, if people's pretherapy beliefs and disbeliefs were all they needed to solve their emotional problems, they would not need psychotherapy. RBT holds that to be healthy and therapeutic, therefore, the meaning of *rational* has to go beyond personal beliefs and disbeliefs and refer to an optimal level of mental health. This explains why, when RBT therapists use the word *rational*, they refer to cognitive, emotive, and physical behaviors that simultaneously obey at least three of the following five rules for optimal mental health:

1. Healthy behavior is based on obvious fact.
2. Healthy behavior best helps you protect your life and health.
3. Healthy behavior best helps you achieve your short-term and long-term goals.
4. Healthy behavior best helps you avoid your most undesirable conflicts with other people.
5. Healthy behavior best helps you feel the emotions you want to feel, without alcohol or other drugs.

Now change the word *healthy* to *rational* in those rules, and you will have the five rules used in RBT to describe rational thoughts, beliefs, attitudes, emotional feelings, and physical actions.

Remember, though, that it is not enough for cognitive, emotive, and physical behaviors to obey one or two of those rules. To be rational, behaviors must obey at least three of the five rules at the same time.

The five rules for rational behavior make it easy to recognize irrational behaviors. In RBT, irrational behavior means cognitive, emotive, and physical behaviors that simultaneously disobey three or more of the five rules.

You may wonder: What about a behavior that obeys one or two of the rational rules, disobeys one or two, and is irrelevant to the others? The behavior cannot be rational in the RBT meaning of the word; at best, it will be *nonrational*. But nonrational behavior is not good enough to produce optimal mental health, so RBT therapists reject it as readily as they reject clearly irrational behavior.

CLINICAL APPLICATIONS

THE THERAPEUTIC RELATIONSHIP

Our research on the therapeutic relationship in RBT (Maultsby, 1975b) indicated an interesting fact. There is good reason to doubt that there is an objective thing in RBT that can be reliably recognized as a "therapeutic relationship." Instead, it seems more logical to talk about therapeutic *interactions*—interactions between therapists and clients that help clients help themselves.

That research finding led us to conclude that consistent therapeutic interactions in RBT have three essential features: (1) efficient teaching of effective self-help concepts and techniques to clients; (2) a friendly, competent therapist; and (3) a cooperative patient. For a detailed discussion of this topic, see chapter 9 in *Rational Behavior Therapy* (Maultsby, 1984).

STRATEGIES OF TREATMENT

Some therapists or counselors might ask, "But if attitudes are wordless and superconscious, how can you get people to change them?" The answer is: Easily! Just show them how to convert their wordless attitudes back to their belief forms. Here's how.

First, point out that attitudes and beliefs are simply different forms of the results of the same A perceptions and B thoughts, having been processed differently by the right and left brain. Once people understand this, they usually have no trouble seeing that beliefs are simply the word forms of attitudes, and that attitudes are simply the wordless forms of beliefs. Long before their therapy, most clients have learned that their attitudes and beliefs are intimately related. So they are already well prepared for the next step in converting an attitude to its spoken belief form.

Second, tell clients to ask themselves and then honestly answer this question: "By reacting as I did, what ideas did I imply that I sincerely believed?"

Third, give clients a common yet instructive example of their attitudes in action. A good example is this: Suppose you were driving a car and a child suddenly ran across the road in front of you. You would immediately slam on the brakes and feel afraid, without taking time to think anything first. By reacting that way, you would have behaved as if you had sincerely thought, "I'm about to have a terrible accident; I'd better stop immediately." Well, those ideas would have been your attitudes. They are the appropriate ideas that would have come into your head if you had had the time to think anything before you slammed on the brakes; these ideas express the wordless or unspoken forms of your safe-driving beliefs.

Your wordless or unspoken beliefs exist in your superconscious mind as attitudes. Superconscious attitudes enable a person to react to external situations instantly and seemingly involuntarily, but with appropriate, learned reactions (such as fearful braking), without needing to think conscious thoughts about the situation beforehand.

Now suppose that while driving, you see two children running down the sidewalk parallel to the street. You would probably maintain your speed and continue to feel calm about doing it. Again, you would react without consciously thinking anything. Why? Because your controlling attitudes then would be the unspoken mental equivalent of this belief: "There is no danger; I have no reason to slow down or feel afraid." Those personal examples show you clearly the essential role that attitudes play in rapid, logical, appropriate emotional and physical reactions.

THE NORMAL THERAPEUTIC SEQUENCE IN RBT

First do the initial evaluation. We almost always complete the evaluation in an hour. On rare occasions, however, unusually distressed clients with unusually complicated problems require as much as 3 hours of ventilating before they are ready to get involved in therapy. Here's the two-part rule: When we have heard all we want to hear about a new patient's problem *and* the patient seems ready to start looking for therapeutic solutions, that ends the initial evaluation. Then formal RBT begins immediately.

Normally, the first step in formal RBT is introducing clients to their emotional ABCs. If you are also using the recommended rational bibliotherapy, you would assign your clients chapter 1 in *You and Your Emotions* (Maultsby & Hendricks, 1974); or for alcoholics or other drug abusers, you would assign booklet 1 in the rational bibliotherapeutic series *Freedom from Alcohol and Tranquilizers* (Maultsby, 1979). Depending on how cooperative your clients are, you might spend one or two sessions on the emotional ABCs.

Next you would cover the five rules for optimal emotional health—that is, the five rules for rational behavior. The bibliotherapy assignments would then be chapter 2 in *You and Your Emotions* or booklet 2 in the bibliotherapeutic series for alcoholics and other drug abusers.

Again, depending on your clients' cooperativeness, you might spend one, two, or maybe even three sessions getting them used to thinking of and applying the five rational rules to their problem-related thinking and behavior.

Next, you would explain *cognitive-emotive dissonance* to your clients. Cognitive-emotive dissonance is the unavoidable stage in therapeutic change when ill-prepared clients (regardless of the therapeutic technique) are most likely to want to give up their therapeutic efforts. However, adequate rational preparation enables clients to move rapidly through this stage to the advanced therapeutic change called *emotional insight* (see chapter 13 in *Rational Behavior Therapy*, Maultsby, 1984). Then you would introduce your clients to the idea of doing regular, written rational self-analysis (RSA). For the 80% of clients who will bring at least one written RSA per week to therapy, you would structure the therapy sessions around discussing the RSAs. Up to 20% of your educated clients will not diligently do either bibliotherapy or written RSAs, but they will still benefit from RBT if they keep regular appointments and if you discuss their problems using the ABC format and the five rules for rational thinking. In our opinion, these clients learn most comfortably from vocal rather than written communications. They especially like and benefit from listening to recordings of their RBT sessions.

After your clients discuss with you a well-done RSA, they are ready to start doing daily rational-emotive imagery (REI).

After clients begin doing REIs, they are still given weekly bibliotherapy assignments until they complete the six chapters in *You and Your Emotions* or the five booklets in the bibliotherapeutic series for alcoholics and other drug abusers. Then, only if clients request further reading materials (about 25% do), we refer them to one of the more advanced self-help books: *Help Yourself to Happiness* (Maultsby, 1975a), *Your Guide to Emotional Well Being* (Maultsby, 1980), or *A Million Dollars for Your Hangover* (Maultsby, 1978).

WRITTEN RATIONAL SELF-ANALYSIS

Written RSA is the first major therapeutic technique in RBT. A written RSA between therapy sessions is a structured way for clients to discover the cause-effect relationship between the cognitive, emotive, and physical components of their personal problems, and also the rational changes they must, and can, make at will to start helping themselves to happiness immediately.

For the best results with written RSAs, have your clients use the standard RSA format (Figure 5) and their own everyday language. They should write down their experiences as soon as possible after they occur; that way they will get the fastest, most lasting results possible. Emphasize that people are never too upset to do an RSA, and that actually an RSA is faster and safer than minor tranquilizers for calming people down.

The correct RSA sequence is as follows:

Step 1. Have clients describe A, the activating event, on the left side of their paper. In their usual language, clients are simply to state the facts as they saw and experienced them.

Step 2. Immediately under their A section, clients are to write B, their beliefs. As best they remember, they are to state word for word their sincere thoughts, self-talk, or inner speech about the A event.

Have clients number each B section idea. Then they are to show whether they had a positive, negative, or neutral attitude about each idea by writing "positive" (or "good"), "negative" (or "bad"), or "neutral" in parentheses following each idea. In the B section, clients are to label all unanswered questions as "rhetorical questions." Next, clients are to state the personal beliefs hidden in those questions;

A.	ACTIVATING EVENT: What you perceive happened.	Da.	CAMERA CHECK: If you perceived anything a video camera would not show, correct that to what a video camera would have shown.
B.	YOUR BELIEFS: Your sincere thoughts about A, plus your attitudes about each B sentence.	Db.	RATIONAL DEBATE OF B: Answer yes or no for each rational question about each B sentence. Then write rational alternative self-talk for each irrational B idea. For ideas that prove to be rational, write "That's rational" in the Db section for that idea.
B-1		Db-1	
B-2		Db-2	
C.	CONSEQUENCES OF B: 1. Emotional feelings 2. Actions	E.	EXPECTED NEW BEHAVIORS: 1. New emotional feelings 2. New actions

FIGURE 5. The standard RSA format

then, in the Db section, clients are to debate rationally each of those stated beliefs.

Normally, it takes about six times as much space to correct irrational thinking as it does to write it. So advise clients to leave six times as many blank lines under each B-section idea as it took to write it. That way, they will probably have enough space on the opposite side of the page to debate that idea rationally in the Db section. Of course, clients can always use the back of the page if they need more space for their rational debate.

After clients complete their B section, they are to count up their positives, negatives, and neutrals. Their totals will show them the main types of attitudes that helped trigger their emotional feelings and the other reactions they put in their C section about A, the activating event. This maneuver makes clear how and why clients' superconscious, wordless attitudes can be more important than their conscious, verbal thoughts in some of their reactions.

Step 3. In the C section, have your clients write the behavioral consequences of their B ideas. The C section has two parts: emotional feelings and actions. In the appropriate section, clients are to state simply how they felt emotionally and what they did physically.

Step 4. Immediately under the C section, have clients write the five rational questions. In reality, questions are neither rational nor irrational. "The five rational questions" is just a shorthand way of saying "the five questions that help ensure that your cognitions, emotional feelings, and physical actions will be rational." The five rational questions follow:

a. Is my thinking here based on obvious facts?
b. Will my thinking here help me protect my life and health?
c. Will my thinking here best help me achieve my short-term and long-term goals?
d. Will my thinking here best help me avoid my most unwanted conflicts with others?
e. Will my thinking here best help me habitually feel the emotions I want to feel?

Step 5. Opposite the C section, have your clients write the E section; it contains the new emotional feelings and actions they want to have in similar future A events.

Advise clients not to put wishes of the "Oh, if I only had..." type in their E section. The E section is for wants that they have already decided to make their habits. So they are to list only emotions and actions for which they can honestly say, "The next time I shall...." Remind clients that the E section describes only their own choices of new emotional and physical actions for similar future A events. They are to ignore completely behaviors that others (including their therapist) may want them to learn but that they are not yet convinced are right for them.

Initially, in RSAs of negative emotions, the most rational new emotional goal will be to feel less negative or more calm in similar future A events. But you may wonder, "What if clients want to enjoy an event they now hate or fear?" That is okay; they have that emotional choice, too. But the most rational emotional goals will usually be those that clients are most likely to achieve most quickly. This brings us to an important insight: To replace a strong negative emotion with a positive emotion, people must first pass through the calm or neutral emotions. Calm or neutral feelings are real emotions, too. The opposite of negative emotion is not necessarily positive emotion but can also be neutral emotion.

If, for example, clients want to stop having pre-exam anxiety, they must first get rid of the fearful attitudes that maintain their anxious responses. If they immediately require themselves to love taking exams, they will probably fail, for they will be demanding too much immediate emotional change. Permanent new emotional learning does not occur in such an extreme, dramatic way. That is why their most rational first emotional goal would probably be to fear taking exams less and less until they can take them calmly. That's enough for most people. But after that, if clients still want to, they can learn to love taking exams.

Common examples of hated behaviors clients often want to learn to like doing are studying; doing certain types of work; writing; speaking in public; and refusing to overeat, drink too much, or smoke anymore. Usually though, your clients will not want to like the things they hate or are depressed about. They will just want to calmly forget them.

Sometimes your clients will not be sure what emotions or actions they want to have in future A events. Tell those clients to leave the E section blank but to make sure they put their most sincerely rational thoughts in their Db section. Their sincere rational thoughts will often point them directly to the most rational emotional and behavioral goals to adopt. When they discover these goals, they are to write them in their E sections.

Remind your clients that rational E sections will be logically related to their rationally chosen Db-section ideas. So it will be a waste of time to write "to feel calm" at E if they have Db ideas like "It really is awful. No one in their right mind would stand for it. I will just die if it happens again."

At this point clients often ask, "Isn't it unhealthy for people to stop having emotions?" Yes, to completely stop having emotions would be most unhealthy. Fortunately, though, doing RSAs cannot completely stop people from having emotions. The minds of physically healthy people force their brains to trigger and maintain some type of emotional state every second they are awake. So if people are conscious and have healthy, undrugged brains, they will always have some type of emotion. It may not be the emotion they want; it may even be the one they hate the most; but they will definitely have some emotion.

There are only two things that RSAs do: First, without alcohol or other drugs, RSAs help people have fewer undesirable emotions and physical reactions; and second, RSAs help people have more desirable emotions and physical reactions, also without alcohol or other drugs. So, correct meaningless E-section statements such as "I want to have no feelings at all." No one can achieve that emotional goal and remain healthy and awake.

Step 6. The sixth step in doing an RSA is Da, the camera check of A. Clients are to ask themselves: Would a video camera have recorded the A events as I described them? If their answer is "yes" for each A section sentence, clients are to write "factual" or "all facts" in the Da section and go on to the Db section. But if clients have "no" answers, that means they have mistaken one or more personal opinions for a statement of fact. In the Da section, clients are to correct any such statements to reflect what a video camera would have recorded. For example, you would correct "I cried my heart out all the way home" to "I cried intensely until I got home, but my heart did not leave my body, not even for a second."

Do camera images always accurately describe facts? No, for just like the human brain, cameras can misrepresent obvious facts. But the value of the camera check is not based on what a video camera might have recorded, but on what a video camera could not have recorded. For example, take the self-perception "I cried my heart out." No video camera could have recorded a person's heart leaving, or being out of, his or her body. So, that A-section statement could not pass the camera check, as it would not fit the obvious facts of the person's situation. But to have the most emotionally healthy self-control, people's perceptions must accurately fit the obvious facts of their situations.

Sometimes clients are concerned about how to write the A section of an RSA for an emotional feeling that is not in response to some specific external event. They point out that one cannot do a camera check of an emotional feeling. But emotional feelings are neuropsychophysiological facts; clients either have them, and describe them accurately, or they do not. So they can put simple statements of emotional facts, such as "I was sad" or "I felt depressed" in the A section though they would still write "sad" or "depressed" in the emotion part of their C section. Then, in their Da section, they would simply write "factual" for their camera check of an A section about feelings.

Remember, though, that in RBT, feelings are almost always one-word nouns. If at A clients write "I just died from embarrassment," in the Da section they would correct that to "I did not die, but I did feel more embarrassed than I wanted to feel." Then in their C section they would also write "embarrassed."

Step 7. The seventh step in doing an RSA is Db, the rational check and debate of each B-section idea using the five rational questions. Then, as needed, clients are to replace irrational B ideas with rational ideas in the Db section.

First, clients are to read over their B-1 idea; next, see if they can give three or more honest "yes" answers to the five rational questions about it; if they can, they write "That's rational" at Db-1 and go on to B-2. But if they cannot give at least three honest "yes" answers to the five rational questions, clients write "That idea is irrational" at Db-1. Then they think of different ideas about their situation that have these two features:

a. The clients can give at least three honest "yes" answers to the five rational questions about their new ideas.
b. The clients are willing to make their new ideas into personal beliefs by acting them out in future A situations.

Then, clients are to write those ideas in their Db section. However, remind your clients that it does not matter how rational an idea may be in itself; if they are not willing to make that idea their personal belief by habitually acting it out, it will not help them.

RATIONAL-EMOTIVE IMAGERY

Rational-emotive imagery (REI) is the second major therapeutic technique in RBT. It is the rational technique for healthy emotional practice. Its basis is the neuropsychological fact that imagining (i.e., mentally practicing emotional or physical reactions) produces the same quality of rapid learning as real life experience produces (Beritoff, 1965; Eccles, 1958; Luria, 1966a, 1966b, 1973; Maultsby, 1984; Mowrer, 1966; Razran, 1961). Consequently, every time people mentally picture themselves thinking, emotionally feeling, and physically acting the way they want to, they are using REI, the most efficient form of emotional practice. REI is also helpful for enhancing physical practice. When clients practice REI daily, they teach themselves new emotional habits in the safest and fastest way possible. The following is a list of standard instructions for REI.

1. Read the Da, Db, and E sections of a well-done RSA.

2. Get relaxed using the instant better feeling maneuver (IBFM) (Maultsby, 1984).

3. When you are noticeably relaxed, mentally picture yourself as vividly as possible back in the Da situation described in your RSA.

4. As you vividly picture yourself back in the Da situation, thinking your rational Db thoughts, imagine yourself having your E section emotional feelings and physical behavior. Make the experience as vivid and realistic as possible.

5. Maintain that image and rethink your rational Db thoughts. If B-section thoughts pop into your mind, calmly challenge them with your Db thoughts, and calmly ignore all non-RSA thoughts.

6. Repeat Step 5 over and over for 10 minutes. If you have two RSAs to practice, spend 5 minutes on each. But do not do REI on more than two RSAs during one 10-minute REI session.

Tell clients not to expect an emotional miracle after just two or three REI sessions. It takes both time and repeated practice to extinguish and autocondition new emotional habits. Clients are to practice REI daily using the same RSA until they start experiencing the type of C-section responses they want to have in everyday life. The daily REI routine we recommend is listed below:

1. Advise clients to put themselves to sleep every night with REI. It is cheaper, safer, and quicker than most sleeping pills.

2. Ten minutes before clients get out of bed each morning is the next time for REI. It will help them start their day with the

pleasantly powerful emotional feelings associated with confidence of success.

3. Ten minutes before lunch, or instead of their cigarette break or coffee break, clients are to do REI again. Then they will be fighting irrational emotions, lung cancer, heart disease, and bad breath all at the same time!

4. Especially before their first afternoon cocktail, have clients do 10 minutes of REI. If they do, they will be most likely to stop after only one or two cocktails, then remember eating and enjoying their evening meal.

In addition to the REI routine, clients can also do REI with their eyes open—while driving or riding to work, waiting in traffic jams, or waiting for someone who is late. At those times REI helps keep blood pressure down and prevent other stress-related difficulties, such as tension headaches. Having a daily REI schedule enables clients to autocondition their new, healthier cognitions (which are essential for their new healthier behaviors) in the shortest time possible. In addition, daily REIs reinforce clients' other self-help efforts and increase their commitment to therapeutic change.

OVERCOMING OBSTACLES TO CLIENT PROGRESS

One way of overcoming the obstacles to a client's progress is to follow the normal therapeutic sequence in RBT, as outlined in the strategies of treatment section.

Another method used is *rational bibliotherapy*. Rational bibliotherapy means systematic reading of easy-to-understand self-help reading materials based on RBT theory. This is a simple yet highly effective way to overcome therapeutic resistance and get clients quickly involved in therapeutic emotional self-help. But as with any self-help maneuver, the therapeutic results vary directly with the amount of structured, goal-oriented instructions clients receive. In our experience, the most effective instructions for bibliotherapy include daily reading goals.

Immediately after the initial evaluation, we ask clients to read chapter 1 in *You and Your Emotions* (Maultsby & Hendricks, 1974) once a day, every day until the next appointment. Even clients who read slowly can probably read the chapter in 20 minutes. We emphasize that if clients are not willing to invest 20 minutes a day in solving their problems, they are dooming themselves to slow therapeutic progress. We also point out that clients have the right to progress as rapidly or slowly as they choose.

The reading on the first day is merely to give clients a clear understanding of the material. The second day's reading is to help clients discover ideas with which they disagree. We ask clients to write those ideas down and bring them to the next session for discussion. At first, most clients tend to disagree with almost anything that will require them to change their habitual behavior; thus, showing immediate interest in clients' possible disagreements is an important treatment strategy. It quickly gets those potential therapeutic barriers out in the open where they can be speedily eliminated.

The third day's reading is for clients to find and briefly write down the ideas with which they agree and why they agree with them. Having clients record these ideas aids therapeutic progress in two ways. First, it increases the probability that clients will put those ideas into daily use, and second, it increases the probability that clients will avoid the antitherapeutic game of "fool-the-therapist."

For the fourth day's reading, we tell clients to look for and write notes about events described in the book that they have seen in the daily lives of others. This exercise helps clients quickly get over the self-defeating idea that their lives are uniquely complicated or difficult.

For the fifth day's reading, we have clients look for examples of events in their daily lives in which they applied the insights gained from their bibliotherapeutic reading and the results they achieved. The standard RBT bibliotherapeutic reading *You and Your Emotions* (Maultsby & Hendricks, 1974) describes only basic principles of normal human behavior. Therefore, once people start thinking about them, they readily see those basic principles in action in their own daily lives and the daily lives of others.

Since repetition is usually the royal road to the most rapid learning, for the seventh day's reading we ask clients to review their notes as preparation for discussing them in their next therapy session.

After these instructions, 80% to 90% of our clients will return to therapy having read their assignment at least once; of those, 40% to 60% will have read it twice; between 10% and 30% will have read it six or more times. Many of these latter clients will have moderate to severe problems with obsessive-compulsive behavior. They are usually the most worrisome and difficult clients to treat, but calm persistence usually yields good therapeutic results.

Rational bibliotherapy is not essential for successful RBT; neither are RSA and REI. But these techniques make RBT ideally effective and most enjoyable for both therapists and clients. Still, if psychotherapists discuss their clients' problems, using the ABC model and the five rules for rational behavior, their clients will still make appropriate therapeutic progress. On the average, however, therapeutic progress will be slower than it would have been if clients had used these techniques. Still, 10% to 20% of our clients seem to prefer to let us do all the work.

CASE STUDY

A case is treated according to the normal sequence of RBT outlined earlier. The intake would be obtained as outlined and the client would be given the recommended rational bibliotherapy. The client would be taught the emotional ABCs and the five rules for rational thinking. The concept of cognitive-emotive dissonance would be explained to the client as appropriate. After the intake and up to the RSA phase, therapy is primarily a directive educational process with the therapist serving as the educator. It is only at the RSA phase that the client is doing most of the work.

This example is a client who has already learned her ABCs and the five rules for rational thinking and is currently doing an RSA, which represents the backbone of the work done by clients in an RBT session.

One of the features of RBT is that when you learn how to apply the concepts to one problem you can easily apply them to another, as this case will demonstrate.

Dr. F., a widowed English professor, and her teenage daughter had received RBT to learn how to interact more rationally with each other. About a year after therapy, Dr. F. decided to use her skill in doing RSAs to solve her problem with procrastination. When Dr. F. later described her success, we asked her to let us present her RSA here as a teaching example. Let's now examine each section of her complete RSA. It demonstrates well how and why getting clients to learn to do RSAs helps make RBT a comprehensive, short-term psychotherapy that produces long-term results.

Dr. F.'s RSA

A. ACTIVATING EVENT: For a month now, I have three letters of recommendation hanging over my head and it's driving me crazy.	Da. CAMERA CHECK: Nothing is hanging over my head and I am the only IT that can drive me crazy. But since I don't like the idea of being crazy, I refuse to drive myself there. A month ago, I promised three students I would write letters of recommendation for them. But instead of writing the letters, I'm making myself miserable while I put off doing it.
B. YOUR BELIEFS:	Db. RATIONAL DEBATE OF B:
B-1 What can I say? (negative) That's a rhetorical question hiding the belief that I don't know what to say.	Db-1 My belief gets a "no" for RQs (rational questions) 1, 3, 4, and 5. Rational thinking is: I can say anything I want to say. I don't have to be effusive or dishonest. I can simply say I believe the students have whatever potential I believe they have to do graduate work in English. Then I can describe what they have done in my classes.
B-2 Why should I have to write letters when I don't want to? (negative) That's another rhetorical question hiding the belief that it's unfair that they should expect me to write letters I don't want to write.	Db-2 My belief gets a "no" for RQs, 1, 3, 4, and 5. Rational thinking is: Writing letters of recommendation is part of my job. Therefore, I am obliged to write letters for students if they request them. Three letters is a reasonable number. So to say that I shouldn't be expected to write them is absurd. And it's even more absurd for me to feel angry about it. I'm just trying to justify avoiding my responsibilities. I agreed to work for the university; writing letters is a part of my job. So I calmly choose to write them.

B-3	I hardly know these students. (negative)	Db-3	That idea gets "no" for RQs 1, 3, 4, and 5. Rational thinking is: If I want to know these students better than I do, I can easily schedule conferences with them and get better acquainted.
B-4	I'll be forced to say things about these students that I don't believe.	Db-4	My thinking here gets "no" for RQs 1, 3, 4, and 5. Rational thinking is: I won't be forced to say anything I don't believe. I alone will write the letters. I alone will decide what I say in them. My belief just doesn't make rational sense, so I'll give it up and write the letters.
B-5	I don't want to write letters when I don't know the facts. (negative)	Db-5	That idea gets "no" for RQs 3, 4, and 5. My thought is a fact, but it's irrelevant. If I want more facts than I already have about my students, all I have to do is study their files.
B-6	I don't like being forced to do anything I don't want to do. (negative)	Db-6	That idea gets "no" for RQs 3, 4, and 5. My thought is a fact, but it's irrelevant to this situation. No one is going to overpower me and force me to write the letters. So I don't and won't have to write them. But because it is a part of my job and I choose to do my job well, I will write them.
B-7	I know I shouldn't be procrastinating like this. (negative)	Db-7	That idea gets "no" for RQs 1, 3, and 5. I should be procrastinating, exactly as I am doing. But since I don't like this experience, I'll change it immediately.
C.	CONSEQUENCES OF B: 1. Emotional feelings (a) Anger (b) Anxiety (c) Shame 2. Actions (a) Procrastination.	E.	EXPECTED NEW BEHAVIORS: 1. New emotional feelings (a) Calm, if not positive feelings 2. New actions (a) Immediately write these and future letters of recommendation.

156

Well-done RSAs immediately decrease negative emotions and reinforce rational, positive emotions. Whether clients analyze positive or negative emotions, therefore, well-done RSAs cause them to feel better immediately. What if clients don't get that immediate better feeling? Advise them beforehand that in such cases it's best to check their RSA immediately for (a) accuracy of their camera check of A and (b) sincerity of Db-rational debates of their B-section beliefs. If no improvements in the RSA seem indicated, that RSA is to be a priority discussion topic in the next RBT session.

Why have clients analyze their positive emotions? Analyzing their positive emotions helps clients become aware of their essential contributions to their happiness. That awareness makes clients more appropriately dependent on themselves and less irrationally dependent on their therapists, on other people, or on fate for their happiness. But as we encourage clients to do an RSA on every troublesome negative emotion, we suggest RSAs on positive emotions only occasionally—for instance, when clients seem to be inappropriately ignoring their own contributions to their happiness, or when clients seem to be inappropriately exaggerating the perceived contribution of others or of fate.

Dr. F's well-done RSA is typical of the RSAs cooperative clients start doing after 8 to 10 RBT sessions. Skill in doing RSAs makes clients rapidly and happily self-confident in the most rational sense. That's why terminating in RBT is usually a progressively smooth and mutually pleasant experience.

REFERENCES

Adams, R. D., & Victor, M. (1977). *Principles of neurology.* New York: McGraw-Hill.

Beritoff, J. S. (1965). *Neural mechanisms of higher vertebrate behavior* (W. T. Liberson, Trans.). Boston: Little, Brown.

Bogen, J. F. (1969a). The other side of the brain, 1: Dysgraphia and dyscopia following cerebral commissurotomy. *Bulletin of the Los Angeles Neurological Society, 34*(2), 73–105.

Bogen, J. F. (1969b). The other side of the brain, 2: An appositional mind. *Bulletin of the Los Angeles Neurological Society, 34*(3), 135–162.

Brandsma, J. M., Maultsby, M. C., & Welsh, R. (1979). *Outpatient treatment of alcoholism.* Baltimore: University Park.

DiCara, L. V. (1970). Learning in the autonomic nervous system. *Scientific American, 222*(January), 31–39.

Eaton, M. T., Peterson, M. H., & Davis, J. (1976). *Psychiatry flushing.* New York: Medical Examination Publishing Company.

Eccles, J. C. (1958). The physiology of imagination. *Scientific American, 199*(September), 135.

Ellis, A. (1962). *Reason and emotion in psychotherapy.* New York: Lyle Stuart.

Gazzaniga, M. S. (1970). *The dissected brain.* Englewood Cliffs, NJ: Prentice Hall.

Grace, W. J., & Graham, D. T. (1952). Relationship of specific attitudes and emotions to certain bodily diseases. *Psychosomatic Medicine, 14,* 243–251.

Graham, D. T., Kabler, J. D., & Graham, F. K. (1962). Physiological response to the suggestion of attitudes specific for hives and hypertension. *Psychosomatic Medicine, 24,* 159–169.

Graham, D. T., Stern, J. A., & Winokur, G. (1958). Experimental investigation of the specificity of attitude hypothesis in psychosomatic disease. *Psychosomatic Medicine, 20,* 446–457.

Hudgins, C. V. (1933). Conditioning and voluntary control of the pupillary light reflex. *Journal of General Psychology, 8,* 38–48.

Luria, A. R. (1960). *The role of speech in the regulation of normal and abnormal behavior.* Bethesda, MD: U.S. Department of Health, Education, and Welfare, Russian Scientific Translation Program.

Luria, A. R. (1966a). *Higher cortical function in man.* New York: Basic Books.

Luria, A. R. (1966b). *Human brain and psychological processes.* New York: Harper & Row.

Luria, A. R. (1973). *The working brain.* New York: Basic Books.

Maultsby, M. C. (1975a). *Help yourself to happiness: Through rational self-counseling.* New York: Institute for Rational-Emotive Therapy.

Maultsby, M. C. (1975b). Patients' opinion of the therapeutic relationship in rational behavior psychotherapy. *Psychological Reports, 37,* 795–798.

Maultsby, M. C. (1978). *A million dollars for your hangover.* Lexington, KY: Rational Self-Help Aids.

Maultsby, M. C. (1979). *Freedom from alcohol and tranquilizers* [Series of five rational bibliotherapeutic booklets]. Lexington, KY: Rational Self-Help Aids.

Maultsby, M. C. (1980). *Your guide to emotional well being.* Lexington, KY: Rational Self-Help Aids.

Maultsby, M. C. (1982). Rational behavior therapy. In S. M. Turner & R. T. Jones (Eds.), *Behavior modification in black populations: Empirical findings and psychosocial issues*. New York: Plenum.

Maultsby, M. C. (1984). *Rational behavior therapy*. Englewood Cliffs, NJ: Prentice Hall.

Maultsby, M. C., & Hendricks, A. (1974). *You and your emotions*. Lexington, KY: Rational Self-Help Aids.

Miller, N. E. (1969). Learning of visceral and glandular responses. *Science, 163*, 436–445.

Monrad-Krohn, G. H. (1947). Dysprosody, or altered melody of language. *Brain, 70*, 405–415.

Mowrer, O. H. (1966). *Learning theory and the symbolic process*. New York: Wiley.

Olds, J. (1969). The central nervous system and the reinforcement of behavior. *American Psychologist, 24*, 114–132.

Patton, L. P. (1976). *The effects of rational behavior training on emotionally disturbed adolescents in alternative school settings*. Unpublished doctoral dissertation, North Texas State University.

Razran, G. H. S. (1961). The observable unconscious and the inferrable conscious in current Soviet psychophysiology. *Psychological Review, 68*, 81–147.

Ross, E. D., & Mesulam, M. (1979). Dominant language functions of the right hemisphere: Prosody and emotional gesturing. *Archives of Neurology, 36*, 144–148.

Ross, G. (1978). Reducing irrational personality traits, trait anxiety and intra-interpersonal needs in high school students. *Journal of Measurements and Evaluations in Guidance, 11*, 44–50.

Rotter, J. B. (1954). *Social learning and clinical psychology*. New York: Prentice Hall.

Rotter, J. B. (1966). Generalized expectancies of internal versus external control of reinforcement. *Psychological Monographs, 80,*. 1–28.

Rotter, J. B. (1971). External control and internal control. *Psychology Today, 5*, 37–59.

Schwager, H. A. (1975). *Effects of applying rational behavior training in a group counseling situation with disadvantaged adults*. Counseling Services Report 22. Glassgo AFB, MT: Mountain-Plains Education, Economic Development Programs.

Smythies, J. R. (1966). *The neurological foundations of psychiatry: An outline of the mechanism of emotions, memory, learning and the organization of behavior with particular regard to the limbic system.* New York: Academic Press.

Staats, A. W., & Staats, C. K. (1958). Attitudes established by classical conditioning. *Journal of Abnormal and Social Psychology, 57,* 187–191.

Staats, C. K., & Staats, A. W. (1957). Meaning established by classical conditioning. *Journal of Experimental Psychology, 54,* 74–80.

Tobias, P. V. (1970). Brain size, grey matter and race—Fact or fiction? *American Journal of Physical Anthropology, 32,* 3–26.

Volgyesi, F. A. (1954). School for patients: Hypnosis, therapy and psychoprophylaxis. *British Journal of Medical Hypnosis, 5,* 10–17.

Watzlawick, P. (1978). *The language of change.* New York: Basic Books.

PART II

CULTURAL PARADIGMS

CHAPTER 7

TRANSCULTURAL COUNSELING WITH AMERICAN INDIANS AND ALASKAN NATIVES: CONTEMPORARY ISSUES FOR CONSIDERATION

JOHN JOSEPH PEREGOY

It is the primary goal of this chapter to present factors to consider in planning to provide a helping relationship in a transcultural setting with American Indians and Alaskan Natives. In pursuing this goal, structural biases and myths will be explored as they affect the perception of the non-Indian other when working with the American Indian or Alaskan Native (Indian/Native) client. Components of the American Indian's perception of mainstream America will also be explored through ethnographic interviews conducted by the author. This information is presented as a way to understand historical and contemporary issues that currently affect values and interaction in an increasingly multicultural world.

The first section focuses on conflicting definitions of Indian/Native governmental status. The second section examines spiritual orientations, selected shared cultural value systems, and contemporary social issues. The third section provides a look at educational experiences and opportunities. The fourth section analyzes economic trends and challenges that have affected Indian/Native tribes since the beginning of the "contact era" and hold contemporary meaning in the Indian/Native worlds. With the preceding information in mind, the final section presents several culturally sensitive approaches for use in transcultural settings with Indian/Native clients.

WHO IS THE AMERICAN INDIAN?

American Indian is an ethnic descriptor that refers to all North American Native people, "including Indians, Alaskan Natives, Aleuts, Eskimos, and Metis, or mixed bloods" (LaFromboise & Graff Low, 1989, p. 115). The *Indian* part of this phrase finds its roots in a mistaken label assigned by a wayward sailor in 1492 (Trimble, 1981). In actuality, when contact was made in the "New World" there were numerous tribes of indigenous peoples throughout this "new" land. Estimates of the pre-contact population vary from 10 to 45 million according to some researchers to around 470,000 according to U.S. government estimates (Allen, 1986). In the 1990 census, approximately 1,959,234 persons described themselves as American Indians (U.S. Department of Commerce, 1992a). This estimate is probably conservative because of the number of Indians/Natives who chose to "pass" (Goffman, 1963) on the census for personal reasons. *Passing* is a word Goffman uses to describe the volitional action taken to conceal one's stigma with an unknowing public by a person who is discreditable. This author estimates the number to be 2.5–2.8 million Indians/Natives.

Today in the United States there are 517 tribes recognized by the federal government (LaFromboise & Graff Low, 1989); this number does not include the tribes that died out entirely during early contact times nor the tribes that were terminated in the 1950s and 1960s through what some have called "cultural genocide" (Allen, 1986). Although government efforts have been extended in the recent past to minimize population growth (Dobyns, 1983), Indians/Natives are proportionally the fastest growing ethnic group in the United States. (Herring, 1992).

About 625,136 Indian/Native people are 15 years of age or younger (U.S. Department of Commerce, 1992a). This number represents an increase of approximately 36% from the 1980 census. The median age for American Indians is 22.9 years, for Alaskan Natives it is 18 years, and for Whites it is 31.1 years (U.S. Congress, Office of

Technology Assessment, 1986). At least 32% of the Indian/Native population is 15 years of age or younger; 41% are 20 years of age or younger (U.S. Department of Commerce, 1992a). Based on these statistical increases, it is projected that the population of Indians/Natives will likely double within the next 15 years.

Each tribe maintains its own unique customs, values, traditions, social organizations, spiritual beliefs and practices, and family and clan structures (LaFromboise & Graff Low, 1989). Tribes range from the very traditional, in which members speak their tribal language at home, to the mostly acculturated, whose members use English as their first language.

It is estimated that the 1990 census will show that at least 63% of all Indians/Natives live off the reservation. World War II, economic conditions, and government programs such as the Relocation Act of 1953 have contributed to the off-reservation movement (Burt, 1986). A population shift from the reservation to the city has resulted in an increase in intertribal and interethnic marriages. This diversity is also compounded by the fact that over 60% of all Indians are of mixed background, the result of intermarriages with Black, White, Hispanic, and Asian populations (Trimble & Fleming, 1989). These demographics show that the Indian/Native of today is not isolated in a reservation enclave but is rather a member of the general community (Peregoy, 1991).

Unlike other ethnic or minority groups, there are legal definitions tied for the most part to blood quantum for the Indian/Native. However, there is no single agreed-upon definition. Government services, either treaty-bound or legislated obligations, such as housing, medical and mental health services, educational programs funded under the Johnson O'Malley Act, and other services, are the reason legal definitions are needed. Although funding for these obligated services has risen over the years, it has not kept up with the population growth. Tremendous strains are being placed on the tribes and the federal government to provide adequate services.

The multiple definitions of *Indian* can be understood by examining three different governmental criteria. The Bureau of Indian Affairs (BIA), once under the Department of War and now under the Department of the Interior, defines an Indian/Native as a person whose blood quantum is at least one-fourth. Any less than one-fourth and the individual is not eligible for services from the BIA (Trimble, 1981).

The Department of Education, on the other hand, operates under a more liberal definition of Indian/Native. Its definition includes tribal recognition because some tribes do not subscribe to the one-fourth definition; a descendant in the first or second degree of someone who is a tribal member (child or grandchild of an enrolled member); someone who is considered by the Secretary of the Interior for any purpose; and/or an Eskimo, Aleut, or Alaskan Native (Indian Fellowship Program, 1989).

Finally, we can view the drastic differences in the definition of *Indian* by considering the Bureau of the Census. It relies on self-identification, although census takers occasionally will attempt to verify information with neighbors. Trimble (1981) calls this a "criteria more of a social-cultural affiliation rather than a legal, sanguinolent one" (p. 206).

The confusion of multiple definitions does not stop here. Some people, Indians/Natives or not, feel that if a person is not a full-blood, then the person is not Indian/Native. These differences in blood quantum and "Indianness" are based in "legalistic genetics," imposed largely from the outside, and rooted in an Anglo-Saxon paradigm (Wax, Wax, & Dumont, 1989).

Indian/Native identity is not only a blood-quantum or lineage relationship, but more specifically, a relationship of sociocultural affiliation, embedded in reciprocal recognition. Wilson (1992) recently pointed out someone of mixed descent is no less than a full-blood if the person's heart and soul are intertwined with the Indian/Native community. It is clear that after more than 500 years of contact with Euro-Americans, the Indians/Natives of today have survived with both a distinct identity and a commitment to their people. This survival has not come easily, but with much pain and consequence.

The median annual income for Indian/Native families is considerably lower ($13,869) than the national average ($19,928). Twice as many Indians live below the national poverty level compared with the general U.S. population (May, 1988). The unemployment rate continues to be high among Indians/Natives, ranging from 27.5% in urban areas to more than 80% on some reservations (Neligh,

1990). Suicide rates among young Indians/Natives are more than twice the national average for their age group (May, 1987). In Alaska, Alaskan Natives make up 15% of the population, yet suicide rates among men between the ages of 20 and 24 are more than 10 times the national mean (Herring, 1992).

STRUCTURAL BIASES AND MYTHS

From the foregoing discussion, it is easy to surmise that *diversity* is the word that characterizes Indians and Natives. The concept of *Indian* itself is a myth built upon from the time of Columbus. The stereotype of the Indian in the general public's mind is the Plains Indian, dressed in buckskins and wearing a full headdress, with black hair and brown eyes, accented by high cheekbones. As inter-marriage changes the gene pool, many Indians/Natives of today do not appear as others might expect. There are the blond-haired, blue-eyed Indians of the northern plains and the Black Indians of the Carolinas and Florida.

Viewing social intercourse from a symbolic interactionist per-spective, we can look at meaning for the actors involved in an interchange. Sandy, an Assiniboin-Sioux in his mid-20s, spoke of how he saw himself:

> I get these feelings sometimes. I hate to say it, ...but sometimes I wish I wasn't Indian. But then again, I think about it, and I'm proud to be an Indian. I often wonder what it would be like to be White. I see myself as a young man. I'm aware that I'm Indian. I'm sure others are aware of it also.

This statement presents a view of the self in relation to the *other*, a generalized reference group, this group naturally being the White segment of our society as a result of years of oppression and racism. Whites are held as a comparative group against which other groups can gauge their success as individuals or on a group-versus-group basis. By using a comparative group one develops barriers that may hinder the development of skills for surviving and living in a mul-ticultural world. These barriers are invisible, of course, but as real as walls when all segments of a society allow stereotypes and myths to create false realities.

Stereotypes of the Indian/Native as drunk, lazy, and stupid have proliferated around reservations and seeped into the general public's mind as another set of assumptions with which to view the Indian/Native. These stereotypes have been perpetuated and are portrayed in the media and the movies (Price, 1978). Even more so, these stereotypes are evidenced in interaction between groups, for example, by one group acting out in verbal or nonverbal performances or gesticulations. These actions can be words or phrases used to describe Indian/Native people or actions of exaggerated physical mockery. Violence is an extreme example of the consequence of stereotyping behavior.

An interesting phenomenon appears to take place with stereotyping and overt acts of prejudice: Non-Indians living on or near reservations are perceived to use stereotypes and practice discrimination more overtly than their contemporaries away from the reservation (Wax et al., 1989; Peregoy, 1991).

Gloria, an older Crow woman, talking about discrimination in a Native American studies class said, "We kind of noticed [White] people that live close to the reservation, you know, around reservations, are more prejudiced than people farther away."

Although prejudice may be more overt on or near the reservations, it also becomes visible in the general community. Sandy, speaking of being in public and not being recognized physically as an Indian, has overheard several conversations riddled with racial slurs. At the heart of these slurs is the idea that Indian/Native people are dumb and as a result speak slowly. It seems that the oppressor does not consider that English may be a second language for many. Sandy told the story of being in a tavern one night and the conversation he overheard:

This one girl was talking to a guy one night. And she said something in a real slow, deep voice. And he said, "Come on now, cut that out, you sound like a fucking Indian." And he looked at me, and he didn't know I was Indian at that time. I just thought, God, what an ignorant fucker. I just let it go. I guessed he was from a reservation. The worst ones are from reservations.

For the Indian/Native it is easier to pass off an offensive or blatantly racial slur if it can be placed in an acceptable context (Peregoy, 1991). The context Sandy used was that the non-Indian male in the above situation must have been from a reservation area.

When the remarks are reframed and placed in an understandable context, the situation becomes less anxiety provoking.

Sandy's logic in reframing this exchange is based on this assumption: It is more likely that a non-Indian from a reservation area would be so irresponsible as to make such a comment. This is grounded in negotiated meaning and the belief that non-Indians living on or near reservations are more prejudiced than those who live outside reservation areas.

Here, self-dialogue is instrumental as a coping mechanism and provides an acceptable meaning to the interaction. This is an example of the negotiation of meaning through self-dialogue, or what Blumer (1969) referred to as *self-indication*.

On the flip side of this view of discrimination is the Indian/Native who returns to the reservation after earning a higher education. One who has left and returned with a degree may be viewed suspiciously in the community and considered an *apple*—red on the outside and turned white on the inside through the process of education. This appears to happen on reservations that are more traditional and rurally isolated. As one informant related on the question of education, trust, and returning home after college,

> They think that when you're educated you turn into a White person. Yeah, and if you're...and they think that you're different and you'll use that [education] against them, and they don't trust you. "Yeah, she's White "...they don't trust you after you finish your education.

These are just a few examples of how biases and myths operate in both the Indian/Native and White worlds. Biases and myths are a result of negotiated meaning regardless of whose world they are given social meaning in, because one world overlaps with another. Ultimately they create barriers to communication and suspicion of the other.

Other myths regarding Indians/Natives exist in the non-Indian world. The following discussion highlights only a few of the more prevalent myths. The first is that all Indians receive monthly checks from the government. An event that is shrouded in myth by both actors involved is the discovery of one's Indianness by the non-Indian other and the potential outcomes of that discovery. Finally, the third myth to be explored is what the author refers to as the "expectation of genetic wisdom" (Peregoy, 1991).

The first myth to be explored is that all Indians/Natives receive checks from the federal government. Oh, if it were only true! Indians/Natives do not receive monthly checks from the government. Some Indians/Natives receive social services assistance, just as many other citizens receive such assistance. They may also receive social security benefits. Tribal members may receive per capita payments from their tribe. Per capita payments are like dividends paid to stockholders in corporate America. These payments are generally made once a year from money generated by the tribe through leasing of tribal lands or other income-generating endeavors. These payments are not necessarily large, but can help pay some of the month's bills.

Taxation is another question that has been washed with controversy and myth. Money made by individuals working in the free-market economy is taxable by the federal and state governments. Indians/Natives do pay income taxes. Land holdings through the Allotment Act are not taxable while the land is held in trust by the BIA. Once a parcel of allotted land is patented, it becomes taxable. The tribe generally gets the first crop or cutting of timber, or a portion thereof, which is another avenue for generating tribal general funds that are used for per capita payments to members of some tribes.

The second myth to be explored is that of discovery and the expectations of the other when finding out one is Indian/Native. Being *fingered* is being the object of public discovery, whether it has positive or negative connotations ascribed to it by the viewer. This discovery is not related to the effort one takes in passing and being found out in what Goffman (1963) refers to as "an embarrassing incident" (p. 75). Rather, being fingered refers to an individual who operates under the assumption that one's Indianness is known, when it is not. When discovery occurs there is a recognition that a change in perception or action by the other may take place (Peregoy, 1991). This is not an unusual occurrence for the biracial individual who is not necessarily physically identifiable as a member of a racial or ethnic minority group.

Lori, a 22-year-old Assiniboin-Sioux, described her experience of being discovered by one of her classmates. While she was reading a book on American Indians, he asked, "Are you Indian?" Lori said, "Yeah, I am. You didn't know that?" He said, "I guess that's how well I know you." Lori continued about being fingered as an Indian/Native,

With some people it's obvious, and with other people, they don't even pay attention. But I was just thinking there, when he asked—he asked the question, will that change our relationship? I hope not. But I also wonder about that because I am an Indian.

Fear of different treatment arises in the one who has been fingered or discovered. This concern is grounded in past changes in behavior by others who have made the discovery and operated under false myths and assumptions once discovery has been made.

Another situation can arise when one is fingered as an Indian/ Native. People make assumptions about one's knowledge and understanding about other Indian/Native tribes. The author views this assumption on the non-Indian's part as grounded in an expectation of *genetic wisdom*—expecting the Indian/Native who has been fingered to be an expert in Indian/Native affairs and other realms with which he or she may have no experience or familiarity (Peregoy, 1991).

Jay, a Blackfoot Indian, shared with me his perception of discovery and being fingered:

...they [non-Indians/Natives] assumed that I knew everything about all Indians. And I don't know. ...Like I said, some people assumed ...because once people did discover I was Indian, that I should know everything [about all Indians]. But that was not the case. I still don't know. Like how could I know everything?

Myths, assumptions, and stereotypes interfere with open and honest communication. They become barriers to meaningful interaction between people, whether engaged in transcultural settings or in understanding people like themselves. When ethnicity and cultural identity are shrouded in myths held by another, meaningful interaction can be lost.

SPIRITUAL ORIENTATIONS, VALUE SYSTEMS, AND SOCIAL ISSUES

The non-Indian/Native counselor may need to engage in a paradigm shift when working with the Indian/Native client, depending upon the client's level of acculturation (Berry, Minde, & Mok, 1987;

Sue & Sue, 1990) and Indian/Native identity (Atkinson, Morten, & Sue, 1993; Zitzow & Estes, 1981). This paradigm shift can be understood as paralleling the one required in shifting from an individual counseling approach to a systemic approach (Goldenberg & Goldenberg, 1991). The systemic approach views behavior not as individually motivated, but rather as motivated through the interconnection with others. Rather than a Lockean approach (A causes B, which in turn causes C), the systemic approach takes into account the reciprocal effects of actions and changes in the entire system.

The traditional Indian/Native's system of life is intertwined with the tribe and extends further into a metaphysical belief system. These two systems, the worldly and the otherworldly, operate hand in hand on a daily basis. In essence, the interplay of these two systems creates a single, functioning system. Quite often attention to both of these worlds is necessary to yield any long-lasting and effective changes for the client. Trimble and LaFromboise (1985) pointed out that this consideration "is quite at odds with the individual rootedness, personality-permanence, and the self-containment of psychological process embodied in Western notions of therapy" (p. 258).

The worldview held by the Indian/Native sees "actions as linking what happens in the ritual performance, in the cosmos, in the spirit world, in human existence, and in the animal and vegetable life" (Courtney, 1986, p. 50). When the Indian/Native performs the proper ritual correctly, all of life and the universe is renewed and put into balance. Indian/Native religions can be described as *continuing* religions because they are not necessarily traced to a founder, like Jesus for Christianity or Buddha for Buddhism (American Indian Religious Freedom Act of 1979).

Indian/Native cultural values, grounded in a spiritual orientation, differ from the Western values that dominate mainstream society. Some of the most common values shared across tribes and identified in the literature include the family structure; giving, sharing, and cooperating; time orientation; and harmony with nature (DuBray, 1985; Ho, 1987; Sue & Sue, 1990; Thomason, 1991).

The Indian/Native family structure often includes an extended network system with parents, siblings, uncles, aunts, and cousins. These relationships are grounded in tradition and are developed through clans and social society relationships, depending on one's tribe of origin. This extended family system provides a wide array of social supports for its members. There is also a cultural emphasis on keeping family matters within the family (Atkinson, Morten, & Sue, 1989). Mouseau (1975) has characterized the Indian/Native family as an open-family, closed-community pattern. The function of the family as a resource network and as a structure for intervention or mental health delivery should not be overlooked (Attneave, 1982). Protocol within the family needs to be determined because specific people within the family system will have designated roles. The extended family can play an important role in intervention and treatment (Everett, Proctor, & Cartmell, 1983).

Giving, sharing, and cooperation are values that have their roots in hundreds of years of tradition. Sharing material wealth and oneself is at the core of being for the traditional Indian/Native. The family and group take precedence over the individual (Ho, 1987). This concept of collaterality extends to a worldview that holds that all people, animals, plants, and objects in nature have a place in the universe, creating a harmonious whole.

The value of sharing is captured in the practice of the *giveaway*. Material items are given away to honor others for assistance rendered, for achievements, or to acknowledge kinship ties. Momaday (1974) characterizes the giveaway as a means of recycling the good of honored dead and showing respect for the living.

Indian/Native people have a time orientation based in the rhythms of nature. The importance of time is grounded in the immediate, not the future. Contrary to the myth that Indians/Natives have no concept of time, their concept of time is partially grounded in the "nature of traditional Indian/Native economies and the need to focus on daily survival, [and] it is also related to the worldview of events moving through a rhythmic, circular pattern" (Ho, 1987, p. 71).

The value orientation of harmony with nature stems from the recognition that human beings are only one part of the universe. In this universe, everything—plant, animal, and rock—has a living spirit and warrants respect. Many ceremonies and rituals recognize and express this respect through reverence to nature's forces in an effort to create balance between all spiritual beings. The concept of stewardship stems from this recognition that all of the universe is occupied by a variety of spiritual beings. The values presented are only a few of the values shared across tribes; for a more detailed look, see Courtney (1986), DuBray (1985), Everett et al. (1983), and Trimble and Fleming (1989).

These values and the historical and contemporary clashes that have developed with mainstream American values and society have led to the manifestation of a number of current social issues. Many social issues are at the forefront of concern in Indian/Native America, including unemployment, alcohol and substance abuse and its effects, education, economic development, and maintaining cultural integrity while working within the mainstream fabric of America, to mention only a few.

Alcohol and substance abuse is one of the major social issues affecting Indian/Native America today. Alcohol-related death rates for Indians/Natives have ranged from 4.3 to 5.5 times the national average (Gurnee, Vigil, Krill-Smith, & Crowley, 1990). Many Indian/Native deaths, including accidental deaths, homicides, and suicides, are attributed to alcohol and substance abuse (May, 1988). Nearly one third of all outpatient visits to Indian Public Health Services are related to alcohol or substance abuse or dependence (Sue & Sue, 1990).

A consequence of alcohol abuse is *fetal alcohol syndrome* or *effects* (FAS or FAE). If a mother consumes large amounts of alcohol during pregnancy, her child can suffer from neurosensory and developmental disabilities (Plaiser, 1989). While FAS occurs in every cultural community and socioeconomic group, it varies by subpopulations. FAS is estimated to occur in the general population at approximately 1 in 750 births. A study conducted by May, Hymbaugh, Aase, and Samet (1983) found that the incidence ranged from 1.3 in 1,000 live births for the Navaho tribe to 10.3 in 1,000 live births for the Southwestern Plains tribes.

There are a variety of explanations for the high use of alcohol and substances among Indians/Natives. Berlin (1982) suggested that drinking provides a release of emotions that arise from boredom and frustration, allowing Indian/Native people to express emotions that are normally under control. Other theories point to alienation caused by cultural clashes between Indian/Native values and mainstream American values, ecological stressors, and socioeconomic variables, including education, status, and salary (Silk-Walker, Walker, & Kivlahan, 1988).

EDUCATIONAL EXPERIENCES AND OPPORTUNITIES

The context of the Indian/Native experience in education can be found in the history and structural biases of Indian/Native–White relations. There are four recognized eras of this contact: genocide and warfare, assimilation, federal domination, and self-determination (O'Brien, 1989; Szasz, 1984).

During the early years of contact, from the 16th century to the 19th century, Euro-American contact with indigenous peoples stemmed primarily from two influences. The first was the missionary movement, which was seen as the work of God saving the souls of the poor savages in America. The second influence, and probably the most significant, was that the missionary movement facilitated Euro-American economic and political goals (Scheirbeck, Barlow, Misiszeck, McKee, & Patterson, 1976).

The French and Spanish switched from genocide and warfare to forced assimilation as a means to deal with the "Indian problem." Directed culture change became the ethos of Indian/Native–White relations during the missionary era (Szasz, 1984). This ethos carried over into the early and middle parts of this century. It is unclear in some minds that forced assimilation of the Indian/Native in America today has ended (D. Lester, personal communication, June 1992).

The U.S. government embarked on a final series of efforts in the 1800s to "either exterminate them [Indian/Native peoples] as separate people or assimilate them forcibly into the general population" (Wax et al., 1989, p. 2). During this time, churches were cooperating with the federal government to achieve state goals of education and assimilation.

During the 19th century the reservation system succeeded in breaking the power of sovereign tribal nations and brought them under control of the military and corrupt federal Indian agents (O'Brien, 1989). The reservation system, an extension of the Removal Act of 1830, forced Indians/Natives from homelands and relocated them in generally undesirable areas. This relocation included the surrender of independence by the tribes. It also induced surrender of control over Indian/Native education.

During the latter part of the 19th century Indian/Native children were forcibly removed from their homes and essentially incarcerated in church-run boarding schools hundreds of miles from their families and cultures. The intent of the boarding schools was to strip Indian/Native children of their culture and turn them into Whites (Wax et al., 1989).

During this era of assimilation, the Dawes Act of 1887 divided reservations into quarter sections of land. These quarter sections, carved from communal holdings, were then redistributed to heads of households. The idea behind this redistribution of land was to change the Indian/Native from a communal savage to a civilized individualist (Wax et al., 1989).

The mission schools and boarding schools were replaced in the early part of this century by BIA schools. Criticisms of these schools were highlighted in the Meriam Report of 1928. This report concluded that boarding schools were "overcrowded, unsuited to Indian students in terms of work and study programs, deficient in health and food services, and excessively rigid in discipline" (Thompson, 1978, p. 5). Not until the Wheeler-Howard Act of 1934 were large numbers of Indians/Natives hired to work in the BIA educational system.

The era of Indian self-determination began in the early 1970s with the passage of the Indian Education Act of 1972. With this act and the Indian Self-Determination and Educational Assistance Act, Indian/Native people regained the opportunity to shape their children's futures and provide direction and leadership for them (Sahmaunt, 1973).

Many tribes have since responded by establishing tribally controlled community colleges. The mission of these colleges is to help the tribes with cultural preservation, to assist local tribal members in addressing educational and economic development needs, and to provide for training for the tribes. There are now 23 tribally controlled community colleges across the United States.

Dr. Joe McDonald (personal communication, July 1992), President of the Salish Kootenai College on the Flathead Reservation, has indicated that the community colleges have also touched an unserved segment of the reservation population. This segment is composed of those students who because of finances, cultural conflict or discontinuity, academic integration, or lack of adequate precollege preparation have dropped out of 4-year institutions and moved home.

During the 1970s, the number of college-age (aged 18–24) Indians/Natives more than doubled. By 1980, 60% of the Indians/Natives in this age group had graduated from high school. This was a 9% increase over the high school graduation statistics in 1970 (Fries, 1987). Only 6% of the Indian/Native population (aged 25 years and older) were college graduates during the period from 1971 to 1981. During this same period, Whites had a 23% graduation rate and Blacks a 12% graduation rate (Astin, 1982).

Although the Indian/Native population is proportionally the fastest growing minority population, there has not been an appreciable increase in graduate degrees earned by Indians/Natives. The number of doctoral degrees conferred on Indians/Natives in 1975–76 was 93; in 1978–79 there were 104; and in 1980–81, 130 (Fries, 1987). In 1991, only 128 doctoral degrees were conferred on Indians/Natives (Leatherman, 1992).

Wax et al. (1989) have pointed out that reservation schools have less access to finances needed to adequately equip and pay teachers. High turnover rates for teachers in reservation schools disrupt continuity in the educational system. Perspectives of Indian/Native people about the educational system's commitment to Indian/Native education can influence parental support for the educational process (Peregoy, 1991). One of the informants, Gloria, spoke about how she viewed the school system on the reservation:

> And the school systems [here, away from the reservation], they're willing to help Indian students a lot. But back home, they'd rather just put them back, so they wouldn't have to be bothered with them. That's how they deal with the Indian kids back home.

Finances are the number-one barrier to higher education for Indian/Native students. This barrier, with a shift in current federal financial aid policies from grants to loans, will have a dramatic effect on the ability of Indian/Native students to attend colleges away from home and complete a baccalaureate degree in the traditional 4 years.

Despite the structural biases in Indian/Native education, more children are going to school, and more adolescents are graduating from high school. With national trends toward the recognition and appreciation of diversity and the inclusion of culturally appropriate teaching methods, advancement in educational attainment for Indians/Natives cannot be far behind. The tribally controlled community colleges will have an appreciable impact on transfer students to 4-year colleges. This impact will be realized by an increase in graduation rates for Indian/Native students.

ECONOMIC TRENDS AND CHALLENGES

Reservation areas are generally isolated and have been said to be long on scenery and short on resources. This isolation, in tandem with government dependency, hindered early economic development. In an interview in June 1992, Don Whorton, a lawyer with the Native American Rights Fund in Boulder, Colorado, stated

Clearly, Indian country has been left out of what the dominant majority culture calls economic development. Not only have Indians/Natives been left out of it, they were excluded from it, institutionally, legally, and as a matter of dominant cultural practice. ...This was done by the majority culture by viewing Indians/Natives not as people, but seeing them in terms of their natural resources.

In 1983, under the Reagan administration, funds to reservations were cut by 22%, from 3.4 to 2.7 billion dollars (Rawlinson & Heiser, 1983). This cut in economic assistance lent further momentum to the movement of tribes toward self-determination and away from federal dependency.

An analysis of economic trends in Indian/Native country is no simple task. Economic development is intertwined with structural barriers in the form of cultural values, federal legislation, law, and myth. Overcoming these barriers to economic development requires a "creative process which melds politics, financial packaging, and hard nose negotiations" (Rawlinson & Heiser, 1983).

Resources on reservations vary by location. There are generally three types of resources: nonrenewable resources, such as oil, coal, and other minerals; renewable resources, such as agriculture, fisheries, and timber; and human resources. Without economic development on the reservations, money will continue to flow out, and no returns will be realized in the community. This can be understood by viewing the reservation community as a system that has little business or industry. For example, when tribal members shop for food, the money they turn over is outside the system. There are few turnovers within the system. An economic system like this is riddled with economic leakage, which contributes itself to high unemployment rates.

When planning for economic development the tribes have to look at some basic questions (D. Lester, personal communication, June 1992). What are the short- and long-term benefits to tribal members? What are the social and cultural influences going to be today and tomorrow? How will this economic development affect our cultural fabric as a people? And finally, how will this development affect surrounding towns? In the case of exploiting renewable or nonrenewable resources, the questions need to be asked: Where will the revenues go? Will they be paid back in per capita payments or reinvested in the tribe?

The Ak Chin Pueblo, 30 miles south of Phoenix, Arizona, is one tribe that has assessed itself, its needs, and its opportunities. The process this tribe went through was to analyze its strengths, its history, and its future. In so doing, the tribe committed itself to economic development in the form of agriculture. The BIA said that the project would fail and did not provide any assistance (Rawlinson & Heiser, 1983).

At Ak Chin, the tribe grew cotton as its main crop. From 1962 to 1983 the tribe focused its development efforts on this agricultural endeavor. By 1982, the tribe's unemployment rate was only 2.5%. Tribal employees are required to commit 200 hours of labor a month. In exchange, not only do they receive a paycheck, but also their housing expenses are covered and paid vacations are provided (Rawlinson & Heiser, 1983).

This tribal economic endeavor was initiated by the tribe for the tribe. It appears that successful economic development in Indian country comes from the tribes themselves and is not imposed from the outside by trendy government programs.

Another successful tribal enterprise is the Chata Development Company, created in 1969 by the Choctaw Nation in Mississippi. By the late 1980s, the Choctaw industrial park had 300,000 square feet of industrial manufacturing space housing six separate plants and employing over 1,000 people. Chata Enterprises supplies General Motors Corporation with electrical harnesses and has a higher acceptance rate of its product than all other manufacturers of the same product (O'Brien 1989).

Chata Enterprises, the third-largest greeting card production company in the world in terms of volume, began operating in 1982 (O'Brien, 1989). This endeavor was funded by industrial revenue bonds issued by the city of Philadelphia, Mississippi. Philadelphia had to be the issuing authority because the law does not allow tribes to issue bonds (Rawlinson & Heiser, 1983). This is an example of the creative financing needed for economic development on reservations. It also shows the importance of reinvesting profits back into tribal development efforts.

In 1988, the tribe completed the Choctaw Shopping Center, a tribally owned development (O'Brien, 1989). With the opening of this development, tribal members had a choice of where to shop and gained added control over the outflow or economic leakage from their reservation. These are only two examples of tribes that have been successful. Other tribes have also been successful, and still others have failed drastically.

Successful tribes share some common elements. First and foremost is reinvestment of capital gains into tribal development. Another influencing factor for success is a tribal commitment to success.

Management skills are another necessary factor in economic development. Managers are sought after because of a proven track record and have typically been non-Indians/Natives. This will change in Indian country as more young people study business and finance.

One of the major trends in economic development is gaming on reservation lands. The path to gaming on tribal lands is shrouded in federal legislation and state cooperation. Federal law allows bingo (a Class II designation) on reservations without limits and permits casino-style gaming (a Class III designation) on reservations in states that allow similar gaming off the reservation. This is only allowed after the tribe and the state have negotiated a compact allowing gaming (Rawson, 1992).

The Indian Gaming Regulatory Act (IGRA) of 1988 is federal legislation that provides the process tribes need to gain gaming privileges on reservation lands. The act intends Indian/Native gaming "as a means of promoting economic development, self-sufficiency and strong Tribal government" (Minnesota Indian Gaming Association [MIGA], 1992). IGRA holds regulatory authority over Class III games, which include blackjack, baccarat, slot machines, and electronic facsimiles of any game of chance.

Peregoy (1992) summarized the requirements of instituting Class III games on reservation lands: a negotiated state-tribal compact; the state's negotiating in good faith to enter into a compact; the state's not taxing gaming enterprises or refusing to negotiate a compact because it cannot tax the tribe. The burden of proof is on the state to establish good faith; and, if the court finds the state did not negotiate in good faith, the court can order a compact within 60 days.

These requirements are control issues hampering economic development on reservation lands. Gaming as a form of economic development, like other economic development efforts on reservation lands, requires political action and creative financing. One of the structural biases pointed out by Giago (1992) is the reluctance of state governments to extend the same government-to-government relation to tribes that they extend to the federal government and other state governments.

The benefits of Indian/Native gaming are multidimensional. A recent study of economic benefits of tribal gaming in Minnesota (MIGA, 1992) pointed to six major benefits to the tribes and to the state: increased tribal revenues to support Indian/Native government services; economic development and self-sufficiency; increased jobs and employment; reduced public-assistance expenditures; increased jobs from secondary spending and construction; and increased out-of-state visitor spending in Minnesota.

This study documents that tribal gaming in Minnesota has produced 4,700 new jobs, some in remote rural areas. "Of these jobs, Indians/Natives hold approximately 20% of the new jobs and non-Indians/Natives have benefited from 80% of the new jobs" (MIGA,

1992, p. 2). In addition, public assistance in the form of Aid to Families with Dependent Children decreased 16% in four nonurban counties containing major tribal gaming operations. This is a significant decrease when compared to the state of Minnesota as a whole, which had an overall increase of 15% during the study period between 1987 and 1991 (MIGA, 1992).

Within Indian/Native America, a developmental process is taking place that lends itself to a growing sophistication in economic development, self-sufficiency, and tribal government. This sophistication is supported by education of Indian/Native youth, the growth and understanding of tribal leadership, and the involvement of tribal members in all aspects of economic development. Economic development is not a separate entity from the tribe, its cultural values, or its history or future, but rather a component, a part of the universe, to be dealt with on a conscious basis for today and tomorrow.

TRANSCULTURAL COUNSELING WITH INDIANS/NATIVES

The goal of transcultural counseling with Indians/Natives is to create a dialogue of growth within individual clients and their communities and across mainstream cultures. Embedded in this goal is a respect for culturally specific indigenous value systems that interact and transcend dominant cultural values. The operative concept in transcultural counseling is the intent of creating balance, or helping the client develop bicultural skills in a necessarily multicultural world.

To accomplish this task the counselor needs to develop an open-mindedness toward the client's worldview (Pedersen, Fukuyama, & Heath, 1989; Ibrahim, 1991). Worldview serves as the backdrop for the collage of identity (Sanford & Donovan, 1984) one develops, grounded in the individual, group, and universal levels of human behavior. The identity collage, with varying components being salient and dependent upon the environment and stimulus of the time, is dynamic. Identity influences the processes of interpersonal communication and one's ability to send and receive messages accurately. The complexities of verbal and nonverbal communication and their appropriateness in the counseling relationship go beyond context to include cultural communication styles anchored in worldviews (Ibrahim & Kahn, 1987).

Thomason (1991) has described the shared worldviews of the Indian/Native perspective of health. In this description the need for balance in all domains of the individual's life, social and community, spiritual, and right living are considered components of a whole that cannot be divided into its parts. This relates to the earlier discussion in this chapter on spiritual orientations.

A traditional client who seeks assistance from an indigenous healer looks to the healer to identify the cause of the problem and work the cures. Part of ritual ceremonies may involve members of the family and community taking an active role. This type of intervention is generally contrary to Western techniques and interventions of psychotherapy.

Indians/Natives are affected by several cultures. Thus, to rigidly classify them would establish yet another prejudicial system and contribute to a variation of oppression (Peregoy, 1991). Several studies have indicated that Indian/Native clients are looking for someone who understands the practical aspects of tribal culture and can give sound advice about their lives (Dauphinais, Dauphinais, & Rowe, 1981). Peregoy concluded that although cultural similarity of the therapist was not necessary, potential Indian-Native clients preferred a therapist who possessed a general awareness of Indian–White relations, some specific tribal knowledge, and an understanding of Indian/Native family relationships. Informants in this study indicated that they wanted a therapist who was culturally sensitive.

The initial interview is key to developing the therapeutic alliance and establishing rapport with Indian/Native clients. This is where the counselor establishes credibility and trustworthiness. More traditional clients may view the counselor as an elder, expecting the counselor to speak more than they do. It is suggested that the counselor briefly discuss the counseling process and confidentiality of the relationship and give an example of a typical session.

This discussion achieves several things. First, it provides clients with an understanding of the counseling process, which they may have had no contact with before. Second, it highlights the importance of confidentiality, which may enhance clients' trust in the relationship. Third, it indicates to clients what their expected role in therapy might be.

It is important to bring the Indian/Native client into the counseling relationship. Early in the counseling relationship the counselor may make the client more comfortable by practicing/modeling some self-disclosure and indicating the desire for reciprocity (LaFromboise & Bigfoot, 1988). The client should not be pushed to make self-disclosures or assume a familiarity that perhaps is not there.

Considerable time should be spent being *with* the client. That is to say, time needs to be spent formulating the problem or issue from the client's perspective and within the context of the client's worldview. Simultaneously, the counselor needs to assess the client's level of acculturation (LaFromboise, Trimble, & Mohatt, 1990; Peregoy & Chapman, 1989) and position within the Minority Identity Development Model (Atkinson, Morten, & Sue, 1993). This will help the counselor understand the issues and tasks the client may be facing. Soliciting the client to assist in the definition of the problem and to provide input for establishing counseling goals may increase comfort levels during the early stages of counseling. The therapeutic problem, when defined through cognitive and behavioral assessment, would involve exploring the client's thoughts or self-talk and cues or reinforcements for the undesired behavior or thoughts.

Arredondo (1986) has proposed a systematic model for working with refugees that is also applicable to working with Indian/Native clients. This model is holistic, in that it encompasses six dimensions of the client's life: the historical era, sociopolitical factors, sociocultural factors, individual variables, developmental tasks, and esteem and identity themes.

By using these six dimensions and combining them with social cognitive interventions, the counselor will be using a framework that is considered less culturally biased than other theoretical approaches (LaFromboise & Rowe, 1983). This approach is considered less biased because it recognizes the impact of culture on personal and environmental variables and allows each culture to define its own appropriate behaviors or targets for intervention. It is culturally sensitive in that it provides for the differences across tribes.

Included in social cognitive interventions is an examination of the belief systems associated with target behaviors; in so doing they have heuristic appeal for accommodating cultural values and expectations (LaFromboise & Bigfoot, 1988). Group skills training with Indians/Natives has been used as an effective means for teaching new behaviors and skills (LaFromboise & Bigfoot, 1988). Group work using social cognitive interventions has been particularly effective with Indians/Natives because it reduces the emphasis on individual disclosure, which is difficult for some Indians, and introduces collective responsibility (LaFromboise & Graff Low, 1989). Because a collective approach is characteristic of some tribes, this may be a very culturally appropriate intervention.

Cognitive therapies differ from the disease model of psychopathology. Cognitive therapies maintain that most psychological problems are learned within a social milieu and continue through cognitive reinforcement (Meichenbaum, 1977). LaFromboise and Graff Low (1989) pointed out that when working with Indian/Native clients, the therapist must be aware of the influence the dominant culture may have on a client's self-depreciating beliefs.

Likewise, beliefs that are irrational by standards of the dominant culture may be perfectly legitimate given the course of Indian-White relations or within the specific cultural context (LaFromboise, Trimble, & Mohatt, 1990). For example, mistrust of the educational system and even counseling may be rooted in historical mistrust based in assimilationist policy (Locust, 1988).

The counseling goal then would be to influence the client to change his or her irrational thoughts, internal dialogue, and negative self-assessments. This goal would be facilitated by self-monitoring, behavior change, and social validation. These could be accomplished by using social skills training and rehearsal of potentially stressful events. In addition, positive self-affirmations can be used after defeating self-statements are recorded in a daily log.

Another culturally appropriate technique is the use of guided imagery. For example, an Indian/Native woman comes to the counseling center with presenting concerns related to her self-concept. The counselor may want to use guided imagery techniques to have the client visualize herself as she perceives herself to be, and then, have her visualize how she would ideally like to be. Once this is done the client then develops steps, with the assistance of the counselor, to work toward the goal of how she would like to perceive herself in the future.

The strategies presented here are not intended to replace Indian behaviors with mainstream behaviors unless this is what the client desires, nor is the suggestion of using cognitive behavior therapy as a replacement for other therapeutic processes intended to deny the credibility of other theories. Cognitive behavioral interventions are presented as a means of enhancing the Indian/Native's repertoire of coping options.

This section has presented social cognitive interventions as culturally sensitive interventions. Along with social cognitive interventions, guided imagery was also presented as a culturally sensitive technique to use with the Indian/Native client. The importance of bringing the client in early in the counseling relationship was underscored.

CONCLUSION

This chapter has presented factors to consider when engaging in a helping relationship in a transcultural setting with American Indians or Alaskan Natives. In view of the diversity of the different federally recognized tribes and the socioeconomic status of urban and rural Indians/Natives, any discussion of therapy runs the risk of overgeneralizing or developing another set of stereotypes. However, there are shared elements in the lives of Indians/Natives. These include structural biases and myths that were presented and operate in both the Indian/Native world and mainstream society. These myths serve to create barriers to communication and to perception of the other. Furthermore, structural biases are an impediment to self-determination.

Value differences were provided to stimulate counselors to think about what assumptions they may operate under and to give a glimpse into the Indian/Native worldview. Social issues were presented that revolve around economic development and the maintenance of cultural integrity in a necessarily multicultural world. Tribally controlled community colleges were mentioned as one avenue in Indian country to contribute to cultural preservation and community education.

David Lester, executive director for the Council of Energy Resource Tribes, summed up the self-determination of Indian peoples succinctly in an interview with the author in June 1992. We're not the vanishing American—the reservations are not halfway houses for assimilation or extermination. Indians/ Natives are an integral part of 20th century America. As long as there are human beings in the Western Hemisphere, we're going to have Indian people governing themselves, making their own decisions for their own future.

REFERENCES

Allen, P. G. (1986). *The sacred hoop.* Boston: Beacon.

American Indian Religious Freedom Act of 1979, PL 95-341.

Arredondo, P. M. (1986). Immigration as a historical moment leading to an identity crisis. *Journal of Counseling and Human Service Professionals, 1*(1), 79–87.

Astin, A. W. (1982). *Minorities in higher education.* San Francisco: Jossey-Bass.

Atkinson, D. R., Morten, G., & Sue, D.W. (1989). *Counseling American minorities* (3rd ed.). Dubuque, IA: Brown.

Atkinson, D. R., Morten, G., & Sue, D. W. (1993). *Counseling American minorities* (4th ed.). Dubuque, IA: Brown.

Attneave, C. (1982). American Indian and Alaskan Native families: Emigrants in their own land. In M.McGoldrick, J. K. Pearce, & J. Giordano (Eds.), *Ethnicity and family therapy* (pp. 55–83). New York: Guilford.

Berlin, I. N. (1982). Prevention of emotional problems among Native American children: Overview of developmental issues. *Journal of Preventive Psychiatry, 1*, 319–330.

Berry, J. W., Minde, T., & Mok, D. (1987). Comparative studies of acculturative stress. *International Migration Review, 21*, 491–511.

Blumer, G. H. (1969). *Symbolic interactionism: Perspective and method.* Englewood Cliffs, NJ: Prentice Hall.

Burt, L. W. (1986, spring). Roots of the Native American urban experience: Relocation policies in the 1950's. *American Indian Quarterly, 10*(2), 89–99.

Courtney, R. (1986). Islands of remorse: Amerindian education in the contemporary world. *Curriculum Inquiry, 16*(1), 43–64.

Dauphinais, P., Dauphinais, L., & Rowe, W. (1981). Effects of race and communication styles on Indian perceptions of counselor effectiveness. *Counselor Education and Supervision, 21,* 72–80.

Dobyns, H. F. (1983). *Their number becomes thinned: Native American population dynamics in Eastern North America.* Knoxville: University of Tennessee Press.

DuBray, W. H. (1985). American Indian values: Critical factor in case work. *Journal of Contemporary Social Work.* January, 30–38.

Everett, F., Proctor, N., & Cartmell, B. (1983). Providing counseling services to American Indian children and families. *Professional Psychology: Research and Practice, 14*(5), 588–603.

Fries, J. E. (1987). *The American Indian in higher education: 1975–1976 to 1984–1985.* Washington, DC: Center for Education Statistics, U.S. Government Printing Office.

Giago, T. (1992, May 22). Indian gaming is a good bet for the states. *Char Koosta News*, p. 2.

Goffman, E. (1963). *Stigma: Notes on the management of a spoiled identity.* Englewood Cliffs, NJ: Prentice Hall.

Goldenberg, I., & Goldenberg, H. (1991). *Family therapy: An overview* (3rd ed.). Belmont, CA: Brooks/Cole.

Gurnee, C. L., Vigil, D. E., Krill-Smith, S., & Crowley, T. J. (1990). Substance abuse among American Indians in an urban treatment program. *Journal of the National Center for American Indian and Alaskan/Native Mental Health Research, 3*(3), 17–26.

Herring, R. D. (1992). Seeking a new paradigm: Counseling Native Americans. *Journal of Multicultural Counseling, 20*(1), 35–43.

Ho, M. K. (1987). *Family therapy with ethnic minorities.* Beverly Hills, CA: Sage.

Ibraham, F. A. (1991). Contribution of cultural worldview to generic counseling and development. *Journal of Counseling and Development, 70,* 13–19.

Ibrahim, F. A, & Kahn, H. (1987). Assessment of world views. *Psychological Reports, 60,* 163–176.

Indian Fellowship Program (1989), Final Regulations, 34 CFR Part 263.

LaFromboise, T. D., & Bigfoot, D. (1988). Cultural and cognitive considerations in the prevention of American Indian adolescent suicide. *Journal of Adolescence, 11,* 139–153.

LaFromboise, T. D., & Graff Low, K. (1989). American Indian children and adolescents. In J. T. Gibbs & L. N. Huang (Eds.), *Children of color:*

Psychological interventions with minority youth, (pp. 114–147). San Francisco: Jossey-Bass.

LaFromboise, T. D., & Rowe, W. (1983). Skills training for bicultural competence: Rationale and application. *Journal of Counseling Psychology, (30)*, 589–595.

LaFromboise, T. D., Trimble, J. E., & Mohatt, G. V. (1990). Counseling intervention and American Indian tradition: An integrative approach. *The Counseling Psychologist, 18*(4), 628–654.

Leatherman, C. (1992, May 13). After 10 year decline, number of black Ph.D.'s begin to increase. *The Chronicle of Higher Education, 38*(36) 1, 18A.

Locust, C. L. (1988). Wounding the spirit. *Harvard Educational Review, 58*(3), 315–330.

May, P. A. (1987). Suicide and self-destruction among American Indian youths. *Journal of the National Center for American Indian and Alaskan/ Native Mental Health Research, 1*(1), 52–69.

May, P. A. (1988). The health status of Indian children: Problems and prevention in early life [Monograph]. *Journal of the National Center for American Indian and Alaskan/Native Mental Health Research, 1*(1) 244–289.

May, P. A., Hymbaugh, K. J., Aase, J. M., & Samet, J. M. (1983). Epidemiology of fetal alcohol syndrome among American Indians of the Southwest. *Social Biology, 30,* 374–387.

Meichenbaum, D. H. (1977). *Cognitive behavior modification: An integrative approach.* New York: Plenum.

Minnesota Indian Gaming Association (1992, March). *Economic benefits of tribal gaming in Minnesota.* Minneapolis: KPMG Peat Marwick.

Momaday, N. S. (1974). I am alive. In N. S. Momaday (Ed.), *The world of the American Indian.* (pp. 29–47). Washington, DC: National Geographic Society.

Mouseau, J. (1975). The family, prison of love. *Psychology Today, 9,* 53–59.

Neligh, G. (1990). Mental health programs for American Indians: Their logic, structure and function [Monograph]. *American Indian and Alaska Native Mental Health Research: The Journal of the National Center Monograph Series, 3,* 3.

O'Brien, S. (1989). *American Indian tribal governments.* Norman: University of Oklahoma Press.

Pedersen, P. B., Fukuyama, M., & Heath, A. (1989). Client, counselor, and contextual variables in multicultural counseling. In P. B. Pedersen,

J. G. Draguns, W. J. Lonner, & J. E Trimble (Eds.), *Counseling across cultures* (3rd ed., pp. 23–52). Honolulu: University of Hawaii Press.

Peregoy, J. J. (1991). *Stress and the sheepskin: An exploration of the Indian/ Native experience in college.* Unpublished doctoral dissertation, Syracuse University.

Peregoy, J. J., & Chapman, R. J. (1989, March). *The invisible minority on campus: Counseling the American Indian.* Paper presented at the annual meeting of the American Association for Counseling and Development. Boston, MA.

Peregoy, R. M. (1992, July). *Tribal sovereignty and Indian gaming.* Paper presented at the Tribal Resource Institute in Business and Engineering Sciences, Colorado School of Mines, Golden, CO.

Plaiser, K. J. (1989). Fetal alcohol syndrome prevention in American Indian communities of Michigan's upper peninsula. *Journal of the National Center for American Indian and Alaskan/Native Mental Health Research,* 3(1), 16–33.

Price, J. A. (1978). *Native studies: American and Canadian Indians.* New York: McGraw-Hill Ryerson.

Rawlinson, C. (Producer), & Heiser, S. (Director). (1983). *The new capitalists: Economics in Indian country* [Film]. Portland, OR: Odessy Productions.

Rawson, W. F. (1992, May 15). FBI raids five Indian casinos; Yavapi set up blockade. *Char Koosta News,* p. 1.

Sahmaunt, H. (1973). An Indian education leader speaks out. *Education Journal, 1,* 4–10.

Sanford, L., & Donovan, M. (1984). *Women and self-esteem.* New York: Penguin.

Scheirbeck, H. M., Barlow, E. J., Misiszeck, T., McKee, K., & Patterson, K. J. (1976). *Final report to the American Indian Policy Review Commission.* Washington, DC: U.S. Government Printing Office.

Silk-Walker, P., Walker, D., & Kivlahan, D. (1988). Alcoholism, alcohol abuse, and health in American Indians and Alaska Natives [Monograph]. *American Indian and Alaska Native Mental Health Research: The Journal of the National Center Monograph Series* 1(1) 65–93.

Sue, D. W., & Sue, D. (1990). *Counseling the culturally different* (2nd ed). New York: Wiley.

Szasz, M. C. (1984). *Education and the American Indian: The road to self-determination since 1928.* Albuquerque: University of New Mexico Press.

Thomason, T. C. (1991). Counseling Native Americans: An introduction for the non-Native American counselor. *Journal of Counseling and Development, 69*(4), 321–327.

Thompson, T. (Ed.). (1978). *The schooling of Native America.* Washington, DC: American Association of Colleges for Teacher Education.

Trimble, J. E. (1981). Value differentials and their importance in counseling American Indians. In P. B. Pedersen, J. G. Draguns, W. J. Lonner, & J. E. Trimble (Eds.), *Counseling across cultures* (rev. ed., pp. 203–226). Honolulu: University of Hawaii Press.

Trimble, J. E. & Fleming, C. M. (1989). Providing counseling services for Native American Indians: Client, counselor, and community characteristics. In P. B Pedersen, J. G. Draguns, W. J. Lonner, & J. E. Trimble (Eds.), *Counseling across cultures* (3rd ed., pp. 177–204). Honolulu: University of Hawaii Press.

Trimble, J. E., & LaFromboise, T. D. (1985). American Indians and the counseling process: Culture, adaptation, and style. In P. B. Pedersen (Ed.), *Handbook of cross cultural counseling and therapy* (pp. 127–134). Westport, CT: Greenwood Press.

U.S. Congress, Office of Technology Assessment. (1986). *Indian health care.* OTA-H-290. Washington DC: U.S. Government Printing Office.

U.S. Department of Commerce. (1992a). *Census bureau resources for the Congress.* Washington DC: U.S. Government Printing Office.

U.S. Department of Commerce (1992b). *Census of population and housing characteristics—1990 summary.* Washington, DC: U.S. Government Printing Office.

Wax, M., Wax, R., & Dumont, R. V., Jr. (1989). *Formal education in an American Indian community* (rev. ed.). Cooperative Research Project No. 1361. A Study of Social Problems Monograph. Prospect Heights, IL: Waveland Press.

Wilson, T. P. (1992). Blood quantum: Native American mixed bloods. In M. P. Root (Ed.) *Racially mixed people in America* (pp. 108–125). Newbury Park, CA: Sage.

Zitzow, D., & Estes, G. (1981). The heritage consistency continuum in counseling Native American students. *Proceedings from the Conference on Contemporary American Indian Issues, 3,* 133–142. Los Angeles: UCLA Publications Services.

CHAPTER 8

TRANSCULTURAL COUNSELING FROM AFRICAN-AMERICAN PERSPECTIVES

HERBERT A. EXUM AND QUINCY L. MOORE

INTRODUCTION

African Americans are currently the largest ethnic minority group in North America. Their impact on the history of the United States has been unmistakable. Although African Americans are a highly diverse group in terms of physical appearance, geographical preference, and socioeconomic status, they are still a culturally distinct group bound by an ideological unity and a functional system of values and beliefs. Their cultural ethos and worldview are inextricably woven together to give meaning and order to both their historical and contemporary experiences, and an appreciation of these cultural elements is a prerequisite to understanding and interpreting their patterns of behavior (Butler, 1992).

African Americans have historically been underserved by traditional counseling programs. Several reasons have been suggested for this gap in service. Among these are poverty, lack of accessible facilities, lack of awareness of service facilities or their purpose, and the absence of culturally acceptable treatment models (Dillard, 1983). Acceptable treatment models are those that recognize the African-American worldview, behavioral and life-style patterns, and coping and problem-solving methods.

This chapter presents a discussion of fundamental African-American social characteristics in their historical and contemporary contexts as they pertain to effective transcultural counseling interventions. The principal objective of the chapter is to increase practitioners' awareness and understanding of the core elements of African-American culture as they relate to the practice of counseling and psychotherapy in both remedial and preventive modalities.

VALUE SYSTEMS AND SOCIAL ISSUES

The historical experience of African Americans has generally been characterized and described in terms of interactions and responses to interactions with European Americans and in terms of their own internal dynamics, both as individual personalities and as a group (Butler, 1992, p. 25). Despite massive assaults on their humanity, consistent psychological disorientation, and horrendous levels of social and economic deprivation, African Americans have remained resilient and have clung to their cultural heritage. Traditional norms have remained, sometimes intact and sometimes in reinterpreted forms, but the core elements of African-American culture and their African antecedents still persist. This is particularly significant because most African Americans found their way to the Western Hemisphere through the diaspora as chattel property—totally stripped of humanity.

As Nobles (1972) states, African Americans derive their most fundamental self-definitions from several cultural and philosophical premises we share with most West African "tribes" (p. 23). White, Parham, and Parham (1980) discuss several elements of African-American culture that are indicative of the African frame of reference. These include the oral transmission of knowledge, emphasis on the group rather than the individual, and experiential rather than numerical time. Woodson (1968) cites antecedent cultural elements such as folklore, adult-child relationships, sense of justice, and hospitality.

The worldview of African Americans represents their general design for living and patterns for interpreting reality. It is how they make sense of their world and their experience as it determines which events are meaningful and which are not. It provides the process by which those events are made harmonious with their lives. More accurately, the African-American worldview might best be conceived of as an ideological perspective determined by history (Asante, 1988).

COGNITIVE AND BEHAVIORAL STYLES

The African-American worldview is made apparent in language, symbols, values, ideals, and the behaviors and behavioral styles of the people. Behavioral styles represent consistent approaches to the organization of human experiences and to the use of the environment. The work of Hillard (1976) suggests two basic styles characteristic of contemporary American culture: atomistic-objective and synthetic-personal. Although the work of Hillard focused primarily on high-achieving African-American children, his findings seem to generalize well to the African-American population as a whole.

The *atomistic-objective* behavioral style is one in which habitual patterns of approach to experiences involve an attempt to break down the experience into component parts that can then be understood. The observer using this style perceives himself or herself as separate from the phenomena being observed. "These observers also manifest a preference for permanence, regularity, predictability and environmental control" (Hillard, 1976, p. 31). The atomistic-objective behavioral style is similar in form and operation to the analytical cognitive style described by Hale-Benson (1986). The atomistic-objective style is also characteristic of European Americans. However, neither the atomistic-objective behavioral style nor the analytic-cognitive style is a mode of information processing preferred by the majority of African Americans.

Users of the *synthetic-personal* style, on the other hand, tend to perceive themselves as "an integral part of the phenomena which are being observed" (Hillard, 1976, p. 31). Accordingly, high value is placed on divergent experimentation, improvisation, and harmonious interaction with the environment. These individuals also tend to be relationship oriented (Akbar, 1981; Exum, 1979). The synthetic-personal style is very similar to the relational cognitive style described by Hale-Benson (1986) and reflects many of the trends indicative of African-American behavioral patterns described by Akbar (1981). Although various cognitive styles transcend cultural grouping to some degree, data from several sources suggest that the synthetic-personal behavioral style or the relational cognitive style is characteristic of African Americans (Akbar, 1981; Cohen, 1971; Hale-Benson, 1986; Hillard, 1974, 1976).

A summary of Hillard's findings illustrates well several core elements of the African-American worldview. Hillard (1976, pp. 38–39) suggests that

African Americans tend to prefer to respond to and with "gestalts" rather than to or with atomistic "things." There is an impatience with unnecessary specifics. To African Americans, it seems that the predominant pattern of mainstream Americans is the preoccupation with particulars, along with a concomitant loss of a sense of the whole.

African Americans tend to prefer inferential reasoning to deductive reasoning.

African Americans tend to prefer approximations over accuracy in minute detail.

African Americans tend to prefer to focus on people and their activities rather than on things.

African Americans tend to seek acceptance and integration with the environment.

African Americans tend not to be world-bound. Great emphasis is placed on nonverbal communication. Style of presentation is often more highly valued than content.

Ironically, current American educational systems tend to be analytic, obsessive-compulsive, and essentially atomistic-objective (Exum, 1979, p. 315). As Butler (1992) notes, the extent to which educational systems are compatible with the African-American cultural cosmology determines whether the systems will yield positive results (p. 47). The learning styles of any cultural group are an extension of its worldview and cultural ethos. In the case of African Americans, the relational learning style has been found to maximize the potential for academic success better than the less characteristic but more common traditional analytic style of the larger American culture. This fact has had grave consequences for many African-American children and adults in many aspects of their social welfare (p. 47).

ETHNIC IDENTITY DEVELOPMENT

Besides other developmental tasks majority group members experience, ethnic minority group members in American society have the additional task of resolving their own levels of personal identification with their culture of origin. Several authors have suggested that the successful development of a positive sense of self in people of color involves progression through a sequential arrangement of stages (Atkinson, Morten, & Sue, 1980; Cross, 1970; Jackson, 1975; C. Thomas, 1969).

Although there is some variation in the conceptions about identity formation in African Americans, most sources agree that the initial stages of development (*pre-encounter*) are essentially conformist (outside the self and referenced toward others). Individuals at this level attempt to gain approval, sense of worth, money, power, and so forth by accepting and conforming to European-American cultural and institutional standards, which require the rejection and devaluation of that which is Black (Jackson, 1975). In the initial stages of development, the individual's worldview is dominated by European-American beliefs and values. Hence, individuals in these stages are politically naive and usually distrust Black-controlled businesses and organizations (Jackson, 1975).

The behaviors associated with this stage are often used to support the "self-hate" hypothesis relative to African-American collective personality. Researchers (Ausubel & Ausubel, 1967; Deutsch, 1967; Goldberg, 1967; Vontress, 1966, 1969, 1971) suggested that African Americans viewed themselves with self-hatred, negative self-esteem, and self-deprecatory attitudes. This position is best illustrated by Vontress (1966), who states that "the most significant component of Negro personality is his self-hatred for being a member of a downtrodden group" (p. 210). This is surprisingly consistent with Kardiner and Ovesey (1951), who state that the "Negro has no possible basis for healthy self-esteem and every incentive for self-hatred."

Kardiner and Ovesey's indictment of an entire ethnic population was based on a sample of 25 subjects, half of whom manifested symptoms of psychological pathology (A. Thomas & Sillen, 1974, p. 50), and the empirical evidence for Vontress's conclusion remains unclear. Perhaps these researchers sought to create sympathy for African Americans by attributing the "plight of the Negro" to environmental factors rather than genetic deficits. Nonetheless, the conclusion that it is normal for African Americans to hate themselves is not accurate. This view is most probably the result of gross over-generalization and failure to differentiate between deep-seated pathology and the transient episodes of self-deprecation that often accompany depression.

The second general stage (*encounter*) in the development of positive African-American identity and psychological maturity involves confrontation and active resistance to European-American cultural values and orientations. Cross (1970) suggests that both guilt and rage are dominant emotional states during this period of development. Guilt is the result of the individual's reflection upon his or her former unquestioned embrace of European-American culture and its underlying assumption of Black inferiority (Cross, 1970). Rage is experienced when the oppressive aspects of that culture are exposed. Confrontation and rejection of European-American culture is a confrontation as much with self as with external forces that have limited the development of an authentic self or facilitated a distorted perception of self. By removing all White influence, the African American is better able to identify these influences and their negative effects (Jackson, 1975).

European-American counselors meeting African-American clients while the clients are in this phase of identity formation are most likely to be threatened, least likely to be trusted, and most likely to be rejected. Thus, if these clients are students, they are then most likely to be punished or expelled from school. Because the special developmental needs of African-American students are largely ignored, a great educational injustice continually recurs.

The final stage (*internalization*) of African-American identity formation involves Black people acknowledging both African and American influences in their development. Understanding of self and one's place in the world, eliminating racism and other forms of oppression, and helping other oppressed people in their quest for personal freedom are the dominant goals of African Americans occupying this stage of identity development (Atkinson et al., 1980).

Not all African Americans experience this entire range of stages. Some retain primary identification with Anglo-Saxon culture and values; others become fixated at one stage and then regress; but some African Americans are born into families that already function

at the highest levels of ethnic identity development and consequently have no need to traverse the stages.

EDUCATIONAL EXPERIENCES AND OPPORTUNITIES

One of the most serious issues confronting American school systems
relative to the education of African Americans during the decade has
been the declining social, economic, and educational status of young
African-American males (Garibaldi, 1992). Census data present
alarming facts: 40% of young African-American males in big cities
drop out of high school (U.S. Department of Commerce, 1991),
whereas in 1980 only 16% of African Americans dropped out of
school (U.S. Department of Commerce, 1981). In 1988, 60% of African
Americans 15–24 years old lived in poverty, as did 25% of those
25–34 years old. Increasingly, young African Americans are likely to
come from single-parent homes: Nearly two out of every three
African-American children are now born to unwed mothers.

These statistics are alarming, but more disturbing is the impact
these data have on teachers' and counselors' expectations for performance of young African-American males. Garibaldi (1992) reported that in his survey of more than 2,250 African-American
males, 95% reported they expected to graduate from high school, but
40% reported they believed their teachers did not set high enough
goals for them. When Garibaldi randomly surveyed 500 teachers and
asked them whether their African-American students would go to
college, 6 of every 10 teachers said no.

This is even more troubling because 60% of the teachers taught
in elementary schools, 70% had 10 or more years of experience, and
65% of them were Black (Garibaldi, 1992, p. 7).

Unfortunately, these results support the conclusions drawn
from the teacher expectancy literature and confirm that no teacher
is immune to holding negative, self-fulfilling prophecies about the
children they teach (Garibaldi, 1992, p. 7). These results also support
widely held opinion, which suggests that public education merely
reflects the attitudes, values, and beliefs of the general population.
Although African Americans have experienced increased gains in
educational attainment, much more needs to be done.

RELIGIOUS AND SPIRITUAL INFLUENCES

Spirituality and religion are essential elements of the African-American worldview. Although the majority of African Americans are Christians, the religious practices of African Americans still contain many elements of African spirituality, including the belief in the direct link between the natural and the supernatural, the significant ability of music to invoke the supernatural, the importance of human intervention in the supernatural world through possession and spiritual control, and the importance of participatory verbal performance (e.g., the call-and-response pattern) (Jules-Rosette, 1980).

African-American churches have always been more than houses of worship, and the African-American minister has always been more than a preacher. The African-American church has historically served as the spiritual, intellectual, and political focal point of the African-American community, and ministers have traditionally served as teachers, counselors, and political activists. The role of the African-American minister in the civil rights movement is well documented.

As Locke (1992) notes, African-American churches are agents for the transmission of traditional values, for strengthening family ties, and for providing opportunities for African Americans to learn about and appreciate their own ancestry (p. 24). African-American religious beliefs run the gamut from Baptist and Methodist, which are the largest denominations, to Roman Catholic, Seventh-Day Adventist, Holiness, Islamic, and Judaic. The influence of spirituality and the African-American church is pervasive and enduring in all African-American communities.

THE TRANSCULTURAL COUNSELING PROCESS

CLIENT CHARACTERISTICS

African Americans bring several psychological strengths to the therapeutic process that are a function of their cultural ethos and worldview. Perhaps the most important of these strengths are flexibility, forgiveness, resilience, and persistence.

200

African Americans have always had to remain flexible and adaptive to survive in historically hostile environments. They have been successful by making the most of whatever resources they had in each situation. African Americans are very open to new ways or better ways of accomplishing goals or solving problems. The source of client resistance among African Americans is most likely to be an issue of mistrust on the part of the client or countertransference on the part of the counselor or therapist. Change is an integral part of the African-American worldview.

Collectively, African Americans have a great capacity to forgive both in-group and out-group members for transgressions. This capacity is sometimes wrongly interpreted as passivity, indifference, or even cowardice, and it is sometimes exploited by unethical politicians and bureaucrats. However, forgiveness and tolerance both stem from the African concept of acceptance and are supported by the contemporary belief that "what goes around comes around." This belief is similar to but not identical with a belief in karma. Accordingly, the transcultural therapist has a great advantage in working with African-American clients because errors in the counseling process are not necessarily fatal if they are accompanied by a sincere apology.

A third strength is resilience. African Americans are capable of withstanding very high levels of stress for long periods. They are also capable of rapid recovery from personal crises. This is not to say that African Americans experience less emotional pain or suffering than do other ethnic groups. The pain may just not be as evident in the client's verbalizations. It is important for the transcultural counselor or therapist to expect early recovery from African-American clients and to accept that they want to move on.

Persistence, like flexibility, is one of the cornerstones of African-American psychological strength. African Americans exhibit great determinism in achieving their goals once they have been clearly defined. Unfortunately, because African Americans also have great faith in the motivations of others, they sometimes persist in ineffective or negative relationships longer than they should. Accordingly, persistence is positive when applied to focused goals and objectives but negative when used to support nonproductive behaviors and strategies.

COPING MECHANISMS

African Americans use a variety of ego defenses or coping mechanisms that arise from their cultural ethos. Although these coping mechanisms are used primarily during the pre-encounter (conformist) and encounter (dissonance) phases of ethnic identity development, they do generalize to issues other than racism and they do persist in some form through other phases. Distortions of predominant elements in the African-American worldview result in the use of these mechanisms to return the individual to a sense of oneness with the environment. The most common coping mechanisms are denial, isolation, repression, and introjection.

Denial occurs when an individual refuses to admit the existence of something disturbing. This is what happens when an African American who has sought the friendship of an out-group member learns from another source that the out-group member has been telling "nigger jokes," and the African American refuses to believe an otherwise reliable source. It didn't happen.

Isolation is failing to perceive or recall links between related information, thought associations, or identifications that might arouse anxiety. This is what happens when an African-American man fails to recall that every time he walks into a particular office alone, the receptionist leaves her desk to speak with another secretary, but whenever he enters the same office accompanied by his European-American colleague, the receptionist never leaves her desk. Just coincidence. There is no link. He sees no pattern.

Repression involves censoring memories, feelings, or perceptions that have high anxiety-producing potential. In the preceding example, repression would involve the African American not remembering there was a receptionist in the office.

The most serious and self-defeating coping mechanism typically used by African Americans is *introjection*. Introjection involves defending against disillusionment in another by accepting blame or responsibility. Aggression is directed toward oneself in the form of either guilt or depression rather than toward the true object. Introjection occurs when an African-American woman who is not accepted for the all-European-American cheerleading squad because she does not meet the height and weight guidelines (she is "too heavy for her height" or just "too fat") fails to question whether the guidelines are racially biased and fails to even tell her parents about the outcome of the tryouts. Instead, she internalizes the notion that she is too fat, believes she is not pretty enough, and initiates the behaviors that will eventually lead to an eating disorder. Fortunately, introjection is seldom used as a coping mechanism beyond the pre-encounter levels of identity development. Nonetheless, transcultural counselors should be on alert for its presence and be prepared to challenge client ideation that blames the client for racist or otherwise oppressive behavior.

The values usually taught in African-American families center on thinking the best about everyone, trying to get along with others, believing that everyone is a child of God, and believing that no one is really a bad person. For this reason, many African Americans unconsciously engage in denial, isolation, repression, and introjection when confronted with negative issues and particularly with racism.

THE THERAPEUTIC ALLIANCE

The most important aspect of the transcultural counseling approach is creating trust between the counselor and the client. It is already well established that clients are more likely to trust counselors they perceive to be like themselves. What, then, may a highly motivated but culturally different counselor do to be consistently effective in transcultural situations?

There is no substitute for practical experience with a variety of ethnic or cultural groups to achieve competence in working with these groups. Supervised practicums and internships are the ideal methods for increasing competence. Realistically, few professional counselors have opportunities for advanced practical training. Very few programs provide this service. Counselors are able, though, to increase their practical understanding of various ethnic and cultural groups through workshops, conferences, and the professional literature.

Although we recognize that reading about a culture does not in itself make an individual competent within that culture, reading does serve as a basis for building competence in the culture and also provides insight on the worldview of the members of that culture. In addition, it demonstrates respect for the culture to the members of that group and also demonstrates the sincerity of your willingness to learn about another culture. It should not be overlooked.

It is generally agreed that counseling is a social-influence process (Corrigan, Dell, Lewis, & Schmidt, 1980), and when a counselor agrees to work with clients, the counselor implicitly assumes the role of expert (Pietrofesa, Leonard, & Van Hoose, 1978, p. 73). Because it is the client's expectation that counselors are in fact knowledgeable people of authority, it is the counselor's responsibility to behave in a manner consistent with this expectation. Counselors must acknowledge their limitations and, if necessary, advise the client of these limitations while they seek additional training to upgrade their skills. Some transcultural competencies, such as fluency in a second language, are more difficult to acquire than others. However, a second language would seldom be necessary for working with African-American clients. When presenting problems are well beyond the effective capacity of the counselor, an effective counselor would still be expected to have procedures for proper referral.

In addition to further reading and professional training, there are four basic strategies counselors may use to minimize the effects of being an out-group member when working with African-American clients. These are to (1) rely on the core conditions, (2) use directive rather than passive or nondirective methods, (3) attend to nonverbal behavior, and (4) be available.

1. *Rely on the core conditions.*
The counselor who wishes to be successful in helping clients will look beyond a knowledge of client behavior and counseling techniques (Pietrofesa et al., 1978, p. 2). Techniques are secondary to the counselor's attitudes (Corey, 1977). Active listening, reflection of feeling, and clarification of perceptions are essential to the counseling process. The relationship—the therapeutic alliance—is still the vehicle that facilitates problem solution, positive change, and personal development.

The relationship that the counselor provides for the client is not an intellectual relationship (Patterson, 1980, p. 497). The qualities of the therapist that characterize any effective counseling relationship, and particularly a transcultural relationship, include authenticity or genuineness, nonpossessive warmth, empathy, unconditional acceptance and respect for the client, permissiveness, caring, and the communication of those attitudes to the client (Corey, 1977).

Congruence or genuineness, empathy, unconditional positive regard, and the communication of these attitudes are sometimes called the *core conditions* of counseling. Rogers (1951) considered these attributes also to be the ideal characteristics of counselors. *Authenticity, congruence,* and *genuineness* are all terms used to describe the condition in counseling in which the counselor is unified, integrated, and consistent: There is no contradiction between what the counselor says and what the counselor is (Patterson, 1980, p. 498).

The *authentic* counselor is aware of his or her own feelings as they are experienced in the counseling relationship and is able to verbalize them when necessary. Most important, authentic counselors are comfortable with themselves and do not feel the need to change their personality to seek acceptance when they are with different people. This does not mean that the authentic counselor is rigid or inflexible. On the contrary, the effective transcultural counselor will modify his or her style to be consistent with the expectations of the client. It does mean, however, that the motivation for the counselor's behavior is consistent. Without consistency, counselors seldom establish trust—the key to successful work in transcultural counseling.

Empathy means an accurate understanding of the client's private world as if it were one's own, but without losing the "as if" quality (Patterson, 1980, p. 498). Empathy has been identified as the single most important dimension of establishing a counseling relationship (Carkhuff, 1969). Despite dissimilarities between client and counselor, high-empathy counselors are more effective than low-empathy counselors (Banks, 1969). In transcultural situations, *empathy* means evaluating the client's situation through his or her own worldview and finding the correct solution by way of the client's own value system.

Unconditional positive regard is the nonevaluative counselor attitude, which may be expressed both verbally and nonverbally. As Patterson (1980) states, the counselor should be accepting of the client as an individual, as the client is, with his or her conflicts and inconsistencies, and good and bad points (p. 497).

However, this attitude is not possible unless the counselor has already learned to accept himself or herself.

Unconditional positive regard is also communicated nonverbally through the physical expression of understanding and caring, communicated nonverbally through gestures, posture, tone of voice, touch, and facial expression (Egan, 1981). The basic philosophy of the counselor is represented by an attitude of respect for the individual, for the individual's capacity and right to self-direction, and for the worth and significance of each individual (Rogers, 1951, pp. 20–21).

It is not possible to be prepared for every variation in client personalty or circumstance. It is possible, however, to be totally available to the client in each session, and it is possible to give your full attention to the client's problem and his or her presence. The issue is not whether you solve the client's problem in each session but whether you are authentic in each session.

2. *Use directive rather than passive or nondirective methods.*
There has been a consistent theme in the research literature that suggests that action-oriented or directive counseling approaches should be used with African Americans (Hollingshead & Redlich, 1958; Kincaid, 1969; Lefkowitz & Baker, 1971; Peoples & Dell, 1975; Tucker, 1973). There also seems to be increased support for the use of behavioral models (Harper & Stone, 1974; Morgan, 1971; Workman, 1974). Cognitive-behavior modification (Meichenbaum, 1977) may also be an effective approach for working with African-American clients, primarily because it is active, time limited, and solution oriented. The interventions are designed to enlist the client (and in some instances, significant others, such as spouse, parents, or peers) in a collaborative process whereby the client becomes her or his own "personal scientist" (Mahoney, 1974).

The cognitive therapist works with clients to

- Help them better understand the nature of their presenting problems.
- View their cognitions ("automatic" thoughts, images) and accompanying feeling as hypotheses worthy of testing rather than as facts or truths.

- Encourage them to perform "personal experiments" and review the consequences of their actions as "anomalous data" or "evidence" that is contrary to their prior expectations and beliefs.

- Learn new behavioral, interpersonal, cognitive, and emotional regulation skills (Meichenbaum, 1986, p. 347).

The cognitive-behavioral approach does not focus on intrapsychic pathology, nor does it promote dependence. It assumes that the client has psychological strengths that can be used in problem solution, focuses on collaboration in problem definition, and freely allows the client to develop the best approach to problem solution. It also acknowledges the importance of feelings and thoughts in developing problem solution. While no counseling approach is value-free, cognitive-behavior modification minimizes the value distortions of the counselor while providing a concrete course of action for the client. Cognitive-behavioral approaches reinforce self-efficacy and self-sufficiency.

3. *Attend to nonverbal behavior.*
   Traditional counselor education programs place a very high value on verbal intellectual behavior in the counseling process. However, people of color in general, and African Americans in particular, are very attentive to nonverbal behavior. African Americans have learned that intellectual interactions are less trustworthy than the nonverbal messages sent by participants (Sue, 1981, p. 51). Posture, gestures, and facial expression are all essential elements in communication with African Americans. Because nonverbals are often the message themselves, it is essential for transcultural counselors to present consistent verbal and nonverbal behaviors. Sue (1981) notes that for African Americans, conversing with a person dictates a much closer stance than is normally comfortable for Anglos (p. 41). If the counselor were to move backward when approached by an African-American client, the client could interpret this movement negatively. Mistrust would heighten and meaningful communication would cease. Moreover, attire and setting also influence how African Americans receive messages. How furniture is arranged, where the seats are located, where one seats

the client—all have implications for the counseling process (Sue, 1981).

4. *Be available.*
To establish credibility, the transcultural counselor needs to be visible in the world of the client. Counselors interested in helping African Americans must leave their offices and become involved in their clients' communities by spending time there. The flow of the client's community is an essential part of the client's culture. The sights, the sounds, and the colors all have meaning for the client, and it is only in this nonformal environment that the counselor will discover what *normal* actually means for the client. An effective relationship involves a commitment, and there can be no greater demonstration of commitment than active participation in the community of the African-American client.

CONCLUSION

African Americans are a widely divergent group occupying all rungs of the socioeconomic ladder but still not fully integrated into mainstream American culture. Therefore, effective counseling interactions with African Americans require knowledge of the cultural ethos of this group. The challenge for the effective transcultural counselor or therapist is to recognize the individual humanity of each African-American client while simultaneously knowing that the client is a member of an ethnic group that, in many instances, will have a very different way of perceiving the world.

The therapist must balance his or her own stereotypic beliefs against the reality the client presents and prize a member of a devalued group without being patronizing or defensive. The therapist must be willing to accept that she or he will probably be mistrusted but realize, too, that trust can be established. To be effective, transcultural counselors or therapists must be fully open (and vulnerable) to the interaction between themselves and their clients. It is only through authenticity that trust, empathy, and truly therapeutic relationships can be developed.

REFERENCES

Akbar, N. (1981). Cultural expressions of the African-American child. *Black Child Journal*, 2(2), 6–16.

Asante, M. K. (1988). *Africentricity*. Trenton, NJ: Africa World.

Atkinson, D., Morten, G., & Sue, D. (1980). *Counseling American minorities: A cross-cultural perspective*. Dubuque, IA: Brown.

Ausubel, D., & Ausubel, P. (1967). Ego development among segregated Negro children. In J. I. Roberts (Ed.), *School children in urban slums* (pp. 231–260). New York: Free Press.

Banks, W. M. (1969). *The effects of race, social class, and empathy on the initial counseling interview*. Unpublished doctoral dissertation, University of Kentucky.

Butler, J. (1992). Of kindred minds: The ties that bind. In M. Orlandi (Ed.), *Cultural competence for evaluators: A guide for alcohol and other drug abuse prevention practitioners working with ethnic/racial communities*. Rockville, MD: U.S. Department of Health and Human Services.

Carkhuff, R. (1969). *Helping and human relations, Vol. 1: Selection and training*. New York: Holt, Rinehart and Winston.

Cohen, R. (1971). Conceptual styles, cultural conflict and nonverbal tests of intelligence. *American Anthropologist, 71*, 828–856.

Corey, G. (1977). *Theory and practice of counseling and psychotherapy*. Monterey, CA: Brooks/Cole.

Corrigan, J. D., Dell, D. M., Lewis, K. N., & Schmidt, L. D. (1980). Counseling as a social influence process: A review. *Journal of Counseling Monograph, 27*, 395–441.

Cross, W. E. (1970). The Negro-to-Black conversion experience. *Black World, 20*, 13–25.

Deutsch, M. (1967). Happenings on the way back to the forum: Social science, IQ, and race differences revisited. *Harvard Educational Review, 39*, 523–557.

Dillard, J. D. (1983). *Multicultural counseling: Toward ethnic and cultural relevance in human encounters*. Chicago: Nelson-Hall.

Egan, G. (1981). *The skilled helper: A model for systematic helping and interpersonal relating*. Monterey, CA: Brooks/Cole.

Exum, H. A. (1979). Facilitating psychological and emotional development of gifted black students. In N. Colangelo & R. Zaffrann (Eds.), *New voices in counseling the gifted*. Dubuque, IA: Kendall/Hunt.

Garibaldi, A. M. (1992). Educating and motivating African-American males to succeed. *Journal of Negro Education, 61*(1), 4–10.

Goldberg, M. L. (1967). Education for the disadvantaged. In S. H. Passow, M. L. Goldberg, & A. J. Fannenbaum (Eds.), *Education of the disadvantaged*. New York: Holt, Rinehart, and Winston.

Hale-Benson, J. E. (1986). *Black children: Their roots, culture and learning styles*. Baltimore: Johns Hopkins University Press.

Harper, F. D., & Stone, W. O. (1974). Toward a theory of transcendent counseling with Blacks. *Journal of Non-White Concerns in Personnel and Guidance, 2,* 191–196.

Hillard, A. A. (1974). A helping experience in African education: Implications for cross-cultural work. *Journal of Non-White Concerns, 2,* 133–144.

Hillard, A. A. (1976). *Alternatives to IQ testing: An approach to the identification of gifted minority children* [Final report to the California State Department of Education]. Sacramento: California State Department of Education.

Hollingshead, A. B., & Redlich, F. C. (1958). *Social class and mental illness: A community study*. New York: Wiley.

Jackson, B. (1975). Black identity development. *MEFORM: Journal of Educational Diversity and Innovation, 2,* 19–25.

Jules-Rosette, B. (1980). Creative spirituality from Africa to America: Cross-cultural influence in contemporary religious forms. *Western Journal of Black Studies, 4,* 273–285.

Kardiner, A., & Ovesey, L. (1951). *The mark of oppression: Explorations in the personality of the American Negro*. New York: Norton.

Kincaid, M. (1969). Identity and therapy in the Black community. *Personnel and Guidance Journal, 47,* 884–890.

Lefkowitz, D., & Baker, J. (1971). Black youth: A counseling experience. *School Counselor, 19,* 200–293.

Locke, D. (1992). *Increasing multicultural understanding: A comprehensive model*. Newbury Park, CA: Sage.

Mahoney, M. (1974). *Cognition and behavior modification*. Cambridge, MA: Ballinger.

Meichenbaum, D. (1977). *Cognitive-behavior modification: An integrative approach*. New York: Plenum.

Meichenbaum, D. (1986). Cognitive behavior modification. In F. Kanfer & A. Goldstein (Eds.), *Helping people change: A textbook of methods* (3rd ed.). New York: Pergamon.

Morgan, E. (1971). *Behavior theory counseling with culturally disadvantaged underachieving youth.* Unpublished doctoral dissertation, Columbia University.

Nobles, W. (1972). African philosophy: Foundations for Black psychology. In R. H. Jones (Ed.), *Black psychology.* New York: Harper & Row.

Patterson, C. (1980). *Theories of counseling and psychotherapy* (3rd ed.). New York: Harper & Row.

Peoples, V. Y., & Dell, D. M. (1975). Black and white student preferences for counselor roles. *Journal of Counseling Psychology, 22,* 529–534.

Pietrofesa, J. J., Leonard, G. E., & Van Hoose, W. (1978). *The authentic counselor* (2nd ed.). Chicago: Rand McNally College Publishing Company.

Rogers, C. R. (1951). *Client-centered therapy: Its current practice, implications, and theory.* Boston: Houghton Mifflin.

Sue, D. W. (1981). *Counseling the culturally different: Theory and practice.* New York: Wiley.

Thomas, A., & Sillen, S. (1974). *Racism and psychiatry.* New York: Citadel.

Thomas, C. (1969). Boys no more: Some social psychological aspects of the new black ethic. *The American Behavior Scientist, 12,* 38–42.

Tucker, S. (1973). Action counseling: An accountability procedure for counseling the oppressed. *Journal of Non-White Concerns in Personnel and Guidance, 2,* 35–41.

U.S. Department of Commerce, Bureau of the Census. (1981). *1980 census of the United States.* Washington, DC: U.S. Government Printing Office.

U.S. Department of Commerce, Bureau of the Census. (1991). *1990 census of the United States.* Washington, DC: U.S. Government Printing Office.

Vontress, C. E. (1966). The Negro personality reconsidered. *Journal of Negro Education, 35,* 210–217.

Vontress, C. E. (1969). Cultural barriers in the counseling relationship. *Personnel and Guidance Journal, 48,* 11–17.

Vontress, C. E. (1971). Radical differences: Impediments to rapport. *Journal of Counseling Psychology, 18,* 7–13.

White, J. L., Parham, W. D., & Parham, T. A. (1980). Black psychology: The Afro-American tradition as a unifying force for traditional psychology. In R. L. Jones (Eds.), *Black Psychology,* 56–66. New York: Harper & Row.

Woodson, C. G. (1968). *The African background outlined.* New York: Negro Universities Press.

211

Workman, E. A. (1974). *A comparison of behavioristic and humanistic procedures on the achievement of success in a sheltered workshop.* Unpublished doctoral dissertation, University of Southern California.

CHAPTER 9

TRANSCULTURAL COUNSELING AND THE HISPANIC COMMUNITY

MARIA J. BEALS AND KENNETH L. BEALS

CULTURAL AND DEMOGRAPHIC BACKGROUND

Hispanic: (a) pertaining to Iberia in general; (b) pertaining to Spain in particular; (c) U.S. Census Bureau term including multiple peoples, such as Cubans, Mexicans, Puerto Ricans, Chicanos, Central and South Americans, and others of Spanish ancestry or descent.

The overwhelming majority of publications, research papers, and stereotypes about Hispanics are actually based only upon some particular subgroup as listed above, but the perceptions become generalized in the ideas that Anglos have and are extended to Latinos in general. The reality is that Hispanics in the United States are extremely heterogeneous. What is typical and expected from one Hispanic client is not necessarily relevant to another. Basic, general knowledge of Hispanic communities, identification of a client's background, and recognition of the cultural variation that exists are critical to appropriate and effective counseling.

The first part of this chapter is a brief survey primarily intended for Anglos who have professional responsibilities such as school counselors, educators, psychologists, and employees of the gamut of agencies who interview, evaluate, and sometimes incarcerate Hispanics. The focus is on relatively unacculturated clients and individuals whom an Anglo counselor will encounter at least occasionally. Anglos who have Hispanic clients begin not

213

with an assumed Latino personality type but with an assessment of acculturation, class, language, education, and subgroup.

CULTURAL RELEVANCE AND THE DIVERSITY OF THE HISPANIC POPULATION

The major challenge of transcultural counseling of Hispanics is that of cultural relevance to the client. However, little congruence exists with variables of nationality, race, cultural history, or language. The key element is an increasing diversity among the Latino populations of the United States. European heritage is one part of a common tradition among all the peoples affected by Spanish colonialism. However, Spain itelf was not at the time of American conquest (and is not today) a homogeneous nation. Today, Spain's principal minority groups and languages include Catalan, Galacian, and Basque (a language unrelated to Indo-European). A client from Spain is a European in cultural orientation, not a Latin American, and shares with the latter only a part of the American Hispanic tradition. The situation is roughly comparable to the culture shared by a Navaho who speaks English and a citizen of Scotland.

The traditions of Spain have indeed permeated its former empire, but they are themselves multicultural—formed from an Iberian Paleolithic, to a circum-Mediterranean foundation, to a Carthaginian outpost, to a Roman conquest, to a Gothic conquest, to an Arabic conquest, to the *Reconquista* (when the Arabs were expelled), to a Golden Age, to a European backwater status, and presently to an economic revival.

One cannot understand the culture of Latinos without knowing its Spanish traditions. However, that foundation is not at all like the relationship between England and the dominant Anglo population of the United States. In this nation, Native American and European descendants remained relatively separate, whereas throughout the New World colonies of Spain much more fusion of indigenous and colonial peoples occurred—with its concurrent syncretism in the formation of a new society.

Millions of Hispanics (as citizens of Latin American nations) are not of Spanish or Indian descent. Particularly in countries such as Argentina, Panama, and Costa Rica, relatively large numbers of people derive from European or Antillean nations. Despite common assumption, tens of thousands of American "Hispanics" (mostly outside the United States) have traditions from China and Japan—brought to Middle and South America by the slave trade and later settlement and economic opportunity.

What frequently happens in this nation is that some client, police suspect, or social agency service recipient is bureaucratically determined to be Hispanic because of physical appearance, passport, work permit documents, or language and then thrown into a collective pot, in which a Spanish-speaking translator (often from a different cultural background) is supposed to solve the language and culture relevance problem.

Who knows how many Hispanics in the United States are psychologically, psychiatrically, and legally assessed without a reasonable effort to provide cultural and linguistic relevance? The answer is that no one knows, because statistics are impossible to gather. However, many people believe that such instances are extremely common, and some of their impressions have found their way into print. For example, the *National Law Journal* quotes Carlos Astiz (a political science professor) as saying "it would be possible to win a new trial for 95 per cent of those convicted who are non-English speaking." "The basis? Bad court interpreting that denied them due process" (Williams, 1985).

If 95% of convicted U.S. Hispanics are inadequately interpreted in court, what must the figure be for Anglo counselors having unacculturated Hispanic clients, in a situation where the consequence of misunderstanding is much less? Surely a 95% inadequacy rate (Astiz's impressionistic judgment based on language alone) is too high for any reasonable and practical forensic or counseling circumstance in the United States, but the clear reality is that unacculturated Hispanics do have severe communication problems with Anglo institutions, service providers, and counselors.

Millions of Hispanics do not have Spanish surnames. Particularly in this nation, intermarriage, surname inheritance pattern, and immigration generational sequence operate to alter assumed ethnic identification of individuals. In addition, it is common for U.S. Hispanics to be known by some English name (or nickname), as are Jim Plunkett, Richie Valens, Jane Watson, or Mary Beals. Despite their common use in statistical surveys, surnames are rather poor indicators of Hispanic cultural identity. For example, most Filipinos have

Spanish surnames but are not considered Hispanic in census data. As another example, in the authors' own extended family, some members have Spanish surnames, and others have English surnames. This is totally a function of English pattern name inheritance, with little connection to being Anglo or Hispanic by cultural heritage.

Millions of Hispanics do not speak Spanish, particularly among the Indian populations in regions of Mexico, Guatemala, and Bolivia. Despite the identification of millions of Americans as "Spanish-speaking," there is in reality no one Spanish language; it is more realistically considered a family of languages, some of which are almost dialectically unintelligible. The majority of Spain's citizens speak *Castellano;* the majority of Chicanos speak *Pocho*—these differences are by analogy less than that between English and German, but greater than differences between dialects of English spoken by, for example, Jamaicans and Pakistanis (both a part of English colonial influence). Intermarriage has created millions of Americans who have one parent of Hispanic descent and another of a different race or cultural background. In such cases, Spanish may not be spoken at home, and so the language tends to be lost among the children.

Some folk names of racial/cultural mixture are *Mestizo* (Indian × White), *Mulatto* (White × Black), *Zambo* (Indian × Black), and *Cholo* (Mestizo × White). These are not just biological terms of hybridization. They are associated with the cultural subgroups to which Hispanics belong. In the Spanish-speaking Caribbean, the native Arawak population became virtually extinct within a generation after European contact. African slaves were brought to the islands as a labor force, and as a result Caribbean Hispanics today share part of their cultural heritage with Africa—and have very little Native American influence. In Mesoamerica, about 50% of the native population survived the conquest, and as a result the great majority of Hispanics from Middle American countries are *Mestizo*—having a syncretized Indian-European background. (The predominant Mestizo population is called *Ladino* in parts of Central America, particularly in Guatemala.) Panama has a large population of Blacks, who are descendants of workers from the Caribbean brought to work on the canal; most are bilingual, speaking English and Spanish. Other Hispanics, especially along the Atlantic and Caribbean coast of Central and South America, are descendants of Indians and African Blacks.

All Hispanics symbolically belong to *la raza* (the race), but *la raza* has no definable anthropological, psychological, or sociological concrete identity: It applies to members who identify with it. This word extends to everyone of its tradition—regardless of race, class, nation, knowledge, subculture, or belief. *La raza cosmica* (the cosmic race) is a philosophical concept of self-identity, particularly in reference to the intermingled biology and culture of Mestizos.

The nationality of a Hispanic client is not a particularly good indicator of the client's values or life history. For example, a family residing in Texas over several generations has changed its nationality six times: from citizenship in New Spain, to Mexico, to the Republic of Texas, to the United States, to the Confederate States, and back to the United States. Puerto Ricans and Chicanos are U.S. citizens, not immigrants. Many millions more, from all areas of the Hispanic world, have become naturalized U.S. citizens, and their descendants, citizens by birth, sometimes for many generations.

Many Anglos in the United States regard Latinos as aliens or foreigners. The reality is that most of the U.S. Hispanic population traces its roots to settlements in New Mexico, Texas, and California before Anglos arrived on the continent.

SPIRITUAL AND RELIGIOUS VALUES

Religion is not a determining factor in being Hispanic. It is true that the proportion of Catholics in the population averages more than 90% in Latin American nations. However, Catholicism is often nominal or syncretized with Native American beliefs. Some Hispanic ethnic groups, such as the Miskito of Nicaragua, are Moravians. In the United States, many Hispanics belong to Protestant churches, particularly those having a fundamentalist and evangelical orientation. *Espiritualismo* is relatively common—an ecstatic religion of altered states of consciousness and folk healing (Kearney, 1978). Particularly among the Antillean peoples, African religious influence exists. In recent years, evangelical Christianity has made major inroads into the traditional Catholicism of Hispanics. For example, in modern Guatemala, almost 30% of the population is now claimed (to some extent) by evangelical Protestantism. Despite recent missionary claims of conversion, the Indian population of Guatemala (some members of which appear in the United States as immigrant

217

workers) combine evangelicalism with elements of ultraconservative Catholicism—and with ancient and native religious belief.

The evangelical movement is spreading throughout Latin America, and it derives mostly from diffusion of sects within the United States. The movement appeals primarily to the lower class, and sociologically results from the perceived failure of the upper and middle classes to solve the problems of the impoverished majority. Evangelicalism is not an orientation to the world that most U.S. Hispanics have, but it is growing in influence. Fundamentalist Christianity is a sensitive issue in Latin American nations. For example, Chamulan Indians recently exiled 10,000 villagers for rejecting traditional beliefs in favor of Protestantism.

Tens of thousands of U.S. "Hispanics" are Native Americans from Spanish-speaking nations, who are primarily migrant farm workers. Most are unacculturated and speak Spanish to various degrees, and little English. The majority retain religious beliefs that do not correspond to European concepts. For example, among the Zapotec, animal guardians (*tonos*) are acquired at birth. If a child is not baptized, he or she automatically acquires the power of turning into an animal (a *nahual*).

Throughout Latin America, Catholicism is divided between conservative and liberal factions. Some priests, families, and individuals are highly committed to social activism; others are committed to the preservation of the traditional value of compassionate authoritarianism. In general, a Hispanic client is less likely to be socially militant than a Black or Native American client, but more likely than an Asian American. Hierarchy, and the respect for it, runs deep in the character of Latino values.

In summary, the Hispanic community of the United States is its most diverse ethnic minority. This reality crosscuts any stereotype of personality type, race, religion, class, citizenship, language, values, or culture. Hispanic clients range from migrant and monolingual Indians from Mexico and Central and South America, to wealthy and upper-class exchange students from other nations, to physicians who have fled Cuban socialism, to juvenile gang members in U.S. slums, to the highly internationally oriented upper class. There is no one Hispanic personality type, value system, or culture, any more than there is one human shoe size or political affiliation.

Race, language, religion, and citizenship are poor predictors of what is relevant to Hispanic clients on any overall basis. Acculturation and class affiliation are far better indicators of values and beliefs.

By far, the numerically dominant U.S. Hispanic population is Chicano, and so some specific information is given below. Chicanos range from prominent U.S. national leaders in many areas of society to monolingual members of small and isolated communities in the Southwest. In speaking among themselves, Chicanos often identify themselves as *Mejicanos*, but the word applies to distinction as a group separate from the Anglo majority and other Hispanic subgroups rather than to a national citizenship.

Chicanos are very different from other U.S. Latinos. Along with Puerto Ricans who live on the mainland, nearly all are products of Anglo-oriented elementary schools. As a result, they usually do not have the formal education in Spanish grammar and national background they would get by attending school in a Latin American country. The senior author (Maria Beals) was reared in a tiny, remote, and monolingual Texas village, with no knowledge of English before age 10, when she was placed in an Anglo school (at the first grade level). She was later a barrio resident in a major California city, then a staunch Catholic (centering her life on mass and prayer), then a migrant worker nurse, and finally a member of an Anglo-Hispanic intermarriage and of the academic community.

Few Hispanics go through such extreme life changes, but all of us know and identify with the roots of our cultural traditions and family orientation. However, a counselor cannot assume that a Hispanic client fits into some assumed typological category. The key element is where an individual falls within the kaleidoscope of acculturation and its associations with class and education.

Most Anglo Americans realize that Chicanos are often regarded as second-class citizens of the nation, but not that they are also now (in effect) aliens in Mexico as well. To be Chicano (the word derives from Pocho *Mejicano*) means that the majority of U.S. Hispanic citizens face confusing cultural and educational barriers when they visit Latin American nations—for example, dealing with kilometers, currency exchange rates, *la mordida* (bribes), and even hat sizes (measured in centimeters around the inside of the brim).

Most Chicanos speak a language (Pocho) regarded as substandard throughout the Latin American world. It contains archaic phraseology, locally unique words and meanings, and many anglicisms (such as *los Crismes*, the Christmas season). The reality is that Pocho is not a corrupted Spanish dialect, but a regional language. However, translators educated in so-called formal Spanish are quite likely to assume the client's speech reflects limited mental capacity or ignorance. As a result, the translation in such cases almost always involves elements of what the translator thinks the counselor wants to hear from the client.

POPULATION TRENDS

Census reports are affected by complex factors of self-identity, undercounting of migrant workers, illegal immigrants, sampling procedure, mixed and intermarried citizens, Spanish surnames, and typological racial and cultural categories (such as White, Black, Native American, and "other"). Census approximations for Hispanics in the United States do exist: Chicanos, 61%; Puerto Ricans, 15%; Central and South Americans, 10%; Cubans, 6%; "other," 9%.

Puerto Ricans and Cubans are disproportionately urbanized within the United States as ethnic enclaves in major metropolitan areas (such as New York and Miami). In fact, despite the popular image of U.S. Hispanics as a rural, farm labor peasantry, only a small minority fall into that category. However, Hispanics do form a majority in certain rural areas of Texas and New Mexico. Rural values, along with romanticization of the rural life-style, remain strong despite increasing urbanization.

Asian Americans were the fastest growing major minority group during the 1980s. However, the Hispanic community added far more members because of its higher population at the beginning of the decade. The U.S. Hispanic growth rate (53 per 1,000) is 4 times higher than that of African Americans and 9 times higher than that of Whites. America is turning Brown. During the 1980s, 8 million Hispanic members were added to the population. Los Angeles is now the second-largest Hispanic city on the continent. The largest minority group in the nation will soon be Hispanic rather than African American.

Population trends are summarized in the Census Bureau's *Projections of the Hispanic Populations: 1983 to 2083*. With the projected high immigration rates, the number of U.S. Latinos will reach 99 million by 2080; with low rates, 50 million. The population is younger in median age (28 years as projected for 2000) than the general population (36.3 years for the same time). Crime and social service requirements are correlated with demographic age structure. Hispanics are growing older (in the population pyramid meaning), but will remain a relatively young national subgroup. The dependency ratio (workers to nonworkers) is high because of age structure and employment factors, but it is expected to decline over time.

Regardless of subgroup, all Hispanics in the United States live in a *Gabacho* (Anglo-Germanic) world, as minority members. Particularly among the unacculturated, they are statistically more likely to be incarcerated, to be forced into unwanted and culturally irrelevant psychological assessment and therapy by forensic and social service agencies, and to underuse counseling, social service professionals, and agencies. From the standpoint of cultural relevance, the key factor is the extent to which the client is *agringado*—not with ethnic status, subgroup membership, language, or race.

Gringo has many connotations, but its primary meaning is an objective description without a value judgment: non-Hispanic, lacking knowledge of Latino society. The word also (in some contexts) conveys a sense of sarcasm, but it is the main word that describes the non-Hispanic world, as used among Spanish speakers.

STEREOTYPES

Gringo images of America's Hispanics derive from a combination of mass-media characters, modal generalities by anthropologists dealing with ethnographic material, Anglo tourism to border towns, and the heavily typological orientations by educators and psychologists. Moreover, Hispanics find it in their interest to promulgate and exaggerate positive images, such as *cariño* (roughly "affection"), *honor*, and *familia*.

Hispanics are dashing, brilliant, and courteous heroes (the Cisco Kid), and simpleminded but loyal friends (his sidekick Pancho). They are also socially dangerous revolutionaries (Che Guevara). They are noble and self-sacrificing (Benito Juárez, Joan Baez, and César

Chávez). They are pompous (Santa Ana), and dictatorial (Porfirio Díaz), but religious (Santa Teresa). American Anglos' images of Hispanics are dominated by portrayals in the mass media and have little relevance to the real diversity of the Hispanic population.

In sociological stereotype, Hispanics are dominated by a complex of folk beliefs and values that explain and create their worldview and personality, such as *machismo, malinchismo, la raza, la Chingada, mordida, patronismo,* and *compadrismo.* Males dominate society; women are either virginal or prostitutes. Hispanics are poor, passive-aggressive victims of society, and share a culture of poverty. Hispanics are voluble and emotional (but stoic and reserved), musical and friendly (but hostile, distant, and alien), fatalistic, fawning, courteous, and deceitful. Hispanics are obsessed with obedience to authority, but revolt whenever authority is applied.

The reality is that Hispanics are more diverse in personality and culture than are Anglos. This diversity derives from an ethnic background ranging from monolingual Indians to members of the international jet set. The reality is that the Hispanic population of the United States is becoming more diverse rather than more homogeneous because of immigration patterns in which more unacculturated immigrants arrive as a result of political and economic circumstances in their homeland—for example, the Mariel Boatload Cubans and Salvadoran refugees.

Hispanics do commonly share a set of stereotypes about Anglos, Asians, Indians, and Blacks. The dominant Anglo population is stereotyped as racist and arrogant, but also efficient. There is also resentment of the many American and European interventions in Latin American governments and affairs.

CULTURAL FACTORS AND COURTESIES AFFECTING COUNSELING HISPANICS

Having argued that there is no one Hispanic type, we must also acknowledge that there are values and beliefs that can clearly affect the appropriateness and outcome of counseling as a practical matter. There are also factors in common among Hispanics (at least statistical generalities among ethnic subgroups) as a result of Spanish colonial history.

Mispronouncing a client's name is a certain way to ensure a client will have little faith in whatever else a counselor says. Families are not pluralized as in English (the Lopez Family are *los LO pes*, not *lo PEZ ez*). The second surname (if given) is the mother's father's surname (i.e., García Hernández). For example, Juan García Hernández is, for the short English equivalent, Mr. (or Señor) García, not Mr. Hernández.

Titles are extremely important, but differ greatly from Anglo usage. Omitting a person's title is considered both ignorant and discourteous; use titles in addressing or referring to individuals. A whole range of titles—*Maestro, Profesor, Doctor, Licenciado, Ingeniero, Don*—have different social applications than exist within Gabacho culture. Use them anyway if a person identifies a title, but be aware that they are sometimes self-assigned as prestige values and may or may not correspond to English cognates or professional degrees.

Most Hispanics, when standing and conversing with others, prefer a shorter physical space barrier than do Anglos—about the length of an elbow, not an extended arm. There are great differences between Anglo and Hispanic traditions of physical space, touching, and greetings. *Abrazos* (hugs) have a specialized etiquette and set of rules. Males in Latin American countries hug, hold hands, and may kiss each other (under certain conditions, such as ceremony and renewal of acquaintance). These customs have nothing to do with homosexual relationship. (Homosexuals in Latin America avoid any public display of affection; such sexual preference is very much undercover and will probably be difficult for a client to discuss. Homosexuality is regarded as a mortal sin among Catholics; among the Aztecs, it carried a penalty of death.) Hispanics in the United States lose much of the touching, embracing, banter, and flirting typical of the ritualized expressions of affection more common throughout Latin America.

Unacculturated Hispanics have a very poor understanding of the role of counselors, psychologists, and psychiatrists. They are often confused with physicians or law enforcement spies. The unacculturated are likely to tell the therapist what they think the therapist wants to hear. They will generally attribute powers of assessment and cure to the therapist that are far beyond the realities of the situation. Among such individuals, the standardized norms of assessment instruments (e.g., MSE, MMPI) are simply invalid. Whether the client and therapist are of the same sex is more important in discussion of personal problems than it is among Anglos. A therapist of the opposite sex can expect great reluctance to reveal actual feelings. A translator is likely to modify and misunderstand what the client has actually said. Spanish is highly *multivalent*—having words and phrases with multiple meanings that can only be understood in context and with the cultural background known.

The movements of political correctness, feminism, ecology, affirmative action, and disabled rights that have recently occurred within the United States are likely to be irrelevant to an unacculturated Hispanic client. Traditional values often conflict with the advice and direction of culturally inappropriate counseling. For example, recommending assertiveness training to a wife in a traditionally oriented family can be a disaster in the conventional family setting, in which females are expected to defer to males.

FOLK DISEASE

Latinos suffer from folk diseases not recognized by scientific medicine. However, such conditions are very real to the people concerned. The extent of folk disease and recommended treatment correlate with educational and cultural background. There are also many local and regional variants to the symptoms and treatment. Many Hispanics (depending on education) have retained a concept of disease derived from Indian tradition and classical Greek medicine (which came to them as the result of the Spanish conquest)—for example, the Greek ideas of humors and the four basic elements of earth, fire, air, and water. Humoral pathology is a diffusion from Greece to Spain (through the Moors) to Latin America. Associated with it are concepts of "hot" and "cold" pathologies and foods.

Hispanic clients are generally pragmatic about medical treatment, seeking whatever means it takes to effect a cure. Many people cannot afford conventional, Western-style medical treatment. As with Anglos, a failure of conventional medicine often leads to an alternative approach through faith healers. Folk diseases (such as evil eye) will appear bizarre to an Anglo counselor. However, they are deeply rooted in tradition. Moreover, the treatment procedures are derived from centuries of practice, are nearly always medically harmless, and usually provide psychological benefit. For example, "curing with eggs" is accompanied by soothing words and affection for the distressed infant. Folk medicine relies on concern for the patient, psychological comfort, the body's natural healing, and herbal remedies.

Hispanics can suffer from many different folk diseases. *Bilis* (depression) is created by frustration and folk-treated by affection and attention to the individual. *Susto* (fright) represents the departure of the soul from the body; the soul is restored by *curanderismo* ritual. *Mollera caida* or *hundida* (fallen fontanel) has symptoms of fever and vomiting; it is corrected by pressing upward on the fontanel of the infant. *Empacho* (colic) is caused by foods that stick to the stomach or by being overheated; the treatment is to pull on the infant's skin, rub oil on its body, and use purgative herbs. *Mal ojo*, *ojo*, or *mal de ojo* (evil eye) results in an upset disposition and is caused by envy of the child by strangers, pregnant women, and Gringos; the cure is prevention by touching the child after praise by others, using *santiguar* (the sign of the cross) and *curar con blanquillo* (to cure with eggs). *Embrujado* (bewitchment) is an illness caused by magic (such as a witch's placing a frog into the body); its treatment is countermagic to remove the evil influence. *Pujo* (gastritis) results from excessive drinking and is treated by herbs that fill the stomach.

Whether a client presents a folk disease to a therapist depends primarily on whether the client believes the therapist is knowledgeable about (and accepting of) the condition. Such folk diseases and treatments are virtually universally accepted among unacculturated Chicanos and Mexicans, but are unlikely to be discussed with an Anglo counselor. The importance of folk conditions, treatments, and faith healing in the Hispanic community is clearly underestimated by Gabachos, because such subjects are not likely to be acknowledged or discussed with them without a long-standing relationship of trust.

SOME OBSERVATIONS

SPECIAL INSTANCES: HISPANICS WHOSE CULTURAL AFFILIATION IS NATIVE AMERICAN

Freed after two years at the . . . State Hospital, Adolfo Gonzales left the . . . County Courthouse . . . flanked by translators, lawyers and a priest. "They blew it," . . . a lawyer . . . said (in reference to the patient's treatment in the mental hospital) . . . They accused him of being mute . . . He has been nearly mute

225

on the ward, even when speaking to a Spanish-English inter-preter. They concluded he was experiencing hallucinations. Gonzales was diagnosed as being afflicted with . . . paranoid schizophrenia. They drugged him up . . . Given powerful anti-psychotic drugs, Gonzales almost died less than two months after he was committed . . .

Later, an independent psychological evaluation...gave Gonzales a clean bill of health . . . Clinical evaluations were fundamentally flawed because of a language barrier . . . Sub-sequent checks with migrant workers and others revealed that his native tongue was an Indian dialect called Trique.

The excerpts above are from newspaper accounts (with identi-ties deleted) and represent an actual case of psychiatric cultural relevance. The patient's records are closed pending possible legal review, and it is therefore not possible to know the details and responsibility for the misdiagnosis. It is, however, possible to inde-pendently evaluate what went wrong.

The patient was a migrant Trique worker having documents of Mexican citizenship. The Trique comprise approximately 20,000 native people of Mexico, concentrated in the state of Oaxaca. Many are virtually monolingual in their own language (as was the patient mentioned above) and relatively isolated from the mainstream of the Mestizo population. Trique is a tonal language; anything the patient said would be completely alien in speech pattern to either an Anglo psychiatrist or a Spanish-English interpreter. It is easy to believe that anything he said under the circumstance of misdiagnosis of schizo-phrenia could have been misinterpreted as psychotic gibberish.

The assumed muteness and missed identity of the patient has a cultural basis. The Trique believe that using a person's name robs the person and invites misuse by malevolent forces. However, Western psychological assessments routinely ask such questions as "What are the names of your children?" Trique do not normally reveal the real names of their children to an outsider. Even the names of adults (such as Gonzales) are a fiction; the Trique randomly assign Spanish surnames to individuals to meet their legal obligations to an alien (first Spanish, then Mexican) society. The Trique believe in witchcraft, and this can produce a bizarre interpretation of beliefs and behavior if translated by an English-Spanish interpreter. Staff at a mental hospital will almost certainly lack the background to assess the cultural framework of such a patient.

Culturally relevant counseling and therapy is not just an idealistic endeavor; failure to provide it can (and does) have great cost to institutions, taxpayers, and the individual misdiagnosed with a mental aberration. Cultural relevance saves money and institutional burden in the long run, even though it may be expensive and difficult to provide to a given person. However, a single case involving such long-term public institutional expense (ultimately paid by taxpayers) costs more than many efforts toward a culturally relevant assessment.

RESEARCH REVIEWS AND RESOURCES

Space limitations do not permit extensive review of the psychological and counseling research literature on Latinos. Moreover, there is a wealth of literature written in Spanish by the many professionals from Hispanic nations. Listed below are a few recent English sources from which an Anglo counselor can obtain references and background in selected topics.

Ponce and Atkinson (1988) discuss Chicano acculturation, counselor ethnicity, counseling style, and credibility. Counselor preference among Mexican Americans has been investigated by López (1991). Criminological literature on Chicanos has been critically examined by Trujillo (1974). Specifically in regard to Mexicans, Díaz-Guerrero (1977) argues that culture can account for significant variance of bona fide psychological and other behaviorial science dimensions, and there is a basis to speak of sociocultural psychologies, such as a Mexican psychology. *National Hispanic Agenda* reports deal with political action recommendations and contain statistical points of summary as they deal with the overall Hispanic population. Research articles on language and ethnocultural barriers include those of Marcos, Urcuyo, Kesselman, & Alpert (1973), Malgady, Rogler, & Costantino (1987), and López (1988). *Out of the Barrio* (Chávez, 1991) is a compendium of many research areas regarding Hispanic assimilation. A general literature review of Latino mental health has been written by Padilla and Ruiz (1973).

Of particular interest to school counselors are the papers on intellectual assessment of Hispanic children (Clarizio, 1982), college preparation (Kavanaugh & Retish, 1991), and social problems in public schools (Retish & Kavanaugh, 1992). Beals (1985) describes standardized norms and multiple regression analyses of Chicano cognitive profiles based upon the Hill Cognitive Mapping Questionnaire (widely used in education to match a cognitive style preference with an instructor or course). Culturally competent assessment services for minority children in general are discussed in many agency reports, such as in the series by the Council for Children with Behavioral Disorders (CCBD) (Executive Committee of the Council for Children With Behavioral Disorders, 1989) and the National Institute of Mental Health, Child and Adolescent Service System Program (CASSP).

CLINICAL EXPERIENCE NOTES AND SITUATIONS

Counseling and psychotherapy, like medical practice, are heavily influenced by the background and experience of the service provider. The following section contains excerpts from the senior author's notes in regard to some specific observations and cases.

As a group, Hispanic professional psychologists have relatively little impact in providing appropriate services to the extremely varied Latino population.

The primary reason is the very limited number of U.S. Latinos with professional credentials (which meet national licensing, academic, or forensic standards). Oregon, for example, has only three bilingual/bicultural Hispanic psychologists for a population of approximately 200,000 Latinos. Most mental health services to Hispanics by agencies are provided by bilingual social workers or paraprofessionals, who have been trained in mainstream psychology and are supervised by an Anglo bureaucracy. One of the frustrations such providers face is the conflict with culturally appropriate recommendations—for example, having a client with *susto* or placing children with foster parents. Those who provide services against official agency policy run the risk of being disciplined or fired for insubordination.

There is another side to the coin. Like all U.S. minority groups, sophisticated Hispanics sometimes exploit cultural relevance programs, statistics, and political action agendas to their own perceived advantage—as with affirmative action, equal opportunity, and the

228

role of playing "dumb and deprived" victims of Anglo society. The reality is that (at least statistically), educated and acculturated Hispanics are doing quite well in the United States (compared to general minority members). Upper-middle-class U.S. Hispanics are on average more sophisticated, more internationally oriented, and more highly educated than their Anglo counterparts. However, such individuals become intermingled with the deprived Hispanic population for culturally appropriate counseling, agency programs, and statistical surveys of the Hispanic population.

There are two simultaneous, but different, trends in the United States. One is the highly successful acculturation rate of middle- and upper-class Hispanics; the other is the influx of new immigrants (mostly unacculturated). Incidentally, the present influx of migration is winning demographically. For example, in 1970, "barely one in five Hispanics was foreign born. Today more than one in three is; of Hispanic adults, one in two was born outside the United States" (Chávez, 1991).

Beware of relying on questionnaires, initial interviews, and admission forms in regard to Hispanic clients.

An example is a 24-year-old Spanish-monolingual man who was referred for an evaluation. The minority counselor asked the client to fill out an initial assessment questionnaire. One question concerned legal matters. The client was being examined for a forensic evaluation. The therapist, after looking at the questionnaire, curiously noted that the client did not circle "legal matters." She asked directly if he had legal problems. The client (specifically referred for forensic reasons) thought about the query and answered no. The counselor then asked if he was having trouble with the law or police, and again he answered no. The counselor did not get a sense of denial on the part of the client and decided to try a different approach. She finally asked, "Have you ever been in jail or prison?" This time, the client responded, "Yes, three times—two times for driving without a license and once when they arrested me this time. I was in jail for two weeks." Such responses to questionnaires are not unusual for unacculturated clients, who have different interpretations for the questions than those in the world of bureaucratic paperwork.

Unlike Yamamoto and Acosta (in Sue & Sue, 1990), who recommend short-term therapy lasting four to five sessions, I have found that in order to do productive work with relatively unacculturated Hispanics, the treatment often needs to be long-term.

Unacculturated Hispanics I have worked with present their problems as they think they are expected to so do—by the slow process of creating trust. It is not unusual for 2 or 3 months to pass before the client develops enough confidence to disclose the real issues.

For example, I once worked with a young Hispanic drug addict who had been incarcerated several times for drug-related offenses. He was intelligent and personable, always joking. In therapy, he expressed a desire to change his life-style, but also said that as soon as he finished a rehabilitation program or was released from prison, he was likely to use drugs again immediately.

This young man was in and out of prison at least three times in a period of about 1½ years, during which time he attended therapy. He finally revealed that his sister had died of a drug overdose in his arms. At that time, he had not been significantly involved with drugs; it was only after her death that he became addicted. In therapy, we discussed how individuals will sometimes emulate behaviors of deceased loved ones.

Before the disclosure, the client was jovial, and the focus of therapy was on breaking the addiction cycle. After the disclosure, he became more serious. The focus of therapy was changed to grief resolution. He has now been out of prison 4 years. To date, he has remained free of drugs. This young man's delayed disclosure is not much different from those of Latino clients with other issues. I personally do not feel that short-term therapy is usually of much value to such individuals unless they are highly anglicized or the situation is a crisis that necessitates only a consultation.

I concur with Torrey (1986) that one of the reasons Hispanics are less likely to seek out therapeutic services is because of the continued cultural adherence to beliefs in folk healing and supernatural theories of medicine.

Such beliefs, however, are not likely to be discussed with those who do not have genuine intimate knowledge of such practices. Contrary to reports by some researchers, such as Karno et al. (in Padilla & Ruiz, 1973), who recognize the existence of faith healing and its practice (but minimize its influence), I have found that practices such as *curanderismo* are prevalent among the less acculturated segment of the population. It is the norm for such Hispanics, when faced with a physical or mental illness, to first seek help through in-group practices of folk medicine. Among Anglos, the reverse is generally true—the physician is usually consulted first for a significant medical condition. Then, when standard treatment fails, patients frequently turn to quacks or unorthodox alternative methods of therapy. On the other hand, unacculturated Hispanics usually seek alternative ethnic practices and, when everything else fails, turn to modern medicine as a last resort.

A knowledge of *curanderismo,* folk medicine, and *brujería* is of great value in working with the large segment of the Hispanic population that endorses such beliefs. It has been my experience (as noted by Torrey, 1986) to initially encounter individuals who deny their traditional folk beliefs because they believe such practices are viewed as primitive by the Gringo mainstream. Clients do sometimes request referral to an alternative method of intervention that may complement the therapeutic process. I make it a point to make referrals only to methods and providers I have personally used and found to be ethical and appropriate. I caution against the use of such adjunct therapies by non-Hispanic counselors. Such referrals should only be undertaken by those who have culturally relevant knowledge in areas such as *curanderismo,* hypnosis, folk medicine, and psychic consultants. Even some Hispanics who traditionally accept such practices may not necessarily benefit from them; some may in fact be traumatized. Some may resort to traditional cures and therapy for conditions that require immediate modern medicinal diagnosis and treatment. There is no standard answer; it depends upon the individual case and the knowledge of the therapist to provide the most appropriate treatment recommendation.

My experience has been that Hispanic clients tend to develop a great reliance on therapy and generally stay in therapy as long, if not longer than Anglo clients, providing they can afford the cost.

Generally a Hispanic client will refer his or her spouse, children, parents, siblings, and other relatives so that the therapeutic linkage includes the extended family (it is not unusual to be seeing several members of a family for a course of therapy lasting 2 to 3 years). If a need arises, clients return and use the therapist much like a family doctor. However, it should be pointed out that standard training programs caution against such practices in psychology because they may give rise to issues of dual relationships—which may be contrary to the ethical standards of the American Psychological Association and the American Counseling Association. Dual relationship conflict is a major potential problem for counselors working with Latino clients—more than among Anglos, because therapy is more often a matter of the extended family involvement.

In working with traditional Hispanics it is not only appropriate that the counselor be bilingual and bicultural (Sue & Sue, 1990) but critical.

It is unfortunate that few therapists fit this description. The problem is not that bilingual and bicultural Latinos lack interest in counseling and psychology, but rather that admission criteria for training programs are based on mainstream, middle-class, language and background educational standards. I am personally aware of numerous Hispanic individuals who (in my opinion) would have become excellent therapists but were screened out early in academic program admission phases. Typical problems that limit Hispanics from entering academic programs are GRE scores, English composition requirements, and formal education outside the United States. It is a problem with no easy solution, because Hispanics are so internally divided over admission quotas and political programs that give preference to minorities.

Hispanic children are often inappropriately removed from families because the family values and life-style do not meet those of an Anglo caseworker assigned to the case.

This is not just a matter of placing Hispanic children in Anglo foster care, but is also a sensitive issue among Hispanic subgroups. All Latinos are symbolic *carnales* (a word not directly translatable into English, but roughly meaning "affectionate members of the same flesh and blood"). However, the social situation is that discrimination and value conflict frequently occur between members of different Latino subgroups. Particularly in the United States, lower-class Chicano and Mexican migrant families often discriminate against each other—although this feeling is rarely expressed to outsiders. Nearly all Mexican citizens who are in the United States have social services and child placements directed by either Gringos

232

or other subgroup Latinos. It is a major problem for them and is especially pressing for children removed from their natural parents and national identity.

My personal experience has been that it is best to see family members individually and in various combinations, to develop a strong sense of how the family functions before bringing them together.

The most beneficial family therapy in my experience has occurred in a subtle manner in the family home, when the family has developed trust in the therapist. On such home visits, the family as a whole becomes engaged in the communication, and it is then that significant issues are usually discussed. Such sessions generally last for 2 to 3 hours and tend to be highly productive.

INFORMATION AND HELP

Below are a few readily available resources in English that can be helpful to an Anglo counselor.

Dozens of instructional videotapes on Hispanic issues exist. For example, several departments of corrections use sensitivity videotapes for employees. Advances in television technology have recently offered major sources of shared information among the international Hispanic community. Most cable companies transmit *Galavision* or *Univision* (or both). These channels are oriented toward generalized Latino culture in the United States. Most of North America can also receive the Mexican Morelos I and II satellite transponders. The importance of television as an instrument of acculturation can scarcely be underestimated. For example, village and community-service satellite dishes are springing into existence throughout remote regions of Latin America. As a result, a client, even from an isolated Latin American village, may know more about certain world events than an Anglo counselor does. At the same time, such a client usually receives a distorted view of the United States, based upon Hollywood movies and the normal news broadcasts, which emphasize social and political problems.

Authoritative English reviews on data pertaining to U.S. Hispanic health issues are available through the American Medical Association's Council on Scientific Affairs. Compared with U.S. Anglos, Hispanics are disproportionately at risk for a multiplicity of pathologies, such as diabetes, hypertension, tuberculosis, human immunodeficiency virus (HIV) infection, alcoholism, cirrhosis, specific cancers, and violent death (Council on Scientific Affairs, 1991). Many of these conditions will reach psychological counselors, and many will involve judgments of traditional (often desperate) folk and family healing efforts.

Heavily unacculturated individuals (mostly migrant workers who are Hispanic Indians) cannot be reasonably assessed without special expertise. Anthropological details of modal cultural patterns are, from the standpoint of forensic, counseling, and psychological practitioners, buried in ethnographic monographs. However, nearly all anthropology departments in major universities have at least one specialist in Latin American culture and can (at least) provide assistance on how to find out more specific information. English summaries of Latin American native cultures are readily available in the Smithsonian series of handbooks, available in any major library and from the Government Printing Office.

Central Intelligence Agency (CIA) and State Department reports contain a wealth of publicly available information regarding all nations, including those of Latin American clients. Overt CIA summaries are available on computer diskettes from shareware vendors, such as TSL (Parsippany, N.J.). CIA and State Department sources include phone numbers and addresses of consulates and embassies, should a point of contact be needed in regard to a culturally relevant assessment and disposition of a Hispanic client who is not a U.S. citizen.

Getting a qualified interpreter can be a major problem, particularly in regions that have small numbers of Spanish speakers. For example, as of 1985, 20 states lacked even one certified interpreter for court cases, and only 262 persons had passed the certification requirements (Williams, 1985). To find a court interpreter, contact the Administrative Office of the United States Courts, Room 776, Washington, DC 20544. Several formal tests of comprehension among interviewees and clients have been devised that may be helpful in assessment, such as the widely used California Test of Basic Skills. Finding and producing a translator for Hispanics who speak Native American languages is a great (and very expensive) problem. However, there is an organization (the Summer Institute of Linguistics) that translates Scriptures into many Native American languages, and is a potential source of technical linguistic assistance—at least in identifying the language. Be aware that general language or cultural identifications (such as *Mayan*) are in actuality cultural clusters of different peoples and specific languages. For example, a half dozen major (mutually unintelligible) "dialects" (separate languages) of Mayan still exist and can occur among Hispanic migrant workers.

La familia, el barrio, el patrón, la iglesia, el compadrismo, and *los otros campesinos* (the family, the neighborhood, the boss, the church, the system of godparenthood, and fellow workers) are invaluable sources of information and help for all Hispanic migrant workers. Make every attempt to contact them in any case of uncertain cultural relevance—as in the case of the Trique worker described above. Migrant workers have their own numerous systems of social support and networks (if they are allowed to access and pursue them).

CASE STUDIES

Case vignettes are widely used in transcultural counseling as a basis for discussion and training. Brief, actual examples from case studies are provided below.

Juanita, a 25-year-old, Spanish-monolingual Mexican girl, was referred for therapy by her attorney. She had been raped by her 25-year-old Mexican fiancé. The girl was distressed, anxious, and in a state of agitated confusion. Her presenting problem was "extreme depression as a result of loss of virginity."

Throughout the gathering of evidence for the fiancé's trial, the attorney was sure the defendant would be convicted, because evidence from the police, medical reports, and the girl's condition all pointed to forcible sexual assault. An all-Anglo jury was selected for the trial. The rape defendant lied in his testimony, and the jury found him not guilty. The apparent reason was that the Anglo jury, because of their cultural background, did not believe that a 25-year-old about to be married to her fiancé would not be involved in premarital sex.

The girl became even more distraught after the verdict. Soon after the trial, she came for a therapy appointment in a state of agitation. She later pulled out an audio recorder and went on to tell the counselor how she had gotten help from a friend, arranged for the defendant to come to her house, and obtained a taped confession of how he had lied in court. The counselor contacted the district attorney's office about the situation, but there was no interest in continuing the legal case.

Hector, a 14-year-old Cuban in custody of the Children's Service Division (CSD) was referred to a counselor after he misbehaved in school and expressed to his Hispanic caseworker that he was seeing the Devil at night.

In the first session, he revealed to the counselor that he had once accused his father of illegal activity. It appeared that Hector's parents were strict. Conflict existed between the state legal authorities, the parents, CSD, and the child. While the counselor consulted with the CSD representative, Hector fled from the waiting room.

At a second session, Hector was asked why he had previously left. He replied that a man with fire pouring out of his eyes had walked by the office window, and that he had wanted to know whether the man was the Devil. He said that the man had disappeared into the air as he was following him from the office. He related having seen the Devil appear in his room at least four times during the past year. The counselor wondered if medication was indicated. However, a Mental Status Exam revealed results within normal range. He decided to ask Hector about folk beliefs. He revealed that when he was very young, his mother had talked about his having the Devil become attached to his back. Later, the family went to a *curandera*, and Hector was "OK" until the past year, when all the problems had occurred.

The counselor asked Hector what he thought might help. He took a religious medal out of his pocket and related that he had gone to a priest to have it blessed, but because of English language barriers he had not got the blessing. The counselor said he would write a note requesting the blessing (in English), which Hector was to take to the English-speaking priest.

QUESTIONS

1. How should a transcultural counselor facilitate the cases above? Are the actions taken above ethical and appropriate to the circumstances?

2. What gender or cultural backgrounds in the cases above are different from the mainstream Anglo set of values?

3. What referral sources (such as local agencies) would you provide to help the client?
4. What resources do you recommend to the counselor that would be helpful to obtain in-depth knowledge of the cultural beliefs as given above?
5. How would you predict the outcome of these cases?

REFERENCES

Beals, M. (1985). *Effect of social status upon Chicano cognitive profiles*. Unpublished doctoral dissertation, University of Oregon.

Chávez, L. (1991). *Out of the barrio: Toward a new politics of Hispanic assimilation*. New York: Basic Books.

Clarizio, H. (1982). Intellectual assessment of Hispanic children. *Psychology in the Schools, 19*, 61-71.

Council on Scientific Affairs. (1991). Hispanic health in the United States. *Journal of the American Medical Association, 265*, 248-252.

Díaz-Guerrero, R. (1977). A Mexican psychology. *American Psychologist, 32*, 934–944.

Executive Committee of the Council for Children With Behavioral Disorders. (1989). Best assessment practices for students with behavioral disorders: Accommodation to cultural diversity and individual differences. *Behavior Disorders, 14*, 263–278.

Kavanaugh, P., & Retish, M. (1991). The Mexican American ready for college. *Journal of Multicultural Counseling and Development, 19*, 136-144.

Kearney, M. (1978). Spiritualist healing in Mexico. In P. Morley & R. Wallis (Eds.), *Culture and Curing*. Pittsburgh: University of Pittsburgh Press.

López, S. (1988). The empirical basis of ethnocultural and linguistic bias in mental health evaluations of Hispanics. *American Psychologist*, December, 1095–1097.

López, S. (1991). Mexican Americans' initial preferences for counselors: The role of ethnic factors. *Journal of Counseling Psychology*.

Malgady, R., Rogler, L., & Costantino, G. (1987). Ethnocultural and linguistic bias in mental health of Hispanics. *American Psychologist, 42*, 228–233.

Marcos, L., Urcuyo, L., Kesselman, M., & Alpert, M. (1973). The language barrier in evaluating Spanish-American patients. *Archives of General Psychiatry, 29*, 655–659.

Padilla, A., & Ruiz, R. (1973). *Latino mental health: A review of the literature.* National Institute of Mental Health. Washington, DC: U.S. Government Printing Office.

Ponce, F. Q., & Atkinson, D. (1988). Mexican-American acculturation, counselor ethnicity, counseling style, and perceived counselor credibility. *Journal of Counseling Psychology, 36,* 203–208.

Retish, P. & Kavanaugh, P. (1992). Myth: America's public schools are educating Mexican American students. *Journal of Multicultural Counseling and Development, 20,* 89–96.

Sue, D. W. & Sue, D. (1990). *Counseling the culturally different: Theory and practice* (2nd ed.). New York: Wiley.

Torrey, E. (1986). *Witchdoctors and psychiatrists: The common roots of psychotherapy and its future.* Northvale, NJ: Aronson.

Trujillo, L. (1974). *La evolución del "Bandido al Pachuco":* A critical examination and evaluation of criminological literature on Chicanos. *Issues in Criminology, 9,* 43–67.

Williams, S. (1985, October). *No comprendo:* The language barrier in the criminal justice system. *Corrections Compendium, 10*(4), 6–9.

CHAPTER 10

TRANSCULTURAL COUNSELING AND PEOPLE OF ASIAN ORIGIN: A DEVELOPMENTAL AND THERAPEUTIC PERSPECTIVE

JIA WENHAO, HILEL B. SALOMON, AND
DOUGLAS M. CHAY

INTRODUCTION

To understand the cultural profile for people of Asian origin, one must understand the influence of the basic Asian philosophy rooted in qualities essential for mutual existence involving self-discipline and hard work. Anyone reared in such a society is certainly influenced by its belief systems, values, and attitudes. Fruitful intervention can be achieved only when counselors develop positive attitudes and appreciate the ways of life of people of varied origins. This chapter provides some developmental information that counselors need to counsel clients of Asian origin. It also introduces issues relevant to therapeutic transcultural interaction with Asian-American clients.

STRUCTURAL BIASES AND MYTHS

Asian Americans are unique among ethnic groups in being perceived as a model minority. Asian Americans are successful in Western society in many ways. They have a higher average income than other minorities. The major Asian-American subgroups have exceeded the national median income. They place high importance on education and claim many academic achievements. Although this is only a small part of the whole, it leads to the belief that Asian Americans, indeed, represent a model minority.

Asians in America are believed to experience few difficulties, to be well adjusted, and to function effectively in American society. This belief is reinforced by their low rates of illiteracy and divorce. Asian families have been able to sustain strict education for their children before they enter school. Such discipline continues until children become adults. The cultural basis for this emphasis on education is the notion that studiousness and virtue are interrelated qualities. For example, Chinese tradition advocates that only through education can one establish oneself with honor and riches and become socially acceptable.

There are other stereotypes of Asian Americans that are incompatible with their model minority status. For example, Asian Americans are considered to be incapable of expressing themselves effectively. A Western stereotype of Asian Americans is that they fail to express themselves psychologically (Rumbaut, 1985).

Asian Americans' difficulty in expression can be attributed to language deficiency as well as a reserved nature. Some Asian immigrants speak limited English before they leave their home countries; others are just beginning to learn English as they arrive in the West. Many have a language differential that partly explains their difficulty with communication. People from Asian countries often maintain a reserved manner. From a Western viewpoint, they are overly shy, but this shyness is due to their natural character. Sometimes these immigrants only hint at their real problems, so the counselor must look beyond what is explicitly stated. Accepting help for physical ailments is not associated with the same dishonor as accepting help for mental problems. Studies suggest that clients express depression and other psychological problems through somatic symptoms such as headaches, weakness, and insomnia (J. M. Lin, Tazuma, & Masuda, 1979).

Counselors with a transcultural perspective work to eliminate myths and stereotypes about Asian Americans. The belief that this population represents a model minority only adds pressure on them. There are some Asian immigrants who have "made it" in society and realized their "American dream," but these people are the lucky few, while most others are still struggling for survival. To most Asians in America, the success story is only a myth.

Myths and stereotypes of Asians in America invariably have functional value for those who hold power. The stereotype of a model minority reduces Asian Americans to an easily classifiable and definable group. As with other forms of racism and ethnocentrism, this stereotype makes it easier for people to attempt to manipulate Asian Americans. As a model minority, Asian Americans experience expectations not only from European Americans but also from other American minorities. In a highly competitive and multiracial society, the concept of a model group can precipitate racial tension and prejudice. Thus, many persons of Asian origin in the United States find themselves feeling nervous, tense, and depressed as they compete with everyone around them.

VALUE SYSTEMS AND SOCIAL ISSUES

The cultural background of any ethnic group is a crucial factor in determining its value system. Understanding a client's cultural background, therefore, is a key element in transcultural counseling.

Asians have a unique cultural heritage, including religious beliefs and practices. Yet they have also made great efforts toward acculturation and adjustment. Their beliefs and values are profoundly rooted in mind and habit. Contrary to the model-minority idea, Asians often have difficulties in adopting new value systems. The embeddedness of a religious belief in sociocultural values, as Tapp (1986) states, dictates against its adoption by those who do not share such values.

Asian Americans recognize that they should adjust in order to mesh with American society. However, it becomes difficult to reconcile American society with Asian cultural heritage. Asians often adopt a new way of life at the risk of experiencing psychological strain. Conflicts of value systems arise in the process of adjustment. By reshaping themselves to fit into new values, Asian immigrants are creating a new identity for themselves while retaining their cultural heritage. One study by Phinney (1989) shows that the identity development pressure is similar across all minority groups in the United States, but the specific problems facing each group are different.

Subgroups within this Asian minority may have differences in values, but their cultural background leads to similarities in family structure, attitude toward marriage, obedience to authority, and emotional restraint, among other things. Asian Americans have a hierarchical family structure in which elders enjoy absolute respect from the young. They believe marriage is the most important event in life. It must be agreed upon by the parents of the couple. When two persons marry, they should keep their marriage vows to the end of their lives. Divorce is considered the greatest possible tragedy.

Asians are capable of controlling their emotions. In the counseling setting, Asian values may come into conflict with those of a Western counselor. According to Kinzie (1985), there are eight major areas in which the Southeast Asian client and the American-trained therapist may differ: (a) the patient's focus on interdependence; (b) structured and appropriate social relationships versus situational ethics, rejection of authority, and equality of family relationships; (c) living in harmony with nature versus mastering nature; (d) attributing mental illness to imbalance in cosmic forces or lack of willpower versus attributing it to mental and physical factors; (e) lack of knowledge of psychotherapy versus strong orientation to values of psychotherapy and personal growth; (f) belief that treatment should be short and rapid versus belief that it could take a long time; (g) belief that the healer should be active and provide solutions for problems versus belief that the therapist should often be passive and that the best solution will be developed by the patient; (h) belief that mental illness represents a failure of the family versus belief that mental illness is like other problems. These conflicts may become barriers to the formation of a therapeutic alliance between the client and the counselor. Southeast Asian clients as well as Chinese-American clients focus on interdependence because they feel they must rely upon each other to survive. Very few of them are comfortable alone in a new country.

VALUE OF EDUCATION IN IMPERIAL CHINA

Chinese males wishing to enter the imperial bureaucracy had to pass a series of civil service examinations, the important ones being held at the county seat, provincial capital, and palace levels. The examinations were extremely rigorous, and a tiny percentage of those taking each level passed and became eligible for the next level. The exams required an almost encyclopedic knowledge of the Confucian classics and the officially designated orthodox commentaries. The government expected successful candidates to know by memory all the official interpretations of the classics, and thus memorization and conformity were rewarded, whereas imagination and originality were unacceptable.

The rewards for passing the examinations were such that ambitious Chinese spent many years preparing for them. However, once they passed, entry into the upper echelon of the Chinese political and social system was guaranteed. Those who passed the palace exams, for example, could petition the throne directly and received specific legal and economic privileges. The children of those who held official degrees enjoyed substantial advantages, but unless they themselves passed the examinations, the advantages did not last beyond the children's generation.

Holding an advanced degree and occupying a bureaucratic office opened the doors to economic as well as social success, and thus the examinations constituted the very real possibility of going from rags to riches. It was not unknown for children of peasants to become important officials and even prime ministers, subsequently achieving wealth as well as power. Such were the rewards for passing the exams that the dream of every household in China was that a child, or even a close relative, would pass them and bring wealth and honor to the family, clan, and even village.

The reliance on these examinations provided a substantial amount of downward social mobility and, in theory, adequate opportunities for rapid upward mobility. In practice, preparation for the examinations required so much tutoring and time to study that wealthy Chinese had distinct advantages. Nevertheless, the examination system created a society that valued education. Governments benefited from the system in that Chinese throughout the country memorized homilies about loyalty and honesty before they became officials. An emperor, therefore, had at his disposal a pool of ambitious but also conformist literati.

The symbiotic relationship between the Confucian literati and China's imperial rulers was, in large measure, responsible for protecting the system from any efforts, peaceful or violent, to change and reform China. In many other countries, revolution was often a consequence of frustrated ambition. In China, success was open to almost anyone who studied and succeeded educationally. The education was so laden with the indoctrination of Confucian values that even those who failed to achieve their goals did not question the legitimacy of those aims. From the time of Empress Wu until the second half of the 19th century, the system survived and even flourished. The challenges presented to China by an aggressive and expansive Western world, however, changed all of this.

CHALLENGES OF COUNSELING CHINESE AMERICANS AND CHINESE STUDENTS IN THE UNITED STATES

More often than not, the students who come to the United States have succeeded in examination systems that are like the former civil service exams. In the People's Republic of China, the Republic of China (Taiwan), and much of Asia, students must take an extremely difficult and crucial high school graduation exam that will determine their future careers. These exams are not intended to encourage originality of thought, particularly in the humanities and social sciences. Many Chinese educators still believe that innovation and creativity are necessary in science and engineering but are dangerous and unmanageable in other areas.

Such students can become very frustrated with instructors who demand creativity in their classrooms. The students have experienced a lifetime of discouragement of innovation, and suddenly they are asked to do what they have conscientiously avoided doing to succeed in their own systems. Counselors should be aware of this problem in helping such students adjust to the American educational context.

Chinese Americans and to a large degree other Asian-American students may also exhibit cumulative attitudes from their parents. The pressures on these students to produce good grades are enormous. Asian-American parents can often accept nothing short of excellence from their children, and many of these students suffer rather traumatically when they are merely average. To Asians and Asian Americans, education is still the only acceptable path to economic success and social acceptability. The age-old prejudices against careers in business have not prevented their parents from becoming successful, but they themselves are driven to become professionals, preferably with postgraduate degrees. Not achieving this goal is viewed by their own societies as tantamount to failure.

Changing this belief system will require considerable time and patience. Educators and transcultural counselors should be aware of the historical and cultural nature of these issues when confronted with nervous and frustrated students. As these students become acculturated, more and more average ones will be noticeable, and counselors will be able to deal with them through standard practices of teaching and counseling. Until that time, however, it helps to understand the historical background of these dilemmas and deal with them with patience and flexibility.

Living in harmony with nature is a well-known ancient Chinese philosophy. Chinese philosophers believed that human beings were a part of nature and had to behave as such. The ideal was for human beings and nature to become one. These philosophers believed that the attempt to master nature was a tremendous mistake on the part of human beings. Traditionally, mental illness has been attributed to an imbalance in cosmic forces or lack of willpower, and the person with such illness is often stigmatized. Therefore the preferred treatment for such illness is short and rapid.

One Western approach is for counselors to be passive and to have clients develop their own solutions. In contrast, Southeast Asian patients expect the healer to be active and provide structured solutions to their problems. They are used to relying wholly on the healer and not developing solutions for themselves—as in the Asian method of teaching. Asian students traditionally are accustomed to accepting passively what the teacher tells them; American students ask questions and often formulate their own opinions. Because of this difference, there could be a conflict between client and counselor. A conflict does not mean that the client is refusing to cooperate; it is simply a matter of custom. Asian clients often believe that mental illness is a symbol of family failure—a disaster for the client and the family. Therefore, the client often feels ashamed and depressed.

Chinese have a leisurely attitude toward life, based on the idea that nature and human beings should be one. That is part of the reason that most Chinese still engage in a slow pace of life. In the Chinese eye, tolerance is a virtue; yet this might not be necessary in Western society. Chinese pay more attention to others than to themselves. There is also ancient precedent for this. Confucius said, "[The good man] does not grieve that other people do not recognize his merits. His only anxiety is lest he should fail to recognize theirs" (Waley, 1945).

Confucius was appalled at the political and social uncertainties of his time. He called for a return to a kind of golden feudal period when everyone knew and accepted his or her place in society. The corollary to this was that birthright-determined status involved obligations as well as privileges. Thus, according to Confucius, a nobleman had to act nobly. Otherwise his birth privileges were invalid, although Confucius did not specify how they might be rescinded. According to Confucius, the guidelines to noble behavior were in the written classics of the time. Thus, a nobleman had to either be able to read these himself, or depend on someone to read them for him. Confucius expected that only the nobility would wish to learn these wondrous guidelines for behavior. He did not rule out the possibility that even common peasants might have questions they would want answered and eventually might even seek education to become better persons. Confucius himself was prepared to teach anyone who wished to learn, as his statement shows. That is why Chinese are often concerned about what others are doing but do not know what they themselves are doing. The Chinese maintain that success and virtue cannot be separated: One cannot achieve success without first establishing virtue. Chinese take pride in their ancestry; Americans take pride in themselves. Myths appeal to the Chinese; Americans prefer success stories.

Cultural knowledge can help the transcultural counselor understand client needs and identify areas of value conflicts. Armed with cultural knowledge, counselors can identify the unique needs of clients. At the same time, counselors should be aware that in many Southeast Asian countries mental health problems are regarded as shameful, and clients may be reluctant to discuss their problems directly. Thus, counselors should explain the role of counseling clearly at the beginning of the therapeutic process.

RELIGIOUS AND SPIRITUAL INFLUENCE

To Asian Americans, religious beliefs and spiritual involvement are important factors in their concept of mental health. Therefore, it is important for the transcultural counselor to have a sufficient understanding of these beliefs and practices. Asian immigrants and refugees bring to a new nation their cultural heritage, the essential part of which is their religious beliefs. Although they are driven to adapt to a new environment, they cling to their cultural traditions, which serve as spiritual support and as a way of maintaining their identity.

The major Asian religions are Buddhism, Taoism, and Confucianism. Chinese cultural beliefs are embedded in Confucianism, with Taoism playing a peripheral role. The sources of Vietnamese religious beliefs are Buddhism, Taoism, and Confucianism. Beliefs of Cambodians, Thais, and Asian Indians are rooted in different schools of Buddhism that originated in ancient India. According to some schools of Buddhism, the world is a place of miseries, and life is full of pain. People should be saved from this miserable place; salvation is thought to be not physical but spiritual. Individuals can free themselves from pain by being tolerant and by rejecting desires. Taoism, having originated in ancient China, advises people to live in harmony with nature. Confucianism is an ethic that stresses order in society. Its concepts also include filial piety; ancestor worship; hierarchical, yet reciprocal interpersonal relationships; and high regard for truth, virtue, education, and social status (Feng, 1983). These beliefs play prominent roles in the lives of Asian immigrants and refugees.

One Asian belief about mental illness is that because no one can avoid pain, no one should resist it. The person with an illness should tolerate it, not feel it spiritually, and the pain will disappear. Another way of dealing with mental illness is to restore physical order to the patient, because mental health is also believed to be closely related to physical health (Sue & Morishima, 1982). People from Southeast Asian countries are not familiar with Western mental health concepts (K. M. Lin & Masuda, 1983). They attach a stigma to mental illness and invariably relate it to internal factors like family disaster or failure, heredity, personal weakness or physical disorder, soul loss, or revenge by fate. Stylistic counseling addresses these factors in its cultural-historical dimension, which has implications for establishing a base for transcultural counseling (McFadden, 1986).

In Asian cultures, the family is the center of life. If something is wrong with the family, it signifies a serious problem. If the parents

247

have mental problems, their children are more likely to have such problems. For that reason, some Asian parents are very careful about the heredity of the persons their children plan to marry.

Beliefs of some Asians include an element of superstition. They may have a profound belief in omnipotent fate, which can take the soul away from the body, resulting in mental illness. However, only those without virtue may lose their souls. That is part of the reason why shame and disgrace are attached to mental illness. In Asian culture there is no distinction between psychological and physical problems. Mental illness is attributed to a disturbance of internal vital energy. The Chinese and Vietnamese historically treated mental illness by using herbal medicine to restore order to the body. They also use acupuncture. In some cases, patients take leave from work to have complete rest. When Southeast Asian clients present themselves at American counseling centers, their condition is likely to be of a mixed psychological and medical nature that may require medical evaluation (Kinzie, 1985). Their physical problems often indicate psychological ones.

CULTURE AND ASSIMILATION IN THE WEST

Sufficient knowledge of the cultural background of the client enables the transcultural counselor to offer effective orientation, as needed, for reasonable and more effective assimilation. The counselor, therefore, should have a clear picture of the major cultural issues facing Asians in America in their adjustment. We may divide these issues into two interrelated categories: physical and psychological. Here, the physical issues are defined as referring to the physical world in which Asian Americans find themselves.

Initially, Asians may have a strong feeling of alienation. A foreigner in Asian countries has high status and acquires certain privileges. However, this is not the case in the United States. Most Asians in America believe that they have come to the most advanced country in the world, and they fear discrimination. They cannot disguise their origins because their physical appearance is different. They may also feel that others regard their countries and culture as inferior. These factors can lead to anxiety or self-hatred for being an Asian.

Unemployment is another major problem, more serious among refugees than among immigrants from Asian countries. Even many with training and experience have difficulty finding jobs because of insufficient preparation or inadequate communication skills. Some Asians in America, especially the young, feel that their own cultures are inferior. This attitude of cultural separatism may cause countercultural behaviors. For example, some young Asian Americans develop a more Western manner merely to cover up what they think is inferior within their own identity. Learning communication skills is the first priority for foreign-born Asian Americans. Learning English is a prerequisite for functioning effectively in the United States: English proficiency strongly influences opportunities in employment and education.

Other important factors in assimilation and acculturation for Asians in America include place of settlement, attitude toward fertility, rejection of cultural biases, and direct interaction with Americans. Living in minority-concentrated areas adds to the isolation of Asian Americans. Increasing suburbanization of Chinese and Japanese may reduce their segregation from Whites (Lam, 1986). Chinese persons will find more opportunities to communicate with citizens of a host country if they do not live in Chinatown because the intensive concentration of one group of people could psychologically prevent others from entering the area for interaction. It is like a Forbidden City within an American city, and other people may go there occasionally but only as tourists. During the process of assimilation and acculturation, members of the younger generation of Asian Americans may regard their own cultures as inferior. There is constant conflict between their Asian origin, which they cannot reject, and the American culture, which they see as appealing. Interaction with citizens of the host country not only reduces probable segregation but helps Asians adapt in America. Both behavioral assimilation and attitudinal acculturation are influenced by direct interaction with members of the host society (Dworkin & Dworkin, 1988).

Finally, counselors should attempt to establish trust and confidentiality between themselves and their clients. Intercultural rapport between the counselor and the client is essential for effective transcultural counseling. Once this objective has been achieved, the counselor should then make necessary distinctions between subgroups of clients, such as groups of different ages, U.S.-born or foreign-born persons, immigrants, refugees, Japanese, Chinese, Koreans, and others. Different subgroups have different problems, which require different approaches to counseling.

AN INTERVIEW WITH CHUN-CHI CHEN
FROM TAIWAN

Q. *Describe some of the basic cultural patterns of Taiwanese.*

A. Everyone is influenced by Confucian thoughts that are viewed as a guide to the way of being rather than a religious belief. Confucian thoughts are our basic spiritual culture. We are educated to follow the ethical standard of Confucian thoughts without exception. Nevertheless, in modern society, all aspects of our lives are influenced by Japan and Western culture. For example, there is an inclination toward materialism in shaping our lifestyle, utilitarianism in our educational practices and livelihood, individualism in our interpersonal relationship. Because Taiwan is open to all kinds of information, Taiwanese culture could be likened to the process of blending various colors of clay—the original piece of clay is gradually blended with other pieces with different colors; although the original color cannot be recognized, the entity of the original piece of clay still exists.

Q. *What is the typical structure of a family in Taiwan?*

A. The nuclear family is the dominant type of family in Taiwan. A typical nuclear family has two children. Although the traditional big family system (three generations living under the same roof or in the neighborhood together with extended relatives) is gradually going out of date, there is a close connection between generations. We believe that we should do our best to rear our offspring, and we also have the obligation to support our parents in reward for what they have done for us. In terms of the distribution of authority and obligation, it is typical that both parents work and share the right of making decisions.

Q. *What are guidance and counseling programs like in your schools?*

A. The functions of school counselors are limited in our educational system. Most students have the impression that guidance and counseling personnel only administer intelligence tests and counsel students who have special problems such as misbehavior or truancy. Small schools might not even have a full-time counselor. Under the tremendous pressure of helping students advance to a higher level of education which permeates throughout our educational system, the important role of school counselors is overlooked. The emphasis is placed on discipline rather than guidance or counseling.

In society, on the other hand, various types of guidance or counseling services mushroom like bamboo shoots after the rain. Most of them are provided by nongovernmental agencies or foundations centering on big cities. These organizations invite helping professionals or scholars in relevant fields to present speeches, workshops, and counseling opportunities such as T groups to the public. Some of them provide guidance or counseling services for certain groups such as adolescents, parents, and persons who have experienced marital difficulties and divorce. Generally, these services are free or available at a low price. However, it is still not common that people would seek professional help when they need it. This conservative attitude toward counseling or psychotherapy is probably due to our belief in the power of religion and fear of disgrace.

Q. *What role do parents play in school activities?*

A. Parents usually supervise their children on a daily basis in order to make sure that they finish their homework and keep up with the class. Students may also attend or participate in occasional activities such as student sports meetings, a garden party, and other youth-related programs. To supervise school activities, parents can attend the teacher-parent meetings to present their opinions. They also work with parent committees to fulfill supervisory duties.

Q. *What do Taiwanese people expect schools to do in educating their children?*

A. For most parents, the major purpose of education is helping children pass the entrance examination for higher schooling. Because of the keen competition for educational opportunities, especially for entering a university, most parents are not offended if schools balance various aspects of student development by implementing moral, intellectual, physical, social, and esthetic education. Therefore, parents, who do not want their children to suffer in a distorted educational system would emigrate to another country. Mothers and fathers believe that schools should provide appropriate discipline to maintain good conduct among their children.

Q. *How does one enter marriage, and what does society expect of a couple in maintaining marriage?*

A. People have freedom to make friends of the opposite sex. However, when they consider getting married, they respect the opinions of their parents and obtain an agreement from them. The prospective groom's family will give presents and/or money to the parents of the prospective bride at a betrothal. In addition, the family of the bride will prepare a trousseau for her.

The rate of divorce is rising in Taiwan because people are beginning to see divorce as an option for dealing with marital problems. For the elder generation, persons who are over 50, divorce is considered to be the worst choice for solving problems in marriage and family. For the younger generation, however, divorce is acceptable as the final option.

Q. *How does the Taiwanese culture perceive interracial marriage?*

A. The elder generation considers that interracial marriage is odd and unacceptable. The young generation has an open mind toward interracial marriage but [is] conservative in terms of their actions. They believe that more social and political concerns are involved in interracial marriage than marrying a person of the same cultural or ethnic background.

Q. *Explain career development and employment in your country.*

A. Our vocational education is well developed quantitatively but not necessarily qualitatively. Eighty percent of the students who graduate from middle school enter a vocational school. According to a recent report, however, one half of the students in vocational schools do not plan to seek a job immediately after graduation because they want to enter a higher level of schooling in order to obtain a degree. A certificate is not as valuable as a degree.

Career development or career counseling services are practiced by public agencies rather than schools in a traditional sense. For example, we have vocational training centers and employment agencies administered by the government to assist in career development. Some middle or large enterprises also provide in-service training for their employees. Generally speaking, it is not difficult to find a job merely to make a living, but it is not easy to find a satisfying occupation for full self-actualization and economic advancement.

Q. *How are Americans and their life-style perceived in Taiwan?*

A. Taiwanese people believe in the "golden mean" of the Confucian school. That is, they believe that too much is as bad as not enough. For them, Americans are inclined to enjoy too much and give too much freedom to themselves. For example, Americans are thought to drink too much, eat too much, have too many sexual partners, and engage in too much violence. In another point of view, Americans are more open-minded and have more respect for individual differences. As a result, they are likely to mind their own business and do whatever they want to do. Taiwanese people are generally impressed by the quality of the environment in America—the spacious dwellings, limited traffic, and fresh air are what they admire.

Q. *What are the issues that would serve as a basis for Taiwanese to seek counseling?*

A. Issues such as conflicts between parents and children, marital problems, relationships between the opposite sex among unmarried people, the pressure of advancing to a higher school among adolescents, and career development serve as a basis for Taiwanese to seek counseling.

Q. *What are some ideas that you would suggest for a counselor in working with Taiwanese?*

A. Taiwanese people need to learn to accept themselves as well as others for who they are. An underlying reason for various kinds of problems is that people place too many unrealistic expectations upon themselves and on others. Because they internalize great ideals of Confucian thoughts, they sometimes are ashamed of admitting that they cannot function well in society. Counselors are not encouraged to confront the individual's beliefs and defenses. However, they can help counselees clarify their beliefs, and explore other alternatives of being. Because Taiwanese people tend to suppress their emotions, transcultural counselors are encouraged to provide a facilitative environment where counselees feel free to express their feelings and behavior.

Q. *Describe your academic expectations and life as a graduate student in an American university.*

A. I hope that I can learn English before I study in English. The reality is that I cannot improve my English proficiency quickly enough in terms of listening, speaking, reading, and writing when I struggle with coursework. I believe that language deficiency is the major barrier to participating in mainstream society for those who do not use English as their first language.

CASE STUDIES

The transcultural counselor should instill in the client's mind an awareness of the need for dialogue in counseling. This may be a long process because Asians in America often lack a clear concept of Western counseling. The counselor should make them aware that the counseling sessions can be as effective as medicines for physical illness. Counselors need to choose appropriate approaches to counseling clients who could be experiencing problems involving cultural differences, as indicated in the following cross-cultural critical incidents.

INCIDENT 1: FROM KINSHIP COMPETITION TO RACIAL COMPETITION

Biodata

Fara Merina is in her mid-20s. She was born and reared in the Philippines and immigrated to the United States in her teens.

Background

Fara just earned her master's degree and is looking for a job. Although she was one of the top students in school, she was not granted a chance that she deserved. Opportunities went to her White classmates. She had to make it herself.

What is more frustrating is the hostility exhibited by people with whom she competes for a position. People asked her why she was here. She was told many times that she had no right to be here and she should go back where she came from. She and many other immigrants were made to feel disadvantaged.

254

Fara asked herself, "Why am I here?" Apparently, she came here with her parents, who moved to the United States because there appeared to be no bright future where they were born. In Fara's country, everything operated on the basis of personal connections or improper profits. For example, if one wanted a job, one had to know or be related to someone influential, and even pay bribes. Otherwise someone else less qualified could prevail.

This is not a just world. People compete with each other all the time. Kinship, connections, race, or some other higher status is the name of the game. Someone like Fara might always be a loser.

Dilemma

Everyone needs to make a living. Fara's parents came to the United States because the survivability in their home country was questionable. However, when individuals in mainstream American society become aware of the pressure for survival, they feel offended by these "aggressive" immigrants. Fara prefers to stay in America, but she does not know how to deal with the complex issues of race, hatred, and economic survivability.

Intervention

Counselors need to acknowledge Fara's desperation, frustration, and alienation. They must be able to help her examine and sort out her priorities and understand that all Americans are not racist pigs. In addition, they might help her explore the positive side of life in this country and develop strategies to deal with the hostile attitudes.

Questions

1. What is/are the underlying reason(s) for race hatred?
2. How can we facilitate the transition from hostility to cooperation, from prejudice to nonprejudice?
3. Probably, it is part of human nature that people are inclined to be partial to their kinfolk or acquaintances of their own race. While we meet people within the broader context of races, on the other hand, we are inclined to work toward the welfare of our own ethnic group. Commonality is too remote to achieve. What should we do as counselors to build trust in others?
4. Besides making a profit, what else can people do when they transplant themselves or their businesses from one country to another?

INCIDENT 2: "I DON'T KNOW WHAT WILL HAPPEN TOMORROW"

Biodata

Sylvan Wang is a Chinese-American, middle-aged, married male.

Background

Sylvan came to America in the early 1970s. He graduated from college in his native country. Conceiving a great dream for the future, he decided to study overseas. Therefore, he enrolled as a graduate student in the master's program in electrical engineering at a U.S. university. After obtaining his degree, he married and found a job with an engineering company. Several years later, he and his wife became permanent residents of the United States.

Mr. and Mrs. Wang have two lovely children, a boy in the eighth grade and a girl in the fourth grade. When their children were younger, Mrs. Wang stayed home. Since their children became more independent, their mother began a part-time job in the post office 3 years ago. The Wangs work hard to rear their children. Besides regular education, these parents support their children in piano, painting, tennis, and swimming lessons, as well as Chinese language classes. Regarding their marriage, although they are not happy with each other, they sustain matrimony by tolerating each other and becoming used to occasional quarrels.

Sylvan is an engineer. He still works in the first company that employed him after graduation from engineering school. He works cautiously and attentively. He has no intention of competing with his colleagues, but he believes that he must work hard to keep his job. Because of current economic difficulties, many employees in his company have been dismissed. He is afraid that it might also happen to him eventually because he is not indispensable. Living in such an unpredictable world makes it hard to know what will happen tomorrow.

Dilemma

Sylvan has great concern about the stability of his job. However, he is unable to discuss the situation and his feelings with his wife. If he loses his job, his family will face financial problems. Can he find a new job? Can he return to his native country? How will his relatives and friends think of him if he becomes unemployed?

Intervention

The counselor should provide opportunities for Sylvan to share his feelings of anxiety and insecurity. It is necessary to help him improve his self-concept and self-confidence. He may need marital counseling as well. Problem-solving skills and behavioral strategies can be applied.

Questions

1. What qualities can a transcultural counselor possess that would help Sylvan with his multifaceted problems?
2. Is Sylvan's fear of job security a typical experience for most people? How can it be approached?
3. What effect does Sylvan's cultural identity have on the probable solution of his dilemma?

INCIDENT 3: LANGUAGE HANDICAP

Biodata

Angela Chen is a 25-year-old, female Chinese immigrant. She is a single graduate student.

Background

Angela immigrated to America with her family. She has been here for a year, but she still feels a barrier to communication. In her country, every student is required to take English in school for a couple of years. The training focuses on reading and writing rather than conversation. She feels frustrated because she has difficulty in communicating with people about everyday life, which involves experiences, thoughts, and feelings.

Angela has been told that if she wants to use English as an effective tool, she has to live with Americans and think in English. It sounds to her as if she has to abandon her roots and plant herself in a totally different world. Nevertheless, it seems that she has no other choice, because she is determined to consider the United States her second home.

She lives with her family, attends a Chinese church, and spends her spare time with Chinese friends. Nothing differs from her former life except attending classes with American classmates and learning more English. She takes much more time than her classmates to finish her assignments and tests. Sometimes she feels that her mind goes blank when she tries to think in English. How can she collect ideas with a limited vocabulary in her memory? She feels as if she can do nothing well as long as she has to use English. She has become aware of what it is like to have a "handicap."

Dilemma

For Angela, it is convenient to continue living in the same way, and it is terrible to separate herself from her own culture. However, if she is not willing to try harder to improve her English proficiency, she could be at a disadvantage.

Intervention

Counselors need to help Angela explore self-awareness and selfacceptance. Counselors can help her understand that learning English does not necessarily mean losing identity. It may take more time to master a language after she passes a certain stage, but she could become bilingual if she invests time and interest. Angela might need academic assistance to help her adjust to a new learning environment. She also may need guidance screening for better ways to learn English.

Questions

1. How could a transcultural counselor help Angela overcome her problem and build self-confidence?
2. On what should the counselor focus to help Angela?
3. To what extent does the term *handicap* influence Angela in forming a communications image of herself?

CONCLUSION

Transcultural counselors can be catalysts for the enhancement of knowledge among mental health providers on behalf of people of Asian origin. The premise that a barrier for one is a barrier for all captures the true meaning of cultural bridge building between counselors and clients. This chapter has offered an understanding of and strategies for providing effective services for Asians and Asian Americans. Inasmuch as Asians constitute a major segment of the world's population, and inasmuch as they encounter a number of dilemmas in the process of acculturation and assimilation in the West, counselors need to examine their own philosophical outlook and counseling orientation to ensure success in working with people of Asian origin. Transcultural counseling promises to help immigrants and refugees from Asia succeed in their new country.

REFERENCES

Dworkin, A. G., & Dworkin, R. J. (1988). Interethnic stereotypes of acculturating Asian Indians in the United States. *Plural Societies, 18*(1), 61–70.

Feng, Yu-lan. (1983). *A history of Chinese philosophy.* Princeton, NJ: Princeton University Press.

Kinzie, J. D. (1985). Overview of clinical issues in the treatment of Southeast Asian refugees. In T. C. Owan (Ed.), *Southeast Asian mental health: Treatment, prevention, services, training, and research* (pp. 113–5, 321). Washington, DC: National Institute of Mental Health.

Lam, F. (1986). Suburban residential segregation of Chinese and Japanese Americans: 1960, 1970, and 1980. *Sociology and Social Research, 70*(4), 263–265.

Lin, J. M., Tazuma, J., & Masuda, M. (1979). Adaptational problems of Vietnamese refugees. *Archives of General Psychiatry, 36*, 955–961.

Lin, K. M., & Masuda, M. (1983). Impact of refugee experience: Mental health issues of the Southeast Asians. In *Bridging cultures: Southeast Asian refugees in America.* Los Angeles: Special Services for Groups—Asian American Community Mental Health Training Center.

McFadden, J. (1986). Stylistic dimensions of counseling minorities. *International Journal for the Advancement of Counseling, 9*(3), 209–219.

Phinney, J. S. (1989, February–May). Stages of ethnic identity development in minority group adolescents. *Journal of Early Adolescence, 9*, 34–49.

Rumbaut, R. G. (1985). Mental health and the refugee experience: A comparative study of Southeast Asian refugees. In T. C. Owan (Ed.), *Southeast Asian mental health: Treatment, prevention, services, training, and research* (pp. 433–486). Washington, DC: National Institute of Mental Health.

Sue, S., & Morishima, J. K. (1982). *The mental health of Asian Americans.* San Francisco: Jossey-Bass.

Tapp, N. (1986). Buddhism and Hmong: A case study in social adjustment. *Journal of Development Societies, 2*(1), 68–88.

Waley, A. (Trans. & annotator). (1945). *Analects of Confucius* (chap. 1). London: George Allen & Unwin.

CHAPTER 11

TRANSCULTURAL COUNSELING AND ARAB AMERICANS

NUHA ABUDABBEH AND MARGARET K. NYDELL

It is important that mental health providers be aware of cultural differences when they work with minority groups. As expressed by Katz (1984):

It is imperative that the psychiatrist be aware that cultural differences do exist, that he seek to become knowledgeable about these differences, and that he attempt to understand the influence of the culture on the patient's ideas, thinking process, ideals, and methods of communication. If the psychiatrist ignores the cultural differences or is unaware of them, he is not just doing nothing about them; rather, he is denying the importance of culture. . . . This results in the establishment of a barrier between the patient and the psychiatrist.

Arab Americans share many of the cultural norms prevalent in other groups, such as African Americans, Hispanic Americans, Asian Americans, and Native Americans, but certain values are specific to Arab Americans. Like other ethnic groups, Arab Americans vary among themselves enough to warrant further exploration of the specific origin of each client. Potential differences include social class (this is significant in Arab society), level of education, language (Arabic has distinct dialects), relative conservatism of the country of origin, time of immigration, and level of acculturation. Despite such cultural variations, sufficient commonalities exist that

261

special attention from service providers is warranted (Abudabbeh, 1992).

There are currently 2.5 to 3 million Arab Americans living in the United States, many having arrived in the last 15 to 20 years (Zoghby, 1990). There are also large numbers of Arab students, between 25,000 and 40,000 (American Friends of the Middle East, personal communication, 1992; Institute of International Education, 1991).

Arab Americans are only now becoming numerous enough to have an impact on their communities and to organize themselves effectively. In some cases their numbers are large enough that they have experienced the resentment and hostility commonly directed toward upwardly mobile ethnic groups. This resentment is exacerbated by the political tension between many Arab states and the West, which leads to a negative image of Arabs as people.

Arab Americans are a heterogeneous group and can be described as a multicultural, multiracial, and multiethnic mosaic population. They tend to divide themselves into Christians and Muslims (relative proportion uncertain, probably about fifty-fifty) because religious affiliation is central to an Arab's identity (Nydell, 1987). They also group themselves by geographic regions in the Arab world, usually considered to be (from west to east) North Africa (the Maghreb), Egypt/Sudan, the Levant (Lebanon, Syria, Palestine, Jordan, and possibly Iraq), and the countries of the Arabian Peninsula.

It must be noted that the term *Arab* is based on a person's language and culture; it is not an ethnic origin, as is the term *Arabian* (meaning of Arabian Semitic stock). Thus there is great diversity among Arabs, and they feel more affinity toward others from the same region and religion. Reflecting societies in the Middle East, there is little or no discrimination based on color or racial origin.

Most Arab immigrants in the 1890s and early 20th century (the first wave) were Christians from Lebanon and Syria, as well as Christians from Iraq (Chaldeans). Later immigrants after the 1940s, especially the large numbers in the 1970s and 1980s (the second wave), have included many Muslims, and they have come from all of the 21 Arab countries (although relatively few from wealthy oil countries). Of the 3.5 to 6 million Muslims in the United States today, a significant number are Arabs. To accommodate them, the number of mosques and student centers has grown from 600 to more than 950 in the last 5 years (Pristin & Dart, 1991). The largest Muslim communities are in metropolitan New York City, Los Angeles, Chicago, Boston, Houston, Detroit, and Washington, DC.

The largest numbers of Arab immigrants are from (in descending order) Lebanon, Syria, Palestine and Jordan, Egypt, Iraq, and Yemen; about 1 million arrived between 1961 and 1989 (*Statistical Abstract*, 1991).

About half of today's Arab Americans are descended from the second wave of immigrants, and it is they who helped form Arab American organizations (Zoghby, 1990). Arab Americans' realization of their identity as a distinct, cohesive group in the United States came about largely as a response to the collective trauma they experienced in the 1967 war between the Arab states and Israel.

Various Arab national groups tend to predominate in certain areas of the United States (and Canada), and most prefer to live in or near large cities. Because of the professional-preference clause in the Immigration and Naturalization Act of 1965, more highly educated and westernized Arabs have been immigrating (*Harvard Encyclopedia*, 1980), and this group now has the second-highest per capita income of all ethnic groups in the United States (Arab-American Institute, personal communication, 1992).

Descendants of first-wave immigrants, Arab Americans born in the United States, tend to be concentrated in the Northeast, whereas second-wave Arab immigrants are present in larger numbers in the western United States (Zoghby, 1990). Both groups of immigrants have had a marked preference for self-employment, and unemployment is low. Arab Americans in general have a higher level of education than the U.S. population as a whole and than other ethnic groups.

First- and second-generation Arab Americans must contend with profound social and cultural differences, especially as they adjust to the relatively liberal and individualistic attitudes in American society. These attitudes are in fundamental contrast to their Arab background of conformity, subordination of individual goals and desires of the family and community, and conservative moral practices, as well as adherence to a collective sense of honor and reputation (Nydell, 1987; Soliman, 1986).

ARAB-AMERICAN CULTURAL NORMS AND VALUES

Arab society is generally conservative, and its values are carried for two or three generations by Arab immigrants. There is little or no difference between the basic values held by Arab Christians and those of Arab Muslims; many Christian Arabs are the product of an Islamic or Islamicized society and way of life.

Keeping in mind the diversity among Arabs, some generalizations can be made. Most Arab Americans share the following beliefs and practices:

1. Marriage and children are essential for a complete and happy adult life.
2. Men are the heads of their families and the designated decision makers. In other words, authority and family identification are patrilineal.
3. The extended family is valued across generations. Young people owe profound respect to their elders, and often even to older siblings.
4. Children are expected to care for their parents and older relatives, usually inviting them to live in their homes, particularly after an older person is widowed.
5. Family honor is most easily damaged by the behavior of women, so they have a great responsibility toward the entire extended family to comport themselves in an honorable way.
6. Family ties and duties have precedence over work or career aspirations.
7. Religious identity and belief in God are essential.

Traditionally, Arabs believe that a person's honor and dignity are an integral part of his or her identity (Nydell, 1987), and if necessary, some families do not hesitate to punish someone to uphold family honor. This strict, traditional attitude tends to be a source of controversy among Arabs themselves and is not universally adopted. It continues to be a source of conflict, especially between generations, as it pertains to parents trying to control their children's activities and the family's social image. The generation gap is often dramatic and painful in Arab families, particularly when younger people have a higher education than their parents, as is often the case. Increased independence of young people has resulted from the influences of modernization, such as the mobility of the family, economic problems that affect the family's ability to care for its members, and basic value and attitude conflicts between the generations (Soliman, 1986).

Many Arabs are very religious, and they aspire to live according to the ideals of their Christian or Muslim faith. They believe that a person should practice his or her religion, and even if not, must acknowledge faith in God and God's power over human events. Many Arab Muslims and Christians are very concerned with maintaining their respective religions when living in the West. They often worry that their children, especially daughters, will marry outside the group. Outmarriage is less of a problem for sons, because children are considered to have the religion of their father.

THE ARAB FAMILY

When people come to an environment totally alien to their way of life, they tend to cling to their own values and traditions. Arab Americans put great value on maintaining solidarity and mutual assistance in extended families. Parents may want their children to live close by and visit frequently, and they want a continuing role in their lives and decisions. Many Arabs experience great loneliness when away from their family. Conversely, those who show a strong desire for independence are often the cause of confusion, hurt feelings, suspicion, and the fear that group solidarity is threatened. Yet many young people who find the home setting unpleasant still do not want to leave home (Soliman, 1986). The influence of an Arab family on its members is profound throughout their lives (Hamady, 1960; Patai, 1976; Sharabi & Ani, 1977).

In traditional Arab society, an individual's self-concept is closely tied to the family and community, and there is less emphasis on personal boundaries than in the West. This fact has implications when developing a counseling or training model (Westwood & Borgen, 1988), and the counselor must realize that he or she will not function effectively without considering the family viewpoint. Individuals owe loyalty to the family, and from it they derive security, emotional support, and financial assistance. People are expected to be supportive of their relatives, even when a relative is in the wrong; the closer the relationship, the more important this becomes (Nydell,

1987). The comparative looseness of family structure and support in American society is often difficult to accept.

THE ROLE OF MEN

In most cases, the men in a family have the entire responsibility for its financial support and for maintaining the family's prestige and honor. Most men feel protective toward women, including their mother, unmarried or widowed sisters, and other female relatives who do not have another man to see to their welfare. As a man grows older, he gains more respect and patriarchal authority, but he also has more responsibility, including financial responsibility, if necessary, for others in the extended family.

THE ROLE OF WOMEN

Arabs generally believe that men and women have significant insurmountable differences and that their roles in society are clearly defined. Women are the stabilizing center of the family, and they owe their primary energies to creating and facilitating a cohesive and happily functioning unit. Women usually have complete responsibility for domestic activities, such as cooking, child rearing, household budgeting, home decorating, and often the arrangement of marriages.

The restricted role of women in traditional Arab societies is misunderstood in the West, in that the motivation is not a desire to repress, but rather the belief that the strength of the family, and by extension the community, will be threatened in proportion to the amount of time and effort a woman spends on outside activities (Mikhail, 1979).

Many Arabs believe that some social ills in Western and American society (child abuse, use of drugs, sexual promiscuity and infidelity, neglect of older people) are the direct result of the increased desire of Western women for more individual freedom, whether manifested as the pursuit of a demanding career or even as the decision not to have children or not to marry at all. If women give up their primary responsibilities, they worry, who will fill them? Or will the family and community fall apart? Many Arabs also believe that by restricting the outside activities of women they are protecting them from the stress and competition experienced by Western women in the workplace, and they point to this protection (which is difficult for Americans and others to understand) as a manifestation of their respect for women.

Arab women, however, have considerable influence in family decisions, and often vehemently disagree with the men in the family and get their way. But this is usually not done in front of others, and not acknowledged overtly.

There is a wide range of reaction by women in Arab society to these restrictions, from complete acceptance and approval (Lamb, 1987) to vehement objection (Mikhail, 1979).

It is significant and interesting that American-born Arab women are twice as likely to remain single as those born in Arab countries (Zoghby, 1990).

THE ARAB MARRIAGE

Given the clear-cut roles traditionally assigned to husbands and wives, there is relatively little adjustment needed in carving out areas of decision making and responsibilities. Many marriages are arranged by families, in the belief that this step is too serious to be based solely on emotional grounds. A person's marriage affects the entire family, and care is taken to match social, educational, and financial backgrounds, as well as to ensure that both partners have good personal and family reputations. Traditionally, marriage to first and second cousins has been common because it keeps the daughters, as well as the money, in the family.

Family involvement in selecting a marriage partner is still practiced by most Arab families (Soliman, 1986), although change has been occurring, particularly in families that have adopted Western values. Many Arabs studying in the West believe that they are not free to select a partner as are their Western friends.

Most Arabs believe that an adult must be married to have a full life, and when they enter into marriage they are looking for compatibility, the social status of being married, and most important, children. The traditional preference for many children, and for sons, is based on the expectation that sons can be most relied on in one's old age.

In contrast to Western practice, Arabs generally approach marriage with more pragmatism, based on group consensus rather than individual choice. They do not expect that their partner will meet all their emotional needs; most of the role of confidant and advisor is still reserved for one's own family, one's parents or brothers and sisters, or close friends in a peer group. Furthermore, men and women participate in many social activities separately and have their own circles of friends. Thus, with more realistic expectations than those of many Americans and the greater probability that one will attain what one is looking for in marriage, these Arab marriages are usually stable and compatible. Great family pressure is exerted on couples who want to separate or divorce, and everyone tries to get involved in counseling them.

ARABS' VIEW OF THE WEST

Arabs share with many other groups a mistrust and fear of Western societal values in general and American values in particular (Lamb, 1987). They believe that training children to be independent and self-supporting may indicate a lack of love and caring, that the free personal and professional association between men and women has led to the lowering of moral standards, that children do not respect their parents, that members of a family are not willing to help each other (this accounts for the large numbers of homeless people), that materialism is overemphasized in the West, that most Americans and Westerners do not have a strong religious faith, and that the idea of older people living in "senior centers" is disgraceful and indicates a lack of love and responsibility on the part of their children.

In the Middle East a crisis of identity and a need to redefine personal goals and values in the fast-changing modern world has led to a reemphasis on the Islamic way of life, which appeals especially to younger and better educated people. This has affected the thinking of many Arabs living in the West as well. They often feel that their values are contradicted and threatened by westernization. Many people experience value confusion, which is viewed as an important rationale for counseling in Arab countries (Soliman, 1987). In Saudi Arabia, *Islamic counseling* is being emphasized, in contrast to Western-style therapies practiced elsewhere (Saleh, 1987).

Some Arabs feel resentment toward Western economic and political domination and lack of sensitivity toward their political plight and their aspirations (the case of Palestine is the most obvious, painful, and frustrating example). It is appealing for many to conclude that returning to a stricter Islamic way of life may lead to a more just, but still competitive, society. Many Muslims living in the West think about these issues as they try to adapt to the Western or "Christianized" world. Practicing Muslim Arabs find a great deal of comfort and peace in Islam as they assimilate into a Western society.

COUNSELING ARABS AND ARAB AMERICANS

As a population, Arabs and Arab Americans have been little studied psychologically (in contrast to anthropologically and sociologically). Historically the Arab-American community has not received much attention from mental health providers. There is almost no literature available on the mental health of Arab Americans, except for a growing body of literature on traumatized Arab populations in or from war zones (Abudabbeh, 1992). Only since the Gulf War and events surrounding it in late 1990 and early 1991 did Arab Americans become a focus of attention as a distinct minority in the United States deserving of attention by mental health workers.

Trauma induced by the Gulf War was identified in several populations, and mental health providers were faced with giving support specifically to Arabs (students) and Arab Americans. The Naim Foundation in Washington, DC, identified Iraqi, Kuwaiti, Palestinian, and Lebanese Arab Americans, each of whom had differing reactions and faced different types of problems, such as loss of employment and income, anxiety about family members, fear of victimization and retaliation in U.S. society, and sometimes guilt about the role of their governments.

To cope with this situation, the Naim Foundation established a hot line monitored by Arabic-speaking professionals, organized workshops to train non-Arab professionals, prepared a crisis intervention handbook adapted to the Arabic-speaking population, organized lectures and support groups, and discussed trauma and posttraumatic stress disorder (PTSD) on a weekly call-in program on an Arabic radio station.

In transcultural counseling literature in the United States, more attention has been given to counseling foreign students (including Arabs) than to family or marriage counseling (e.g., Wehrly, 1986). At this time, many Arab Americans are likely to share the view that this is where the emphasis is needed and are more likely to accept an outside counselor's assistance with problems related to student performance and adjustment rather than family problems.

In the Arab world itself, seeking advice from a trained professional counselor who is an outsider is a new idea, although using mediators within a group is very common. The rationale for counseling and its role are still being developed (Soliman, 1987), and an urgent need for counseling services is recognized (Soliman, 1986).

In Egypt, counseling has been more therapeutic than preventive or educational/vocational (Soliman, 1987). In Saudi Arabia, counseling is developing with an emphasis on Islamic values and doctrine pertaining to all aspects of counseling—personal, psychological, educational, vocational, and social (Saleh, 1987). This is also a basis for counseling in Jordan (Farah, 1992).

The role of vocational and guidance counseling is growing in the Arab world, but slowly. In the 1980s only three Arab countries had counseling services in schools (Soliman, 1987). In Jordan there was a ratio of about 2,000 students to 1 counselor in 1989 (Farah, 1992). Counseling in secondary schools is well established in Kuwait (Abu-Eita & Sherif, 1990).

ARAB INTERACTIONS WITH A COUNSELOR

Confiding anxieties and personal problems to a professional is often painful for Arabs. Airing family matters may be considered disloyal and a threat to group honor (Wehrly, 1986). Admitting personal failure and accepting blame for problems is also difficult and threatens self-esteem and dignity (Laffin, 1975). The counselor must therefore be especially reassuring about professional confidentiality. In many instances individual counseling will be more effective than group counseling, so both types of counseling should be arranged.

Clinical experience has shown the most open groups to be Lebanese and Egyptians, followed by Syrians, Palestinians, and some Saudis. People from North Africa and most of the Arabian Peninsula tend to be more reserved. Men are as likely to seek counseling as women.

Although Arabs respect the counselor's expertise (Soliman, 1986), many believe that counseling is appropriate only for seriously disturbed individuals. The older or more traditional a person is, the more he or she will resist advice from a counselor, often fearing that the counselor reflects Western values and, in the case of disputes, sides automatically with the younger or more liberal party. Thus, those who feel most threatened in a mediation situation are men, husbands, and parents. People whose authority is at stake often resent being involved with a counselor at all, and their expectations will likely differ from those of Western clients (Westwood & Borgen, 1988). Clarifying mutual goals regarding what needs to be changed, and identifying acceptable strategies to achieve change (Harper & Stone, 1986), will help alleviate this tension and should be undertaken early in the counseling relationship.

A counselor must make an effort to appear scrupulously impartial and explain procedures carefully. The counselor should also try to show an understanding of (if not necessarily appreciation for) traditional Arab values and expectations. Many Arabs are defensive about their values and beliefs and feel that Westerners misunderstand and malign them (indeed, Arabs are still the subject of cartoons and negative images more than other ethnic groups). An additional complication arises if there is a difference in religion; this is certainly a factor to keep in mind and possibly discuss. If the counselor is Jewish, this may create additional suspicion, although less so if the counselor is of Sephardic descent.

A counselor must be aware that the strict separation of men and women is one of the last areas where Arabs relax the rules. Men and women do not touch each other in front of others; such touching is embarrassing to an observer, and shocking to some. If the patient and the counselor are of opposite sexes, even more care should be taken not to appear unduly familiar; for example, touching or hugging should be avoided. Indirect eye contact is preferred between men and women.

The differing roles and status of men and women in Arab society usually do not apply to professional women (either Arabs or Westerners). Education is greatly respected, so educated women are generally accorded the respect and deference due their position (professional interactions are quite different from social interactions). Women can be effective as counselors to men. Arab women, however, are generally more comfortable with Western women than with Western men, because there is a tradition of Arab women confiding in each other as friends and seeking each other's guidance, much like sisters. Furthermore, male relatives may be hesitant to approve counseling by a man. It is recommended that if a female patient is married, she be referred to a female counselor.

In Arab society, people of the same sex touch each other more than in Western society; in the Middle East, two male friends or two female friends may walk down the street holding hands. Sometimes a handshake is held for the duration of a (rather short) conversation, and sometimes a person may put an arm around the shoulders of another person when they are sitting together. Arabs often stand or sit very close to someone they are talking to.

The counselor must be patient; many Arabs find it difficult to express anxieties forthrightly or to admit their lack of understanding of an issue. Many will state their intentions and then fail to follow them up with action (words have considerable value in Arab culture; the statement of intentions can be seen as a valid response in itself). The counselor may be obliged to explain and discuss American values and society, in a sense setting up cross-cultural awareness sessions before dealing with specific issues.

Arabs tend to personalize relationships and see people they deal with as individuals, often potential friends. They do not assume roles as readily as Americans do—for example, a teacher-student role or an office colleague role, in which people are cordial but do not expect to know each other well on a personal level. Therefore it is important that the counselor be personable, likable, and genuinely caring; if Arabs for some reason do not like or respect someone, they sometimes simply will not deal with that person. The Arab concepts of friendship and the rights and duties of friends differ significantly from some assumptions in the West (Nydell, 1987). Effort spent in building rapport will be repaid many times over in ultimate effectiveness.

Arabs are more likely than Westerners to show emotion (this varies among national groups) or to deal with situations in a way that is not objective as Americans see it. They may refuse to acknowledge a problem if it is too painful and do not always feel compelled to face issues squarely and objectively, as defined by Western standards. In the West, subjectivity is equated with immaturity, whereas objectivity and rationality are equated with maturity; there are distinct cultural differences in this judgment. Sometimes arguments are won by appealing to emotions or human concerns—for example, describing the effect an act will have on other people or exhorting someone to do something "for my sake," rather than presenting a developed argument. In short, many Arabs may insist on the right to allow subjective feelings to direct their actions.

It is important that the counselor learn to use more formalities than Americans are accustomed to (Wehrly, 1986). For example, one normally stands to greet someone entering a room, shaking hands (although it is best to allow an Arab woman to take the initiative in this), and saying "welcome," in English or in an Arabic phrase.

Arabs tend to judge people by their verbal manners, and also by their grooming and how they are dressed. They disapprove of someone sitting too casually or placing feet on furniture. When standing and talking, they would not lean against the wall or keep their hands in their pockets because this might indicate a lack of respect for the other person or for the occasion. Nonverbal communication is complex among Arabs and symbolic of hierarchy and their social relationships to each other.

Hospitality and generosity are considered by Arabs to be essential attributes, and it is a nice gesture to treat a client as a guest in the office. This specifically means offering something to drink; in Arab offices, guests are offered a choice of coffee, tea, or soft drinks (but no choice about accepting something, because they must not deny the host an opportunity to display generosity). Most Arab adults smoke, and they will be more relaxed if smoking is permitted.

It is useful to plan a course of action, but some Arabs resist attempts to hold them to a specific commitment by a specific time. They may feel pressured, which is demeaning to their dignity, and do not like to be rushed or cornered.

SPEAKING AND COMMUNICATION

It is well known that communication takes place on several levels (Westwood & Borgen, 1988). Arabs' use of language is different from that of Westerners in several ways (Nydell, 1987).

Arabs often talk loudly and vehemently, because this is a sign of sincerity and veracity (Patai, 1976). They raise their voices, use oaths ("I swear by God") and exaggerate or threaten, but this speech should not be taken literally and is not indicative of as much resolution or passion as it appears to be (people from the Arabian Peninsula are, however, generally more reserved). Many Arabs cultivate the art of eloquence and rhetoric, taking a long time to get to the point and possibly never stating their actual beliefs or intentions (Laffin, 1975). In Arab society, decisions are usually arrived at with much discussion and repetition of points of view. *How* something is said is as important as *what* is said.

Traditionally, words are believed to have actual power to affect events, so the use of blessings and benedictions is essential for good manners (it also reinforces the user's image as a believer in God). The counselor should be sure to express good wishes when someone is discussing accomplishments, plans, or future events. This is easy to do in Arabic, using some short phrases listed below, but it is equally effective to give good wishes in English.

When welcoming someone:

Arabic	*English equivalent*
Ahlan wa sahlan.	Welcome.
Marhaba.	Welcome.

When speaking of the future:

Inshallah.	If God wills.
	God willing.

When expressing good wishes about an accomplishment, praising a child, praising a purchase (a new car, a new house):

Mashallah.	As God wills.
	May God keep him/her.
	May God give him/her health and success.
	May you always drive it safely.
	May you live there happily.

Arabs use many euphemisms, especially when speaking about illness, death, or bad events. They often say that someone is tired when the person is sick ("He's in the hospital because he's a little tired"), hesitate to state that someone is growing worse or dying, and hesitate to predict or even discuss bad events. Such events can be discussed more comfortably, however, with appropriate benedictions such as "May he/she soon be better" or "God willing, may this never happen."

Using too much Arabic, or misusing it, can be seen as patronizing, and it seems artificial and unsettling for an American counselor to try to identify too closely. Even Americans who have converted to Islam are first and foremost Americans, and they are more effective if they remain their authentic selves.

TYPICAL MENTAL HEALTH PROBLEMS

The most frequent mental health problems presented clinically by the Arab immigrant population include the following (Abudabbeh, 1992):

- Intergenerational value conflicts
- Parenting problems
- Changes in the role of family members
- Physical abuse
- Cultural agoraphobia (especially among women unaccustomed to going out alone)
- Identity confusion
- Adjusting to a lower social and economic status
- Loss of extended family support system

ASSUMPTIONS THAT ARISE IN COUNSELING ARAB AMERICANS

Pedersen (1988) identified 10 of the most frequently encountered Western-based cultural assumptions in multicultural counseling. Five of these may arise when counseling Arab Americans:

1. *All cultures share a single measure of normal behavior.* Some Arab patients present with symptoms of "depression" that may be the result of the ongoing conflicts in the Middle East and symptomatic of PTSD or may simply stem from culture shock. Diagnosing dysthymia and placing the patient on an anti-depressant may in fact cause more fear and depression. Arab culture does not define depression as it is defined in America, and it provides minimal exposure to psychological

information, so such a diagnosis by a "doctor" is taken as absolute authority and can be quite alarming.

2. *Individuals are the basic building blocks of society.* Among Arabs, the family, the tribe, and the community are the basic building blocks of society. If a family is recently arrived or quite traditional, the therapist must work with the entire family to help an individual.

3. *Independence is desirable; dependence is undesirable.* This assumption pertains to the Western model of mental health; Arab parents and families are supportive of "the children," no matter how old they are, and often overprotective. Although children need to respect their parents' values, the parents also need help in allowing their children to separate from them. The therapist must show understanding and respect for these cultural norms so that parents do not feel that the therapist is leading their child astray.

4. *Western concepts of "good," "bad," "fair," and "humane" are shared across cultures.* Arabs use different criteria in making such judgments. For example, there are differing attitudes toward divulging problems in one's private life (often considered "bad" among Arabs), in the expected roles of men and women, and in the roles of parents and children.

5. *Counselors need to change individuals to fit the system, rather than change the system to fit individuals.* This assumption would discourage many Arabs from accepting counseling as a possible avenue for help in dealing with their problems. They may disapprove of American cultural norms and fear or feel antagonistic toward many Western values.

CASE STUDIES

Vignettes of counseling cases are presented here to illustrate the most common situations and some strategies for dealing with them. It is assumed here that the counselor is a Westerner and the counseling is taking place in the West.

ARAB STUDENTS

1. A Student's Loneliness

A young man in his mid-20s presents himself for counseling, complaining that he is lonely and he cannot achieve successful friendships with Western men or women (especially women).

A young woman presents herself, complaining that she is lonely, she misses her family, and she is concerned that if she attempts more socializing her behavior may be misinterpreted.

Counselors are alerted to pay close attention to this type of student. Some of these students have serious emotional problems that have escaped careful scrutiny. Not having grown up in a society sensitized to mental health issues, students often present with seemingly nonserious complaints such as loneliness.

It is not uncommon, especially after the wars in the Arab world, for students to suffer from anxiety, panic attacks, or depression. The student may be more comfortable presenting as "lonely," but remember that it would take a great deal on an Arab student's part to seek any kind of help. Once he or she approaches an outsider such as a counselor, this may indeed be a cry for help.

An initial thorough history taking is necessary to determine the actual source of "loneliness." Depending on subsequent diagnosis, the student should either be counseled on the premises or referred to appropriate clinicians for treatment.

A frequently mentioned problem for male Arab students is male-female interaction. Some students who are tempted to imitate Western students may become conflicted as they try to make sense of two opposing sets of values. The counselor needs to explore the young man's cultural attitudes toward women, girlfriends, appropriate interaction between men and women, and expectations of behavior toward each other. Many Arabs have grown up in a society that restricts such interaction and do not understand that cordiality between men and women, including frequent direct eye contact, does not always imply personal interest or romantic intentions. Arab students usually lack the skills required for casual Western dating.

The counselor should discuss with the young Arab woman the difference between the relative importance of outward appearance (much emphasized in Arab society) and actual practice (considered more important in the West). She needs to be reassured that

Westerners do not draw conclusions about a woman's character or morality based on what they consider to be normal public interaction with male friends and colleagues.

For most Arab students (away from home and family) college is their first exposure to complete independence and lack of structure and their first opportunity to mix freely with the opposite sex. Depending on the specific home country, socioeconomic background, and religion, college can cause culture shock.

Arabs' loneliness results from their transition from a highly structured, others-oriented culture to an individual-oriented society, where new skills are needed to build close friendships with outsiders. The counselor should explore differing concepts of friendship. There are differences in the intensity and frequency of friends' interactions, the doing of mutual favors, and the relative value of privacy in the West.

2. A Student's Poor Grades

An Arab student (man or woman) is unhappy and confused because of low grades in classes, especially in class participation. The student's grades are also low on some essays and in seminar courses, despite much effort and time spent studying.

The counselor should explain that in the West most teachers encourage and reward original thinking, rather than memorization and repetition of others' ideas. Many teachers expect students to challenge them and to be critical, even of authorities in the field, providing they can justify their opinions. Some teachers judge a student's mastery of material by the student's ability to extrapolate principles and apply them in original situations.

ARAB FAMILIES

3. Conflict Between Parents and Teenager

An Arab-American family comes to a counselor for mediation relating to a teenager's resistance to the parents' attempts to proscribe his or her social behavior, scholastic achievement, and career choice. (Nydell, 1987; Patai, 1976; Soliman, 1986).

Conflicts specific to Arab families include those of curfew hours, types of friendships, different treatment of boys and girls, and amount of parental supervision. More conflict is seen in families that totally reject Western cultural norms. In these families the teenager

278

is expected to conform to the traditional norms of (a) no dialogue with parental figures, (b) no going out unless accompanied by family members, (c) boys being allowed to go out more than girls, and (d) appropriate dress code.

To mediate, the counselor needs to recognize the profound differences between Arab and Western beliefs about individuals and their parents and family (Nydell, 1987). Arab beliefs include the importance of parental authority and filial respect (Mansfield, 1990) and the subordination of individual desires to family expectations. Parents will usually exhibit a strong desire that their children attain a good education in order to make a good living and achieve status (for everyone). Professional and white-collar fields are valued over manual work, the arts, or other pursuits that may in fact lead to more personal satisfaction. There is often a difference of opinion regarding equal educational and career opportunities for women and what constitute appropriate life-style choices.

The emphasis on individual growth and independence in the West conflicts with the conformist and authoritative nature of traditional Arab society. Parents often have specific plans and goals for their children from the time they are very young.

The counselor can provide culturally sensitive guidance by immediately acknowledging the differences between the two cultures. Primary emphasis should be put on gaining the confidence of the parents as well as the teenager by taking a neutral position and respecting both sides of the issues. In most cases the counselor will discover that a family that has already taken steps to come to a counselor will accept advice geared toward finding compromises.

A counselor can justify some compromises here, in that Arab parents must understand that compromises are necessary when they choose to raise their children in a Western society. This acceptance includes recognizing that the West has a "teenage culture," as well as acknowledging a maturing individual's need for personal fulfillment and for making responsible decisions.

A typical case involves conflict between Egyptian Muslim parents who have lived in the United States for 16 years, but who maintain all of the Egyptian Islamic customs and values, and their teenage son, who has begun to disobey them. In addition, he has been doing poorly in school, both academically and behaviorally.

In working with the family, the counselor is impressed that the teenager has already adopted some of his parents' values, in that he prays regularly and respects his father's authority. The counselor works with the family by (a) pointing out to the parents their son's strengths (he was praised for practicing the Islamic religion and also for his sensitivity to his mother while she was ill); (b) counseling the parents and son about the significance of dialogue (the father was counseled about the ineffectiveness of the authoritarian style of parenting in this new society); (c) explaining to the parents the negative effects of their own lack of coordination and how this was being used by their son; (d) negotiating more freedom for the son in return for academic improvement and help with household chores; and (e) setting up a reward system, whereby the son worked to earn what he wanted, including the frequency and length of telephone calls, outings to various places, and driving the car.

4. Conflict Between Parents and an Unmarried Daughter

A family comes to a counselor because of a seemingly irreconcilable conflict between the parents and their daughter regarding the potential husband they have selected for her. She has rejected several candidates in the past, and everyone is becoming increasingly exasperated.

The counselor should realize that many Arab parents are very concerned that their daughter's potential husband have a profession or business that will support her well financially, as well as "good character" (a good reputation), the right social class, and the right religion. These considerations are more important than his age, physical appearance, or personality.

The counselor should attempt to explain to the parents the Western concept of romantic love as the motivation for marriage (whether it can be justified or not) and the belief that an individual has the freedom to select his or her partner, even if this leads to mistakes. Young women usually select someone close to their age, and they think it very important to be in love with a man who is attractive both physically and intellectually.

The counselor can help the parents talk to their daughter about their beliefs regarding marriage—namely, that it is a union of families and that earning power, social class, and religion are important factors in compatibility.

ARAB MARRIAGES

Probably the most unusual or nontraditional type of counseling that Arab Americans would seek is marriage counseling. Generally these matters are handled by the two extended families, and marital issues are considered intensely private. A couple presenting themselves for marriage counseling probably views this as a last resort.

5. Conflict Between Husband and Wife

An Arab or Arab-American couple comes for counseling because of disagreements about the wife's role and aspirations. There is also a problem with the husband's habit of unexplained lateness and absences from the home.

The counselor can expect most marital problems to stem from the wife's desire to increase her role as a decision maker and, in a broad sense, an equal partner. She may also want a fairly demanding career. This will frequently lead to disapproval from her husband, and probably from both sets of parents.

The counselor should be sensitive to traditional Arab expectations for both husbands and wives, the desire for children (particularly male children), the emphasis on the role of mothers in child rearing, and the expectation that men support the family financially. It will be necessary, therefore, to try to find a compromise within this framework.

The Arab husband must understand that in Western society there is a strong belief (at least in theory) in fairness and mutual cooperation between husband and wife. A man's insistence that he should not be accountable to his wife for his activities will lead to stress because it is fundamentally at odds with the ideal of a marriage in Western society.

Many newly arrived Arab husbands are reluctant to allow their wife any autonomy. The husband typically considers his wife sick and asks the counselor to fix her. Without a network of social support, the wife is vulnerable emotionally and begins to show signs of stress. Her complaints may include his not allowing her to learn English, to drive, or to socialize without his permission.

A counselor should assess the wife's strengths during initial intake work. The counselor can then assist her in coaxing her husband to accompany her to counseling. As the situation is explained further, the counselor may discover that the husband is working very hard to maintain adequate financial support and has no time for his wife. Furthermore, her own language and job skills are often no longer applicable in the new society.

Often a wife who has accepted a subservient role for years may need help to deal with her husband, for example, in negotiating specific demands. She should be counseled that in lieu of a drastic solution such as divorce, she can make it clear that she will stay in the marriage on the condition that he agree to counseling. In their country of origin, many couples would have sought this help from members of the extended family, such as an older uncle or an older, respected member of the community, and the counselor can substitute in this role.

DEVELOPING CULTURAL SENSITIVITY

A therapist can test his or her cultural sensitivity and level of awareness in dealing with Arabs and Arab Americans by asking the following questions (Pedersen, 1988):

- Am I able to recognize direct and indirect communication styles?
- Am I sensitive to nonverbal cues?
- Am I aware of cultural and linguistic differences among Arab groups?
- What are the basic values of most Arabs? How do these relate to common counseling situations?
- What are some common myths and stereotypes about Arabs?
- What stereotypes do Arabs have about Americans?
- Am I aware of my own feelings about Arabs and Arab society and culture?

To deal effectively with Arabs and Arab Americans, the therapist must develop basic cultural competence. This can be done through directed reading, training workshops, and sympathetic personal interaction and interest. Most Arabs are so pleased when a Westerner shows interest in them and their culture that they will go to great lengths to become highly responsive clients.

CONCLUSION

It is helpful to know that because Arab society is authoritarian and most Arabs have had similar child-rearing and extended family experiences, they share many values and ideas of proper behavior. Because there is less diversity among Arabs than among Westerners in this regard, effective strategies can be developed and widely applied, providing they are compatible with Arabs' personal beliefs and aspirations.

If a counselor makes an effort to adapt his or her role to Arab expectations where practicable, there is every reason to expect a successful outcome.

REFERENCES

Abudabbeh, N. (1992). Treatment of post-traumatic stress disorders in the arab american community. In M. B. Williams & J. F. Sommer (Eds.) *Handbook of post-traumatic therapy: A practical guide to intervention, treatment, and research.* Westport, CT: Greenwood.

Abu-Eita, S., & Sherif, N. (1990). Counselor competencies and personality traits at secondary schools in Kuwait. *International Journal for the Advancement of Counseling, 13,* 27–38.

Farah, A. M. (1992). Guidance and counseling in the Hashemite Kingdom of Jordan: Some observations. *International Journal for the Advancement of Counseling, 15,* 17–26.

Hamady, S. (1960). *Temperament and character of the Arabs.* (p. 32). New York: Twayne.

Harper, F. D., & Stone, W. O. (1986). Transcendent counseling: A multimodal model for multicultural counseling, *International Journal for the Advancement of Counseling, 9,* 257.

Harvard encyclopedia of american ethnic groups (p. 134). (1980). Cambridge, MA: Harvard University Press.

Institute of International Education. (1991). *Open doors 1990–1991.* New York: Author.

Katz, P. (1984). The psychiatrist and the minority group adolescent. *Clinical Update in Adolescent Psychiatry,* p. 1.

Laffin, J. (1975). *The Arab mind considered, A need for understanding* (pp. 137, 143). New York: Taplinger.

Lamb, D. (1987). *The Arabs, Journeys beyond the mirage* (pp. 137, 139). New York: Random House.

Mansfield, P. (1990). *The Arabs* (p. 500). New York: Penguin.

Mikhail, M. (1979). *Images of Arab women, Fact and fiction* (pp. 11–14, 45). Washington, DC: Three Continents.

Nydell, M. (1987). *Understanding Arabs, A guide for Westerners.* Yarmouth, ME: Intercultural Press.

Patai, R. (1976). *The Arab mind* (pp. 37–40, 56–60, 226). New York: Scribner's.

Pedersen, P. (1988). *A handbook for developing multicultural awareness.* Alexandria, VA: American Association for Counseling and Development.

Pristin, T. & Dart, J. *Los Angeles Times* (1991, January 20). Islam in America, Muslims a growing force in U.S., p. A1.

Saleh, M. A. (1987). Counseling and guidance in the Kingdom of Saudi Arabia. *International Journal for the Advancement of Counseling, 10,* 277–286.

Sharabi, H., & Ani, M. (1977). Impact of class and culture on social behavior. In L. C. Brown & N. Itzkowitz, (Eds.) *Psychological Dimensions of Near Eastern Studies* (p. 248). Princeton, NJ: Darwin.

Soliman, A. M. (1986). The counseling needs of youth in the Arab countries. *International Journal for the Advancement of Counseling, 9,* 61–72.

Soliman, A. M. (1987). Status, rationale and development of counseling in the Arab countries: Views of participants in a counseling conference. *International Journal for the Advancement of Counseling, 10,* 131–141.

Statistical abstract of the United States, 1991 (p. 10). Washington, DC: Bureau of the Census.

Wehrly, B. (1986). Counseling international students: Issues, concerns, and programs. *International Journal for the Advancement of Counseling, 9,* 11–22.

Westwood, M. J., and Borgen, W. A. (1988). A culturally embedded model for effective intercultural communication, *International Journal for the Advancement of Counseling, 11,* 115–125.

Zoghby, J. (1990). *Arab America today, A demographic profile of Arab Americans.* Washington, DC: Arab-American Institute.

PART III

PROFESSIONAL ISSUES

CHAPTER 12

EVALUATION AND ASSESSMENT FOR TRANSCULTURAL COUNSELING

J. RONALD QUINN

INTRODUCTION

For most of the 100 or so years since Binet introduced the notion that something significant could be learned about the internal functioning of human mental activity by observing external human behavior (Binet & Simon, 1916), writers have described this external observing—usually by psychologists and other academics—as *testing*, and more recently college students have been offered undergraduate and graduate courses entitled "Testing," "Tests and Measurement," "Educational (or Psychological) Measurement," or some similar label intended to convey clearly the limits of the subject and the expectations of the potential learners. However, in little over a decade—earlier for psychologists—the terms *assessment* and *evaluation* have been commingled with *testing* and *measurement*, sometimes interchanging with, at other times expanding upon, and in other times differing from, the older, simpler language. This expansion to more and broader terminology seems to have followed roughly the work of Bloom (1956) and others (Harrow, 1972; Krathwohl, Bloom, & Masia, 1964) in more precisely defining ascending orders of thinking from mere knowledge, to understanding, to application, and thence to higher orders of thinking, continuing upward in complexity, ostensibly with the hope of giving greater specificity to the mental function being observed or measured. All of this is to say that, although the terms overlap in their meanings in the literature of the "Science of Psychological Measurement," (Cohen, Montague, Nathanson, & Swerdlik, 1988, p. 47), in this discussion (a) *evaluation* will be used to refer to what counselors and teachers usually have dealt with under the rubric of *testing* or *educational measurement*, and (b) *assessment* will be limited to the processes followed by school psychologists in deciding on special education placement or intervention. Although not precisely true in practice, the separation will help focus the later argument.

The semantic disarray could be even more exacerbated if differentiation were required between *cross-cultural, multicultural,* and *transcultural* contexts. The staff (1992) of the *Social Studies Review* gave some serious and intelligent thought to the question, "Is it possible to be multicultural and Eurocentric?" (p. 15) in attempting to define multiculturalism. The answer seemed a qualified yes dependent upon various "multiethnic contributions" to the Euro-American establishment that seems destined to be in control for a while. In addition, D'Souza (1991) has complicated the task of multicultural counselors by lumping all multiculturalists under the *politically correct* label, there to be attacked as illiberal foes of free speech. Linda Chávez (1991), who has made a political and literary career as something of a conservative maverick, seems piqued by the use of the term *multiculturalism* as just another product of decadent liberalism. One facet of the definitional problem is the question of what prerequisites one must meet to speak for multiculturalism. The editor of this book has simplified the task by his extended definition of *transcultural counseling* as "a new profession that attempts to provide responses to beliefs, needs, and other circumstances prevalent among people of different cultural, ethnic, and economic backgrounds" using various counseling approaches appropriately "in a more flexible fashion ... across cultures" both within and "beyond national borders" (see Introduction). Each usage, from *transcultural* to *multicultural*, with variations between and beyond, belongs here because this discussion is firmly set within the arena of problems and issues of cultural and ethnic pluralism, whether viewed as a worldwide phenomenon or as peculiar to the Euro-American establishment.

A SEARCH FOR RELEVANT LITERATURE

A PUZZLING PAUCITY

It has become a cliché among dissertation authors and even some writers in professional journals to begin discussions with a notice that very little about their chosen topics has appeared in the literature, thereby explaining the need for their attempt to illuminate their chosen subjects. (Having criticized doctoral candidates for using this notation without first conducting a thorough search, I am both surprised and humbled to find myself using the same words even after an intensive review.) There has long been a steady stream of articles by evaluation and assessment practitioners, and recent samples verify that the problems addressed have remained fairly constant (Anastasi, 1992; Bozarth, 1992; Gough, 1992; Karmos & Karmos, 1984). The rising tide of interest in things multicultural can be easily detected in the past 10 to 12 years; for example, Ahia (1984) was concerned with cross-cultural aspects of effective counseling practice; Boateng (1991), with the economic impact of multicultural counseling on clients; Burn (1992), with ethical implications; Hilliard (1992), with multicultural impacts on teaching and learning; Ibrahim (1991), with the need to understand varying worldviews clients bring to counseling; and Diane Ravitch, Assistant Secretary for Educational Research in the Bush administration, and others interviewed by Sanchez (1992) perceived that problems of public policy might be shaped by various cultural groups acting singly or in multicultural configurations. In essence, some from White, Eurocentric cultures like it hot, some not, particularly where vested interests appear threatened. Until recent years the two streams have rarely flowed together, and then gingerly.

LIMITING THE SCOPE

It is even more surprising to review the three American Counseling Association (ACA) publications representing those professionals most likely to have concerns about evaluation and assessment within a transcultural or multicultural context: the *Journal of Multicultural Counseling and Development* (*JMCD*), the *Journal of Counseling and Development* (*JCD*), and *Measurement and Evaluation in Counseling and Development* (*MECD*). This is not to say that interesting discussions and robust debate regarding either multiculturalism or measurement have been absent, but rather that these two broad areas of our collective professional concern have failed to intersect significantly and frequently in the past decade in our own professional journals. Early efforts by Williams (1972, 1974, 1975) to bring about a serious discussion of the effects of culture on testing were rarely taken that way by a measurements establishment whose attitude ranged between condescension and hubris. However, in the past 5 years, considerable introspective thought among multiculturalists (e.g., Carter, 1992; Carter & Helms, 1987; Hansen, 1987; Ponterotto & Casas, 1991) offers portents of an emerging awareness of the technology of tests and measurement, coupled with the skill and knowledge to develop new, more appropriate instruments. The recent review, critique, and recommendations by Sabnani and Ponterotto (1992) provide an excellent beginning for "a science of multicultural evaluation and assessment," to paraphrase Cohen et al. (1988). The imbroglio in the March 1992 issue of *JCD* following McArthur's (1989, 1992) charges that militant feminists had brought about a virtual "book burning" of the Strong Vocational Interest Blank (SVIB) suggests that a not-so-distant drummer may be poised to point out considerably more than that the "SVIB's validity was limited to the *core culture* of the United States" (McArthur, 1992, p. 517 [italics added]). Multicultural scholarship will probably gain respect from establishment scholars to the extent that multiculturists respect and support their own and act collectively on worthwhile research.

Using a content analysis approach, the search of the literature was initially limited to the 5-year period 1987–91 of articles in the multicultural arm of ACA, *JMCD*; the measurements journal of ACA, *MECD*; and the official journal of the ACA, *JCD*. Although a great deal of discussion and debate about issues and usages appeared under the rubrics *cross-cultural, multicultural, transcultural, cultural pluralism, racial and ethnic pluralism,* and so forth, surprise was replaced by mild alarm that a search by the Educational Resources Information Center (ERIC) identified only 22 articles and 5 books that dealt with measurement, assessment, or testing in a multicultural context during the most recent 5-year period for completed journal volumes. Expanding the search forward and backward to include 1982–92 added only 28 cross-referenced publications (i.e., testing versus multiculturalism), for a grand total of 55 publications during more than a decade in the entire field of testing within the context of cultural pluralism.

Of greater concern is the lack of real debate regarding testing issues in a multicultural world. Four of arguably the most influential books addressing counseling in a multicultural world (Herr, 1989; Pedersen, 1988; Sue & Sue, 1990) have been published during the past 5 years. Yet none of these has made a thorough, empirically supported, critical discussion of the role of evaluation and assessment. This is particularly troubling in light of the long history of abuse and misuse of testing on every racial or ethnic minority contributing to these significant and seminal texts. Fortunately, Sue, Arredondo, and McDavis (1992) have brought a much needed, if belated, focus upon "the need for a multicultural approach to *assessment* [italics added], practice, training, and research" (p. 477) in counseling and psychotherapy. As these and other writers in the broad arena of cultural pluralism are beginning to discover, it was not enough to adopt position papers addressed to the professional leaders, most of whom came from what McArthur (1992) calls the "core culture." Change may be initiated by very specific statements, but it almost always takes focused, organized action to bring about substantive change.

An even more puzzling and frustrating situation obtained when the journal literature of ACA devoted almost exclusively to tests and measurement was reviewed. Volumes 20–24 of *MECD* extend from 1987 through 1991 and contain 114 articles, substantive editorials, and book reviews. However, only two articles dealt with multiculturalism at all and then only tangentially. Reynolds (1987) sardonically pointed out that the fourth edition of the Stanford-Binet had failed the industry standard in that its normalization group was heavily overrepresented by upper socioeconomic levels. Then, in an even less controversial article, we were informed by Brown and Duren (1988) that their research indicated limited validity for using the State-Trait Anxiety Inventory to characterize anxiety for Blacks. The real anxiety of African Americans and every other racial or ethnic group member of ACA should have risen considerably at this professional inattention. Possibly the topic was intellectually drained by the excellent special issue on measurement practices in multicultural counseling edited by William E. Sedlacek (1987) immediately preceding Volume 20, with Jo-Ida Hansen (1987, pp. 163–176) giving an in depth study of cross-cultural research on vocational interests and with Carter and Helms (1987, pp. 185–195) introducing the "measurement of racial identity as one of the most important areas of research to be developed in recent years" (Sedlacek, 1987, p. 163). But as useful as that special issue was, it made no critical judgments about the adequacy or applicability to various "noncore" cultures of the bulk of instruments in print and in use.

One would expect to find more articles about multicultural issues in testing and assessment in the *JMCD*, and for the same 5-year period, 1987–91, there was more, but not much more, discussion. In 15 articles spread through the total 92 in 20 issues of the *JMCD* there was at least minimal discussion of the use of measurement instruments, some self-developed, in multicultural counseling settings, but the usage was more practical than theoretical or critical. Here again, Sedlacek, writing with Timothy White (Sedlacek & White, 1987), attempted to open up the debate by examining the validity of the Situational Attitude Scale with African-American males, but that was hardly enough to awaken sleeping giants in the educational measurement establishment or measurement specialists among the multiculturalists.

JCD began the period 1987–91 with far less emphasis on either testing or cultural pluralism as major issues, but the article production in both areas began to increase in the early issues of 1991, culminating in the superior special September/October issue, "Multiculturalism as a Fourth Force in Counseling," edited by an established authority in the field, Paul B. Pedersen (1991). Although apparently unrelated, almost every subsequent issue has featured a full section on "Tests and Assessment," with an excellent lecture appearing in the May/June issue from the eminent authority on psychological testing Anne Anastasi (1992) on what every counselor should know about the proper use of tests. However, Anastasi carefully avoided mention of anything remotely related to multiculturalism in her lengthy and trenchant discussion. One must fear that criticism of the Eurocentric bases for her area of expertise will be left to lesser scholars, because her major concern in this article was how improperly trained practitioners continue to be the main misusers of psychological tests. The earlier cited initiative by Sue et al. (1992) may revive the discussion sooner rather than later; however, it might be hoped that establishment giants will contribute their gargantuan influence and debate regarding multiculturalism's goals, without prompting, as a matter of professional interest and concern.

A REVIEW OF TYPICAL ASSESSMENT TEXTS

In a final look at current literature, an examination of texts commonly used in the education of counselors proved equally disappointing. While the five books named below stray from the Anastasi-Cronbach-Thorndike/Hagen trilogy, they are fairly representative of other high-quality texts used in counselor education programs throughout the United States. They are technically sound, practical, and well written and, to varying degrees, measure up to the scholarly standards of the aforementioned Big Three, but they all hold the issue of multiculturalism and testing at arm's length. Either a cursory review or a thorough scan of the Cohen et al. (1988) *Psychological Testing* text; Noll, Scannell, and Craig's (1982) *Introduction to Educational Measurement*; Hood and Johnson's (1991) *Assessment in Counseling*; Gilbert Sax's (1989) *Principles of Educational and Psychological Measurement and Evaluation*; or Jerome Sattler's (1988) *Assessment of Children* will lead to the general conclusion from each author that the criticisms of tests for their misuse in evaluation and educational placement "have little merit because they are not based on research evidence and fail to consider current assessment practices" (Sattler, 1988, p. 41). What research? And conducted by whom? With mounting legal battles with irate parents convinced of the potential harm to their children from placement based on tests or testing procedures insensitive to language or other aspects of cultural difference, should a 500-page text deal with these problems in less than 30 pages, or as few as 5? Should graduate students in counselor education be prepared to use a "Science of Psychological Measurement" (Cohen et al., 1988, p. 47) still steeped in a Eurocentric model developed largely in the first 4 decades of the 20th century with little more in the way of genuinely new developments than the fourth edition of the Stanford-Binet? A review of the vast number of tests listed in the *Ninth Mental Measurements Yearbook* (Mitchell,

1985), as well as in the *Tenth Mental Measurements Yearbook* (Conoley & Kramer, 1991), reveals that many if not most of the old standards from the first edition of 1938 are still alive in revised editions that often add little more than bells and whistles! Of course, their endurance suggests satisfied consumers, but one wonders if at the turn of the 20th century the science of measurement, reflecting Eurocentric cultural values exclusively, might be overdue for a thorough and skeptical reexamination in light of the quantum increase in racial and ethnic pluralism in the United States. With scholars of the depth and breadth of the text authors cited above, certainly we should expect the same fine scholarship dealing with an issue so immense and pervasive. Sue et al. (1992) have re-sounded the call for action, and multicultural scholars (Carter, 1992; Casas, 1985; Fukuyama, 1990; Helms, 1986; LaFromboise, Coleman & Hernandez, in press; McConahay, 1986; Szapocznik, Scopetta, Kurtines & Arnalde, 1978) are ready with culture-specific instrumentation for testing within a research base rooted in the experiences of various cultures embedded in an overarching multicultural framework (Sabnani & Ponterotto, 1992).

EMERGING MULTICULTURAL LEADERSHIP IN EVALUATION AND ASSESSMENT

Some of the excellent multicultural scholarship in measurement and testing and the research needs peculiar to multiculturalism (Carter, 1992; Casas, 1985; Helms, 1986; Parham & Helms, 1981; Ponterotto, 1988) has begun to expand into the three journals discussed earlier in this chapter as most directly concerned with the professional membership of ACA. A recent article by Sabnani and Ponterotto (1992) in *MECD* is typical of these seminal contributions, and it contains an exemplary model for the scientific scrutiny of multicultural measurement specialists. In brief overview, Sabnani and Ponterotto (a) set out for, and achieved, a thorough evaluation of eight instruments "designed with a minority conceptualization and theoretical base" and (b) integrated the current status of research knowledge in minority-focused instrumentation into "a specific research agenda for the counseling profession" (p. 162).

In accomplishing their task, these authors selected representative instruments from counseling and related interdisciplinary literature of the past decade, sought a balance in type of instrument and ethnic groups focused upon, and then reviewed each instrument in terms of its "theoretical-conceptual base, development, and psychometric properties" (p. 163). The eight instruments chosen included four focused on African Americans (e.g., the Racial Identity Attitude Scale, Parham & Helms, 1981); one on Whites, the Modern Racism Scale (McConahay, 1986); one on Mexican Americans, the Acculturation Rating Scale for Mexican Americans (Cuellar, Harris, & Jasso, 1980); and two for all cultural groups, the Cross-Cultural Counseling Inventory—Revised (LaFromboise, Coleman, & Hernandez, in press) and the Value Orientation Scale (Szapocznik, Scopetta, Kurtines, & Arnalde, 1978).

The rigor and precision of the Sabnani and Ponterotto critique points up some of the blatant technical weaknesses of most of the eight chosen instruments, and the authors judge "minority-specific testing . . . to be considered at an early stage" (p. 179) sorely lacking in the reporting of psychometric properties, particularly reliability and factor analytic procedures. One might infer, although the authors make no such direct statement, that the "core culture" literature on testing is also sorely lacking in providing this same useful kind of professional, constructive criticism of multicultural instruments. The absence of any critical review of any one of these eight instruments in either the *Ninth Mental Measurements Yearbook* (Mitchell, 1985) or the *Tenth Mental Measurements Yearbook* (Conoley & Kramer, 1991) suggests the need for better communication between multicultural and "core culture" specialists in evaluation and assessment. In any case, Sabnani and Ponterotto have shown what needs to be done, albeit they have spoken from a smaller forum than that warranted for their material.

A NONCONVENTIONAL HISTORY OF THE SCIENCE OF MEASUREMENT

More than a decade ago, Stephen Jay Gould (1981) provided a reasoned but devastatingly logical debunking of some time-honored personalities and concepts of the Eurocentric history of mental testing in his book *The Mismeasure of Man*. Because Gould's skeptical revision of the history of testing hit straight at the heart of the profession, the nearly total lack of response in the professional literature begs for explanation. Gould is an evolutionary biologist, and his arguments were part of an attack on the opinions of his biological determinist colleagues at Yale and elsewhere; however, his discounting of much of the work of such testing patriarchs as Terman, Yerkes, and Spearman in his overall discussion demands an equally logical refutation or at least partial acceptance of his rationale. Space does not permit a complete and detailed review of Gould's book, but a representative sample of its major arguments and conclusions follows:

1. It is a myth to view science as a purely objective enterprise "done properly only when scientists can shuck the constraints of their *culture* and view the world as it really is," (p. 21 [italics added]). Rather, Gould insists that science must be understood "as a social phenomenon, a gutsy, human enterprise, not the work of robots programmed to collect pure information" (p. 21).

2. A corollary myth is the notion that science is an inexorable march to truth. Because scientific inquiry is conducted by people, science is an inherently social activity and subject to constant influences from the cultures in which it is enmeshed. Culture sets up our scientific assumptions about ourselves, our intellects, and the world in which they interact, says Gould, but it also forms the questions scientists seek to answer, determines their methodology, and even affects how they react to their own conclusions.

3. The twin myths above lead to two scientific fallacies that Gould says continue to mislead the scientists of mental measurement. The first is the fallacy of *"reification,* or our tendency to convert abstract concepts into entities" (p. 24). For example, mentality has great importance in our daily lives, and our cultural and political systems dictate how we characterize this complex and many-sided collection of human behaviors and capacities. By labeling these complex traits *intelligence,* we have reified them into a single, unitary thing. Having fallen into this fallacious trap, standard scientific procedures virtually insist that the thing must reside in a specifiable location, logically the brain. The second scientific fallacy, according to Gould, follows from the human proclivity for placing complex variation in an or-

296

derly, ascending scale. Since objective numbering provides the criterion for ranking individuals by their proper status on a single scale, both scientific fallacies come together in our scientific quest for quantification—that is, "the measurement of intelligence as a single number for each person" (p. 24). And the gap between scientific error and practitioner mischief is indeed narrow. Societies that "wish to use tests for the maintenance of social ranks" (p. 155), Gould maintains, invariably misuse tests through these scientific fallacies rather than because of some inherent defect in the idea of testing.

4. It is not possible to understand the history of intelligence testing "without grasping the *factor analytic* argument and understanding its *deep conceptual fallacy*" (pp. 25–26 [italics added]).

5. "American psychologists perverted Binet's intention and invented the hereditarian theory of IQ" (p. 157). While conceding as a biologist that intelligence is doubtless to some degree a heritable trait, Gould clarifies the often obfuscated and exaggerated question of how much. Determinist hereditarians fail in their arguments through two fallacies, he maintains. The first is to equate *heritable* with *inevitable*. Genes merely encode a range of possibilities, all of which, including intelligence, are subject to extensive improvement as well as diminution through environmental interventions. Secondly, "variation among individuals *within* a group and differences in mean values *between* groups are entirely separate phenomena. One item provides no license for speculation about the other" (p. 156 [italics added]).

6. Not only does Gould attack fallacious science perpetrated by the mental measurement movement, he goes after many of the fallacious scientists, including Louis M. Terman, H. H. Goddard (1917a, 1917b, 1917c), R. M. Yerkes, Cyril Burt, and Charles Spearman. In his adversarial criticism of Terman, Yerkes, and Spearman, Gould presents facts and reasoning that undermine their basic scientific premises, but he also imputes a degree of intellectual dishonesty to Goddard and Burt, which he documents with their own writings.

One does not have to be convinced by Gould's attacks on the science of measurement and evaluation, but it is inconceivable that

an entire professional community has not responded to his arguments or his facts. Possibly the Eurocentric establishment suffers
from the same self-deceiving hubris found in its earlier reactions to
Williams (1972, 1974, 1975).

RECOMMENDATIONS

To summarize from the preceding points, the time is overdue for
reasoned debate on the role and nature of evaluation and assessment
in counseling with full recognition that we are, indeed, already in a
multicultural world in the United States and rapidly becoming part
of the transcultural world of tomorrow—socially, economically, and
politically. To my colleagues seeking a proper multicultural approach to evaluation and assessment, I recommend the following:

1. We should study more closely, and with great skepticism, the
   history of the so-called science of evaluation and assessment.
   In that regard, I suggest that the review be made, not through
   the traditional texts, but possibly through texts oriented to
   other disciplines, such as *The Mismeasure of Man* (Gould, 1981).
   We will understand our own profession much more clearly
   when we have applied the biologist Gould's kind of objective,
   logical examination of how common scientific fallacies cause
   considerable error and misuse of any technology founded on
   scientific error.
2. We should identify the traps, scientific and technical, into
   which our predecessors in mental testing have fallen. Human
   foibles, as well as scientific fallacies, affected Goddard and Burt
   (Gould, 1981), but multiculturalists have developed some useful screens for sorting and identifying effective techniques to
   guard against error. Pedersen's (1987) 10 assumptions about
   cultural bias suggest some applications to testing and measurement. His very first caution concerned "assumptions about
   normal behavior" that must be accounted for in a culture-specific way if our measurement instruments are to be effective in
   multicultural counseling. Pedersen's fourth assumption relates
   directly to Gould's point about the reification fallacy. Eurocentric psychometricians are not the only ones who assume that
   some abstract thing such as a test score represents a correspond-
   ing single scalable thing in the examinee's brain called *aptitude*

or *intelligence*. Obviously the culture-specific guidelines of Pedersen and other proven multiculturalist scholars should direct the construction of more effective instrumentation and methodology for use in multicultural and transcultural settings.

3. We should select models for research that, like those employed by Sabnani and Ponterotto (1992) and Carter and Helms (1987), are conceptualized in the experiences of a particular culture embedded in a multicultural frame of reference.

4. We should intensify efforts to organize and centralize professional support for the emerging leaders in the new science of multicultural and transcultural evaluation and assessment.

These recommendations are neither profound nor complete and inclusive, but they should be sufficiently provocative to awaken or reinvigorate our own sleeping giants. As with politics, we know that concerted, intelligently driven action is far more effective than shouting, and the time to act in a neglected area of multicultural scholarship is now.

REFERENCES

Ahia, C. E. (1984). Cross-cultural counseling concerns. *Personnel and Guidance Journal, 62*, 339–341.

Anastasi, A. (1992). What counselors should know about the use and interpretation of psychological tests. *Journal of Counseling and Development, 70*, 610–615.

Binet, A., & Simon, T. (1916). *The development of intelligence in children* (E. S. Kit, Trans.). Baltimore: Williams & Wilkins.

Bloom, B. S. (Ed.). (1956). *Taxonomy of educational objectives: The classification of educational goals, Handbook I: Cognitive domain.* New York: David McKay.

Boateng, P. (1991). The role of counseling in a multiracial, multicultural society in an economic context. In E. L. Herr & J. McFadden (Eds.), *Challenges of cultural and racial diversity to counseling: London conference proceedings* (pp. 47–52). Alexandria, VA: American Association for Counseling and Development.

Bozarth, J. D. (1992). Person-centered assessment. *Journal of Counseling and Development, 69*, 458–461.

Brown, M. T., & Duren, P. S. (1988). Construct validity for Blacks of the State-Trait Anxiety Inventory. *Measurement and Evaluation in Counseling and Development, 20*, 321–333.

Burn, D. (1992). Ethical implications in cross-cultural counseling and training. *Journal of Counseling and Development, 70,* 578–583.

Carter, R. T. (1992). Cultural values: A review of empirical research and implications for counseling. *Journal of Counseling and Development, 70,* 164–173.

Carter, R. T., & Helms, J. E. (1987). The relationship of Black value orientations to racial identity attitudes. *Measurement and Evaluation in Counseling and Development, 19,* 185–195.

Casas, J. M. (1985). A reflection on the status of racial/ethnic minority research. *The Counseling Psychologist, 13,* 581–598.

Chávez, L. (1991). *Out of the barrio: Toward a new politics of Hispanic assimilation.* New York: Basic Books.

Cohen, R. J., Montague, P., Nathanson, L. S., & Swerdlik, M. E. (1988). *Psychological testing: An introduction to tests and measurement.* Mountain View, CA: Mayfield.

Conoley, J. C., & Kramer, J. J. (Eds.) (1991). *Tenth mental measurements yearbook.* Lincoln, NE: University of Nebraska Press.

Cuellar, L., Harris, L. C., & Jasso, R. (1980). An acculturation scale for Mexican-American normal and clinical populations. *Hispanic Journal of Behavioral Sciences, 2,* 199–217.

D'Souza, D. (1991). *Illiberal education: The politics of race and sex on campus.* New York: Free Press.

Fukuyama, M. A. (1990). Taking a universal approach to multicultural counseling. *Counselor Education and Supervision, 30,* 6–17.

Goddard, H. H. (1917a). *The Kallikak family: A study in the heredity of feeblemindedness.* New York: Macmillan.

Goddard, H. H. (1917b). Mental tests and the immigrant. *Journal of Delinquency, 2,* 243–277.

Goddard, H. H. (1917c). Review of L. M. Terman: The measurement of intelligence. *Journal of Delinquency, 2,* 30–32.

Gough, P. B. (1992). Double jeopardy. *Phi Delta Kappan, 73,* 739.

Gould, S. J. (1981). *The mismeasure of man.* New York: Norton.

Hansen, J. C. (1987). Cross-cultural research on vocational interests. *Measurement and Evaluation in Counseling and Development, 19,* 163–176.

Harrow, A. J. (1972). *A taxonomy of the psychomotor domain: A guide for developing behavioral objectives.* New York: David McKay.

Helms, J. E. (1986). Expanding racial identity theory to cover counseling process. *Journal of Counseling Psychology, 33,* 62–64.

Herr, E. L. (1989). *Counseling in a dynamic society: Opportunities and challenges.* Alexandria, VA: American Association for Counseling and Development.

Hilliard, A. G. (1992). Behavioral style, culture, and teaching and learning. *Journal of Negro Education, 61,* 370–377.

Hood, A. B., & Johnson, R. W. (1991). *Assessment in counseling: A guide to the use of psychological assessment procedures.* Alexandria, VA: American Association for Counseling and Development.

Ibrahim, F. A. (1991). Contribution of cultural worldviews to generic counseling and development. *Journal of Counseling and Development, 70,* 13–19.

Karmos, A. H., & Karmos, J. S. (1984). Attitudes toward standardized achievement test performance. *Measurement and Evaluation in Counseling and Development, 17,* 56–66.

Krathwohl, D. R., Bloom, B. S., & Masia, B. B. (1964). *Taxonomy of educational objectives: The classification of educational goals, Handbook II: Affective domain.* New York: David McKay.

LaFromboise, T. D., Coleman, S. L., & Hernandez, J. M. (in press). Crosscultural counseling inventory—Revised. *Journal of Multicultural Counseling and Development.*

McArthur, C. (1989). The superiorities of Form M. *Journal of Personality Assessment, 53,* 837–840.

McArthur, C. (1992). Rumblings of a distant drum. *Journal of Counseling and Development, 70,* 517–519.

McConahay, C. J. (1986). The Modern Racism Scale: A construct validation. *Journal of Multicultural Counseling and Development, 14,* 3–15.

Mitchell, J. V., Jr. (Ed.). (1985). *Ninth mental measurements yearbook.* Lincoln, NE: University of Nebraska Press.

Noll, V. H., Scannell, D. P., & Craig, R. C. (1982). *Introduction to educational measurement.* Boston: Houghton Mifflin.

Parham, T. A., & Helms, J. E. (1981). Relation of racial identity attitudes to self-actualization and affective states of Black students. *Journal of Counseling Psychology, 32,* 431–440.

Pedersen, P. B. (1987). Ten frequent assumptions of cultural bias in counseling. *Journal of Multicultural Counseling and Development, 15,* 16–24.

Pedersen, P. B. (1988). A handbook for developing multicultural awareness. Alexandria, VA: American Association for Counseling and Development.

Pedersen, P. B. (Ed.). (1991). Multiculturalism as a fourth force in counseling [Special issue]. *Journal of Counseling and Development, 70.*

Ponterotto, J. G. (1988). Racial consciousness development among White counselor trainees: A stage model. *Journal of Multicultural Counseling and Development, 16,* 146–156.

Ponterotto, J. G., & Casas, J. M. (1991). *Handbook of racial/ethnic minority counseling research.* Springfield, IL: Charles C. Thomas.

Ravitch, D. (1990, October 24). Multiculturalism yes, particularism no. *The Chronicle of Higher Education,* p. A44.

Reynolds, C. R. (1987). Playing IQ roulette with the Stanford-Binet, 4th edition. *Measurement and Evaluation in Counseling and Development, 20,* 121–123.

Sabnani, H. B., & Ponterotto, J. G. (1992). Racial/ethnic minority-specific instrumentation in counseling research: A review, critique, and recommendations. *Measurement and Evaluation in Counseling and Development, 24,* 161–187.

Sanchez, C. (1992). *Is there a national education crisis?* Interviews with Gerald Bracey, Diane Ravitch, Mark Tucker, and Archie LaPointe [Transcript of "Morning Edition" radio broadcast, November 2, 1992]. Washington, DC: National Public Radio.

Sattler, J. M. (1988). *Assessment of children* (3rd ed.). San Diego: Author.

Sax, G. (1989). *Principles of educational and psychological measurement and evaluation* (3rd ed.) Belmont, CA: Wadsworth.

Sedlacek, W. E. (Ed.). (1987). Assessments for minority populations: Traditional and nontraditional approaches [Special issue]. *Measurement and Evaluation in Counseling and Development, 19,* 163.

Sedlacek, W. E., & White, T. R. (1987). A validation study of the Situational Attitude Scale for use with Black males. *Journal of Multicultural Counseling and Development, 15,* 16–24.

Staff. (1992, Spring). Toward a definition of multiculturalism. *Social Studies Review,* pp. 13–15.

Sue, D. W., Arredondo, P., & McDavis, R. J. (1992). Multicultural counseling competencies and standards: A call to the profession. *Journal of Counseling and Development, 70,* 477–486.

Sue, D. W., & Sue, D. (1990). *Counseling the culturally different: Theory and practice.* New York: Wiley.

Szapocznik, J., Scopetta, M. A., Kurtines, W., & Arnalde, M. (1978). Theory and measurement of acculturalization. *Interamerican Journal of Psychology, 12,* 113–130.

Williams, R. L. (1972). *The BITCH-100: A culture-specific test.* Paper presented at the meeting of the American Psychological Foundation, Honolulu, HI.

Williams, R. L. (1974). Black pride, academic relevance, and individual achievement. In R. W. Tyler & R. M. Wolf (Eds.) *Crucial issues in testing.* Berkeley, CA: McCutchan.

Williams, R. L. (1975). The BITCH-100: A culture-specific test. *Journal of Afro-American Issues, 3,* 103–116.

CHAPTER 13

CURRICULUM TRENDS IN TRANSCULTURAL COUNSELING IN COUNSELOR EDUCATION

EDWIN L. HERR AND ELLEN S. FABIAN

Fundamental to the successful application of transcultural counseling and its commitment to bridging cultures are the attitudes and competencies of counselors. Theories, paradigms, and concepts have vitality and meaning only when they are tested and implemented by persons prepared to understand and act on the premises they represent. Thus, a central issue in implementing the multiple elements of transcultural counseling is how these ideas are reflected in the content of the counselor education curriculum and, thereby, in the socialization of counselors to their professional responsibilities and opportunities in transcultural counseling.

This chapter will examine some options by which the counselor education curriculum can emphasize the types of counselor preparation implicit in transcultural counseling by first reviewing broad curriculum trends and then exploring the application of these broad trends through two examples of special interest in counselor education: (a) internationalizing counselor education and (b) incorporating transcultural trends into rehabilitation counselor education.

CURRICULUM PERSPECTIVES

Before addressing transcultural counseling directly as a curriculum issue, it is first useful to think about the meaning of the term *curriculum*. By definition, *curriculum* means "a course of study" (Coulson, Carr, Hutchinson, & Eagle, 1985, p. 208). However, when applied to counselor education, that simple term fails to capture the comprehensiveness of the instructional experiences and environment that make up a curriculum. For example, Hollis and Wantz (1977), in their ongoing attempts to describe the richness and the complexity of counselor education in the United States, have talked about ways to identify the course subsystems that make up counselor education. A frequently used distinction among such courses is *experiential* versus *didactic* courses. In 1977, Hollis and Wantz, using *experiential* to refer to "experiences in working with materials, equipment, or clients" (p. 35), found that the content emphases were ranked by counselor educators as follows in regard to their inclusion of experiential components (p. 38):

1. Internship
2. Field experience
3. Practicum and advanced practicum
4. Techniques and prepracticum
5. Tests, measurement, research, and statistics
6. Career and information processing
7. Theories
8. Principles

From a somewhat different perspective, Hollis and Wantz in 1980 classified the educational experiences provided in counselor education into eight categories. They were ranked and defined as depicted in Table 1.

Although some readers may wish to add or delete subsystems in counselor education from those portrayed here or use other terms more current or descriptive, the point is that the general characteristics of the subsystems that comprise counselor preparation seem to remain stable while the course content or field-based experiences change to reflect counselor specialties or client populations as well as what a particular counselor education program considers important. Expressed somewhat differently, a particular emphasis, such as transcultural counseling, may be relegated by the values or

TABLE 1. CLASSIFICATION OF EDUCATIONAL EXPERIENCES PROVIDED IN COUNSELOR EDUCATION

Rank	Area	Definition
1	Cognitive experiences	Readings, discussions, idea exchange, and presentations
2.5	Student counselor	Serving as a counselor under supervision, as in practicum
2.5	Participative	Serving as a group member, interviewee, or counselee
4	Perceptual	Observations, closed circuit TV, live, and audio tapes, and field trips
5	Vicarious	Audio and video recordings, films, and other canned experiences
6	Situational simulation	Role-playing, socio-drama, psychodrama, decision-making games
7	Conjoint experiences	Working with a professional person and sharing in duties and responsibilities, being a teaching assistant or co-counselor
8	Sole professional	Internship, school or agency setting, research, serving as a consultant or supervisor under periodic supervision

Source: Adapted from Hollis & Wantz, 1980, pp. 94–95.

priorities of a particular counselor education program to a course or a unit in a course; it may be treated as primarily a cognitive matter or an experiential matter; or it may be seen as such a transcendent issue that it pervades all aspects of the counselor education program: the cognitive, the experiential, the mentoring, the role modeling that make up the curriculum.

Of concern in any analysis of counselor education curriculum issues is the potential difference between the overt and the hidden curriculum of the program. The overt curriculum—the printed course syllabi, the announcement of the program's objectives, and the examinations used may all affirm the counselor education program's commitment to a particular emphasis (e.g., to promote transcultural counseling). However, if the faculty does not admit a culturally diverse student body or provide culturally diverse role models, uses only Eurocentric theories in courses, and fails to use culturally diverse examples in course work, the message given to students and to others by the hidden curriculum may overwhelm or defeat those espoused in the overt curriculum. These are issues of curriculum planning as well as of commitment to the array of possible models that will be used to shape the counselor preparation curriculum (e.g., transcultural counseling, systems intervention, life-span approaches, developmental or remedial strategies).

PREMISES OF THE TRANSCULTURAL MODEL

As curriculum elements in counselor education are considered, at least two types of knowledge are necessary before the specific subsystem is planned. One is the set of assumptions or concepts that underlie the emphasis to be incorporated into the program planning. The first basic question is, What is to be taught if this theory, paradigm, or concept is to be included in our counselor education program? What are the experiential or cognitive elements of importance? The second question is, Are there models in the professional literature about how such learning might occur?

Because the various chapters in this book are devoted to the history, the concepts, and the interventions associated with transcultural counseling, there is no reason to write an exhaustive summary of the content of the transcultural approach here. It is, however, worth identifying some fundamental perspectives used in this book:

- The transcultural counseling approach, emphasizing active and reciprocal processes in a mutually acceptable environment for everyone concerned, is an outlook designed to bridge gaps between culturally diverse social groups.
- The ability to face increased complexity and work across and through cultures is the major theme reflected by transcultural

counselors who labor to provide a caring environment that transcends cultural, ethnic, and racial boundaries across national frontiers to develop mutual understanding between people.

- Transcultural counseling is a method of using cultural knowledge and skills creatively to help others survive and live satisfactorily in a multicultural world.

- Transcultural counseling challenges therapists to use their know-how and resources more flexibly and provide counseling across cultures.

- Transcultural counseling does not require that the counselor be an expert in any of the cultures involved or adhere to any school of thought. Rather, transcultural counseling endeavors to develop open-mindedness on issues pertaining to the clients' value system.

- Counselors who plan to deal with issues involving plural societies should have flexible approaches at their disposal to respond effectively to their clients' needs.

- Counselors who deal with multiple cultures can no longer provide counseling that reflects the value systems of only one or two cultural perspectives.

- Traditional counseling procedures have often been grossly contaminated with stereotypes of individuals, groups, and societies of different backgrounds in which ideas and actions by clients or peoples from unfamiliar backgrounds are viewed as inferior rather than different. The transcultural approach stands for self-examination leading to the creation of symmetrical relations between counselor and client, which leads to a better understanding of ways others view themselves and avoids self-righteousness.

- To establish credibility, the transcultural therapist must modify his or her style and be consistent with clients' expectations.

- Transcultural counseling emphasizes readiness to adapt and employ different methods and strategies that promote access to cultural values alien to those of the counselor. The transcultural approach seeks to have counselors understand cultural differences and develop a reciprocal approach between counselor and client.

Although this list is a sketchy portrayal of the models of transcultural counseling discussed in this book, the emphases listed are important concepts. They reflect attention to the self-awareness and attitude of the counselor; a nondefensive openness to values different from the counselor's; a respect for the impact of cultures on the attitudes and behaviors of persons; knowledge differences in cultural value systems, as defined by national boundaries or other variables, such as race and ethnicity; a willingness and ability to match interventions to the cultural characteristics and value systems of the client; and counselor flexibility and openness to a reciprocal relationship with clients.

In planning a curriculum, a counselor education faculty must decide whether the assumptions of transcultural counseling are compatible with their beliefs about counseling and the attitudes and competencies important to counselors. If the assumptions are acceptable, then from a pedagogic perspective the question becomes what preparation models might be employed to embed the attitudes and content of transcultural counseling in the curriculum.

PREPARATION MODELS RELATED TO TRANSCULTURAL COUNSELING

One of the most frequently used models of training counselors or other helpers in multicultural awareness is that of Pedersen (1988). In his book, *A Handbook for Developing Multicultural Awareness*, Pedersen suggests that the three stages of multicultural development are awareness, knowledge, and skill. He identifies concepts, exercises, and strategies that can help a counselor education faculty provide for awareness, knowledge, and skill in different parts or subsystems of the counselor education curriculum.

Pedersen's views about awareness, knowledge, and skill might be summarized as follows:

Awareness. Unlike some other observers, Pedersen does not believe that multicultural awareness is an end in itself. Rather it influences "intentional and purposive decision-making" by helping a person be aware of how cultural differences may affect individual perceptions of behaviors or other responses. Pedersen further believes that "culture is not external, but 'within the person,' and it is not separate from other learned competencies. Developing multicultural awareness is, therefore, a professional obligation as well as an opportunity for the adequately trained counselor" (p. 3). Multicultural awareness is a basic ingredient of multicultural development in the sense that such development proceeds "from increased awareness of a person's culturally learned opinion, attitudes, and assumptions to increased knowledge about relevant facts and information about the culture in question, and finally to increased skill for making effective change and taking appropriate action" (p. 6). Pedersen contends that some programs fail because they "overemphasize awareness through the exclusive use of values clarification or the presumption of simplistic 'good' or 'bad' judgments toward a particular culture" (p. 8).

Pedersen argues that the first stage of developing multicultural awareness comes from asking the right questions about the students' own cultural influences and about other cultures of interest. Such questions have to do with helping students be aware of their prevailing assumptions, the cultural biases they hold, and the values to which they are committed, before developing a knowledge base about different cultures. Much of the learning related to self-awareness of students or faculty will likely require experiential learning, which may be facilitated by such techniques as role-playing, role reversals, simulations, field strips, critical incidents, case studies, and direct contacts with persons from other cultures.

Knowledge. The second stage of multicultural development has to do with the knowledge one has as a basis for understanding. Cultural knowledge takes many forms as it relates to one's own cultural influences, those of various cultural minorities, and cross-national cultural differences. Such knowledge includes how the psychologies of these different cultural groups vary and how culturally defined groups differ in their separate identities, their worldviews, and their beliefs and traditions. Pedersen has suggested that cultural dimensions that separate groups from one another can be viewed at three different levels: international, ethnic, and social role.

To impart multicultural knowledge, Pedersen suggests a variety of methods, including guided self-study using reading lists; the Cultural Grid, which combines personal variables with social system variables to describe a personal-cultural orientation or the cultural aspects of a situation; lecture and discussion; panel discussion; audiovisual presentation; interviews with consultants and experts; and observation (p. 14). One could add to this list knowledge about research on minority groups or mental health interventions used by different cultural groups; existing models of minority identity development; instances of cultural bias in counseling tools (e.g., tests) or in the organization and delivery of mental health services; and the availability of culturally sensitive professional guidelines for program development and accreditation, test use, admissions, or other matters.

Skill. In Pedersen's view, "skill is based both on awareness and on knowledge to bring about appropriate and effective change in multicultural situations" (p. 107). In this context, there are methods of counseling that are preferred in some cultural contexts and not in others. Indeed, Pedersen contends that there are "as many different methods of helping persons as there are cultural groups. Each group defines its own criteria of appropriate helping methods. In a similar way, each culture has its own requirements regarding the formal and informal context in which help may appropriately be provided" (p. 109). Obviously, within such perspectives many culturally relevant skills would be of concern. Among them are behaviors that relate to being accepted by persons from other cultures, identifying appropriate ways to bring about change in collaboration with clients or with the systems they occupy, and ability to receive information about value systems different from one's own and to respect human diversity and personal rights.

One method that Pedersen advocates for training multicultural counselors is the Triad Model as a way of helping counselors discern and be more sensitive to the culturally different client's internal dialogue. In overly simplified terms, the Triad Model includes a counselor-trainee from one culture who works with two coached persons: one a client and the other an anticounselor who tries to make explicit the resistance of culturally different clients. In this model, counseling is a three-way interaction between the counselor, the client, and the problem. The anticounselor represents a personification of the client's internal dialogue or problems and tries to prevent the counselor from creating an alliance with the client to solve the problem. The effort is designed to help the counselor learn to work within the client's perceptual framework.

Besides the Triad Model, Pedersen has suggested other techniques to develop skills in multicultural counseling. They include modeling and demonstration, using video and media resources for feedback, supervising, and practicing a new behavior pattern.

Pedersen's perspectives on multicultural awareness are a major framework for considering the elements of curriculum relevant to transcultural counseling. There are other useful perspectives as well. One of these is helping counselors in preparation to understand and examine the communications issues inherent in transcultural counseling. For example, VanZijl (1985) has listed a broad array of barriers to communication and, in turn, to counseling that sometimes occur between counselors and clients of different cultural backgrounds. They include such processes as transference and countertransference, resistance, values orientation, language, nonverbal communication, ignorance, high levels of anxiety, expectations of the client, and cultural stereotyping. Each of these potential barriers can be examined in depth from a cognitive perspective, and they can be tested in various experiential subsystems of the counselor education curriculum as student counselors interact under supervision with clients from other cultures and engage in culturally different role simulations or similar processes designed to heighten their awareness of the fundamental importance of communications in counseling. Sue (1981) has identified four sets of factors that could essentially be the structure for a counselor education training model: barriers, relationship and rapport factors, cultural identity, and techniques of the culturally skilled counselor.

Other theorists have combined the work of leaders in the field of multicultural counseling into a model for training that is quite comprehensive. One of these is Wehrly (1991), who has used an earlier model of Carney and Kahn (1984) to develop a stage model of counseling training. This model takes students from positions of relative naïveté about other cultural groups and views based on ethnocentric attitudes through stages embodying emerging awareness of their own ethnocentric beliefs and behaviors, conflict associated with feelings of guilt and responsibility, and emerging self-identity as a cross-cultural change agent and participant, to the final stage in which the student assumes a self-directed activist posture in expanding his or her own cross-cultural knowledge, attitudes, and skills and in promoting cultural pluralism in society at large. Wehrly suggests many cognitive processes (e.g., trainees' study of their own ethnic, cultural, and racial heritages, learning about the sociohistorical background and cultures of the non-White people of the United States), process issues (e.g., learning techniques for combining the use of ethnic group knowledge with assessment of unique qualities of each client, developing a wider repertoire of counselor interventions with clients of other cultures while realizing the limitations of cookbook approaches), and needs for experiential learning (e.g., developing a deeper understanding of one's personal racial identity, experiencing counseling supervision by a qualified trainer at an appropriate culturally pluralistic site) that can be incorporated into a counselor education program depending on its goals.

TWO PERSPECTIVES ON TRANSCULTURAL COUNSELING IN COUNSELOR EDUCATION

As one looks at the many implications of transcultural counseling in counselor education, it is probably fair to argue that different emphases within counselor education need to be treated somewhat differently but nevertheless in ways consistent with the principles of transcultural counseling. In addition to the broad perspectives on the curriculum implications of transcultural counseling already discussed, there are subtopics within counselor education that represent examples of the special applications of such perspectives. Two such examples are internationalizing counselor education and, in a more specialized sense, curriculum trends in rehabilitation counselor education that address the cultural differences inherent in disability.

INTERNATIONALIZING COUNSELOR EDUCATION

As counseling has become a process, a program of services, or a mechanism to deal with specific national goals for the allocation or the freeing up of human capital, it has moved from a parochial or limited function to one with worldwide implications and connections. Counseling has become internationalized, and counselor education has no choice but to recognize and respond to international trends, needs, and approaches on the application of counseling.

Each of us has watched in awe as the world's political, economic, and social systems have undergone transformation in the last 5 years in ways virtually incomprehensible a decade or less ago. These transformations are obviously not benign. They have implications for people's choices, achievement images, anxieties, cultural identity, information requirements, and other aspects of their psychological and economic integrity to which counseling can respond. In many countries, counseling has become a major sociopolitical instrument in national development plans designed to respond to the priorities and to the educational, psychological, social, and employment or career issues experienced in a nation.

It has become clear that neither counselors nor the problems people bring to counselors exist in a vacuum. In all nations where mental health services, counseling, guidance, or related processes are available to citizens, these services and their practitioners perform sociopolitical functions. Depending on the specific nation, the resources to support counseling, the definitions of which groups should be served, the conceptions of mental health or illness, the settings in which counseling is provided, and the configuration or substance of counseling, services are likely to be classified, articulated, and provided, directly or indirectly, through government funds and policies. In accordance with the political, economic, and social characteristics of a given nation, the focus of counseling is related to expectations beyond those defined by some set of professional guidelines. As a result, counseling services often differ in purpose and content across national boundaries and across cultures (Herr, 1989). National differences in the provision of counseling extend to the social and political purposes to be served—for example, to preserve the social status quo or to change it, to increase social and occupational mobility or to stratify or preserve existing economic structures, to amplify the individual satisfaction likely to be found in work or in citizenship, or to advocate for, dignify, and facilitate the needs of culturally diverse populations. The associated goals of counseling (e.g, to identify and distribute human capital, to treat what national policies define as particularly troublesome segments of the population—the mentally ill, the violent,

the unemployed—or to facilitate human development and self-actualization) are not fully discrete or mutually exclusive. In any case,
the assumptions on which national policies define by legislation,
statute, and funding who will be served and for what purposes also
typically identify who provides counseling services for whom,
where, and the outcomes expected. Thus, a complex set of cultural
elements interacts in particular nations, including the United States,
to affect what counselors do and why.

Historically, the implementation of counseling services has
been uneven across the world. This has been so primarily because
nations must reach certain levels of industrialization, information,
occupational and psychological diversity, and resource availability
to require formal organizations of mental health or other therapeutic
services designed to facilitate individual behavioral development as
sanctioned within that national context (Herr, 1985). Counseling
services, then, must be understood and appreciated as sociopolitical
processes shaped by the legislation and policies of a specific nation
and by the cultural dimensions that prevail. Of particular importance to the national development of counseling services are such
elements of culture as "the nature and rigidity of the class and caste
structure, the value system, the relationship of the individual to the
group, and the nature of the enterprise system" (Super, 1985,
pp. 12–13). These elements vary from nation to nation and within
nations. But, whatever the combination, they are the mediators of
the available opportunity structure for different groups of people;
of the available career paths and mobility factors; of the social
metaphors that are translated into policy and into achievement
images portrayed by the mass media; of contingencies or reinforcements that shape the individual's cognitive structures, habits, and
information-processing mechanisms; of the in-groups and the out-
groups of society; and of expectations for institutional or personal
loyalties. Regardless of its specific focus, the social structure of a
particular community or nation creates the circumstances in which
people develop as human beings, as workers, and as parents. The
social structure shapes the possibilities for choice, determines the
knowledge available to people about their opportunities, and reinforces the acquisition of specific types of behavior. It is within their
physical, social, and cultural environments that people negotiate

their personal identity, belief systems, and life course. Such political, social, and economic contexts in which individuality is framed and is lived out change across nations, communities, and families, across racial or socioeconomic groups, and, certainly, across time (Herr, 1989). As they change, their ripple effects on individuals and social systems become the content with which counselors serving different subpopulations within different nations deal.

The internationalizing of counselor education, then, as one of several possible applications of transcultural counseling, takes on importance from a variety of viewpoints. Some of these possibilities follow.

1. *Placing into the counselor education curriculum information about how culture affects individual behavior and how counseling varies in its acceptance and implementation from nation to nation.* Including such information not only recognizes the importance of internationalism and the broadening of one's personal paradigms about culture, politics, economics, and other matters that make up the "social ecology" of different nations. It also mirrors, for Americans, the importance of acknowledging that America is a land of immigrants. Therefore, what one learns about other nations and their cultural perspectives has its residual in the worldviews of the waves of immigrants who came to this nation—first primarily from Europe, then in forced circumstances from Africa, and more recently in escalating numbers from Southeast Asia. In counseling theory and practice, we have often taken only a Western psychological view of behavior as linear and individualistic, not an Eastern or Afrocentric view of behavior, which is more likely to be collectivist, group-oriented, and communal in support for people. Or, equally often, the assumptions and techniques of counseling have treated cultural differences as unimportant or ignored them. Thus, counseling models have treated primarily intracultural phenomena, not intercultural or transcultural phenomena.

There has often been the assumption in the national rhetoric that after a person has come to the United States, he or she is almost magically transformed into an American, however that is defined, from whom previous belief systems and culturally mediated behaviors have been purged, and the person's behavior will then be guided by the norms of the adopted culture. However, culture heritages are not extinguished easily. McGoldrick, Pearce, and Giordano (1982) in their modern classic, *Ethnicity and Family Therapy*, have emphasized the continuing, intergenerational effects that family background transmits or reinforces. One's orientation to the past, present, and future; how one views and interacts with strangers and people beyond the family boundaries; how one interprets one's obligations and responsibilities to others; how one views work, marriage, or child rearing; what one defines as a problem and appropriate solutions; and how one copes with a cultural identity or, indeed, the balance between one's adopted cultural identity and one's culture of origin are all affected by one's ethnic, racial, and cultural heritage. Such traditions and their original roots in other nations, cultures, or social structures persist for a long time in people's concepts of who they are and the behavioral norms to which they subscribe—in the ways they conceptualize emotional or mental distress and what they are willing to do with it or with whom they will discuss it. These factors shape behavior, and they lay a base for the interactions likely to occur in a counseling relationship, whether it occurs one-on-one, in a group setting, or within a family therapy context. These views are consistent with, indeed central to, transcultural counseling.

In one sense, then, to understand the variance in behavior and the cultural constructions that motivate the behavior of individual Americans, one's interest in internationalizing counselor education becomes a selfish way to create a framework by which to understand Americans as a microcosm of national differences across the world—a way to take action on the fact that cultures represent expectancies for action, templates and guidelines that give predictability to or explain normative behavior within groups, behavioral sanctions and windows on events, perceptual systems oriented to what one should attend to or not. These perspectives bring vitality to our perceptions that decision making, the development of self-identity, and life choices do not occur in a vacuum. They occur within cultural constructs that reinforce certain types of behavior and try to extinguish others. The occur as a residual, however vague, of the national origins of the traditions by which one's family or subgroup has organized its learning.

Cultural effects do occur at the national level as well as at the community and group levels. Peabody (1985) has summarized a body of research describing national psychological characteristics in which he has been engaged. His research compares psychological characteristics among the English, Germans, French, Italians, Russians, Americans, Northern and Southern Europeans, Swiss, Swedes, Irish, Finns, Dutch, Eastern Europeans, Austrians, Greeks, Turks, Czechs, Hungarians, Spanish, and Filipinos. He also summarizes other major works that examine intercultural diversity across national groups. On balance, his work suggests that when national psychological characteristics are compared, there are partial differences rather than complete differences among groups. Some behavioral manifestations tend to overlap across nations, whereas others are quite distance. Another finding of his study is that national characteristics are created by historical developments, and therefore they can and do change over time. Some national psychological characteristics change rapidly under the onslaught of technology, for example, or occupation by foreign troops, whereas other national character changes are much more subtle and gradual.

Perhaps the most striking finding of the Peabody (1985) study is that psychological characteristics of the national groups investigated are distinguishable and consistent (p. 57). Space and purpose do not permit an analysis of the specific psychological characteristics found in each group or their similarities or contrasts with those in other groups. Suffice it to say that the national groups tended to differ in (a) social relationships, (b) social rules, (c) control of hostility, (d) impulse control, and (e) authority and hierarchical relations. Clearly, the variations in how each of these differences is reinforced and portrayed in a particular nation are internalized by many, if not most, members of that national group. Thus, modal behavior for one national group is likely to be different from that for other groups. Indeed, the rules for interaction or action in a situation are largely cultural with respect to private and public relationships, the formality of communications, and the intimacy or spontaneity by which such relationships are conducted (p. 31).

In such a context, internationalizing counselor education means helping students understand that the human personality and the social structure are interlocking systems. Individual acts are framed within a cultural imperative. Such international perspectives so framed allow students to understand more clearly and forcefully the why of transcultural counseling as an essential tool to counselors in America as a land of immigrants and, increasingly, as professionals in global economy where cross-national migration will increase cultural diversity, not diminish it.

2. *A second dimension of internationalizing counselor education is to recognize again from the experiences of other nations that there are many ways to deliver counseling services.* The American emphasis on individual counseling provided by professionally trained counselors who specialize in specific functions or disorders is not the way of the world. Many nations are more likely to use persons at less than the master's degree as the core of such counseling provisions, or persons we would consider paraprofessionals. Frequently these persons are trained in workshops or certificate programs, not formal academic degree programs. In many nations, counseling is provided to many people by indigenous help-givers, shamans, medicine men, or other natural helpers. For better or worse, these people are not likely to have computer-assisted career guidance systems or dictionaries of occupational titles or batteries of tests to help their clients. They must rely on their personality as the major therapeutic mechanism, on creating expectations in clients that they will improve, and on the use of models in the community or networking or mentoring as adjunctive therapeutic devices. They frequently work with groups of clients, not just with individuals. Such learning from internationalizing counselor education, particularly among Third World nations, again stresses for students that the essence of counseling lies in communication skills, in caring for one's clients, in creating an environment that sets expectancies for improvement of the client's symptoms,

and in causing clients to be sensitive to their self-talk and daily behavior by using diaries and logs.

3. *A third way to internationalize a counselor education program is perhaps the most obvious: to accept and train international students.* However, there are likely to be problems with this way of internationalizing counselor education unless the concepts and cultural sensitivities identified in items 1 and 2 above are first woven into the program. If they are not, counselor education may do international students a disservice by suggesting that American or Western assumptions about personality, techniques, and counselor behavior have universal applicability. As has been discussed here, they do not. They must fit within or be tailored to the cultural imperatives, the resources, and the values of the nation in which they are to be delivered. In the extreme, international students have sometimes been falsely imbued with the idea that American ways are absolutely applicable. They have returned home culturally isolated, frustrated, and unable to translate what they have learned into the realities of their environments. Counselor education programs must be careful to provide processes by which international students can make the cultural transition to American views when they come to this country as well as to help them prepare to make the transition back to their nation and to deal with the culture shock they may experience when they attempt to put into practice what they have learned here.

International students are important elements of internationalizing counselor education, but they cannot be the only elements. They cannot be treated as tokens as Americans who happen to live somewhere else in the world. They must be helped to express their cultural understandings and learnings, how American techniques or technologies may or may not fit within such cultural perspectives, and the bases on which American theories and practices might need to be adapted so that such models can be made elastic and transportable to different cultures—transcultural.

4. *A fourth way to internationalize counselor education is to have American educators participate in international conferences, professorial exchanges, or sabbatical leaves taken abroad.* Each of these situations will test American assumptions and open educators

to new paradigms of practice and new assumptions about human behavior, the impact of social structures on that behavior, and the degree to which individual behavior and aspiration is really as unfettered as Americans profess in their theories and practices. Teaching abroad can be a humbling experience as one copes with the language, economy, bureaucracy, and cultural characteristics of another nation. It makes an American professor unfamiliar with the literature of the host country feel uneducated and incomplete. It helps us understand better the implications of living in a foreign environment as experienced by international students in our counselor education programs. It helps us to recognize that culture is a great mediator of who learns, how, and what.

Attending international congresses of the International Association for Educational and Vocational Guidance, the International Round Table for the Advancement of Counselling, the International Association for Applied Psychology, or one of the ACA Bilateral Conferences with other nations brings one into contact with people and ideas that cause one to think about nations not as abstractions but as places where people one knows live. Similarly, subscriptions to such journals as the *International Journal for the Advancement of Counselling*, the *Educational and Vocational Guidance Bulletin*, and *Applied Psychology: An International Review* provide theory, research, and practices that are used throughout the world, in both developed and developing nations. They report paradigms of counseling and counseling issues that do not usually find their way into the professional counseling literature of the United States.

5. *A final way to internalize counselor education is to host scholars and counselor educators from other nations.* Such persons can help counselor educators in U.S. institutions broaden their horizons and understand that other nations have their own psychologies, theories, and practices. These insights reinforce the premise that U.S. counselor education programs must provide a climate open to transcultural counseling as much more than a set of techniques—as a way of thinking, perceiving, and communicating in a world that is interdependent, yet culturally diverse.

TRANSCULTURAL CURRICULUM TRENDS IN REHABILITATION COUNSELOR EDUCATION

Frequently when curriculum issues are discussed in counselor education, they are cast at a generic level that can be generalized to any counselor education option available—school counseling, community counseling, mental health counseling, college counseling, or rehabilitation. Although such a strategy can be quite useful, it also belies the reality that because the various options provided by counselor education programs differ in the populations and settings that graduates will enter, topics or content, theory, and practice may have significantly different importance for each of these options. So it is with transcultural counseling.

In our example of internationalizing counselor education, we used a broad approach to incorporating transcultural trends into counselor training programs. The following section provides more specific curriculum considerations when incorporating the transcultural perspective into one type of training program.

We use the curriculum implications of transcultural counseling for rehabilitation counselor education specifically to suggest that by definition rehabilitation counselors in training and in practice deal with populations occupying cultures of deafness, visual impairment, and other forms of diversity that differentiate them from the mainstream culture of persons without disabilities. In addition, however, the clients of rehabilitation counselors come from all races, ethnic backgrounds, and socioeconomic and ability levels. In many ways, they are persons of multiple forms of cultural diversity for whom transcultural counseling is an essential process.

The intent here, then, is to examine one specialty in counselor education to explore why and how transcultural trends are incorporated into curriculum development and counselor training. Not only are rehabilitation counselor educators persuaded by the demographics of the 21st century that increasing numbers of people with disabilities will belong to diverse ethnic and cultural groups, but statistics on prevalence of disability suggest that the incidence in some of these groups is higher than among Caucasians. Moreover, recent incidence figures point out the link between disability and poverty (National Institute on Disability and Rehabilitation Research, 1989) as well as the correlation between disability and inadequate training and preparation for the workplace. These figures and the issues they raise have persuaded rehabilitation counselor educators that infusing transcultural perspectives into the core courses of curricula is critical (Crystal & Alston, 1991).

Another reason for examining the development of the rehabilitation counselor education curriculum as it pertains to multicultural training is that people with disabilities who are members of cultural or ethnic minorities may confront a dual stigma: that which arises from social labeling of people with disabilities as deviant, or at least different, and that which derives from ethnic identities different from those of the majority group. That is, like some ethnic groups in American society, people with disabilities have been denied equal access to employment, education, and public services. In addition, some people with disabilities have been denied constitutional rights by some of the abuses that were historically perpetrated through application of state laws for involuntary commitment to mental institutions (Brakel, Parry, & Weiner, 1985). Sociologists and disability rights advocates have long compared the marginal social status of persons with disabilities to that of other minority groups (Sussman, 1969). Even with the passage of the Americans with Disabilities Act, hailed as equal opportunity legislation comparable to major civil rights legislation, negative attitudes toward persons with disabilities, particularly those with severe disabilities, persist. That these attitudes are pervasive is supported by employment statistics: There is probably no other group of adults in American society where unemployment approaches 80%, as it does for people with disabilities who belong to ethnic minorities.

CURRICULAR TRENDS

This brief overview of the social context of disability in American society is important because of its obvious ties to course content and curriculum development in rehabilitation counselor education programs. The central issue of being different and its meaning to the person with a disability has been a significant issue in course content in rehabilitation education for over 40 years. Experiential exercises that encouraged nondisabled students to heighten their awareness of the meaning of disability were incorporated into courses that examined psychosocial aspects of disability, as were didactic discussions of sociological, political, and economic meaning. Yet parallel to the development of multicultural curricula in counselor education, where issues associated with different ethnic groups were initially examined separately from other curriculum concerns and where being different was still viewed as being exotic (Pedersen, 1991), a movement to understand people with disabilities as equal to but different from people without disabilities emerged. This movement led to the beginnings of cultural recognition, awareness, and affirmation of the experiences of people with disabilities.

EMERGENCE OF A CULTURAL CONSCIOUSNESS

Like the paradigm shift in multicultural or transcultural counselor education, which has emphasized infusion of procedures sensitive to cultural diversity into counselor education curricula, understanding disability as a cultural experience has precipitated a growing awareness of the need to recognize the multiple perspectives that confront counselors as they empower persons with disabilities to reclaim their rightful roles (Murphy, 1987; Vash, 1981). This growing awareness of the need for multiple perspectives in rehabilitation counselor education emerged from at least two sources. The first was the political awareness that began to characterize some disability groups, an example being the emerging identity of the deaf culture and their growing political activism on behalf of maintaining their own cultural identity. People with disabilities began to reject the idea of assimilation and adjustment into existing social structures and roles in favor of celebrating their own uniqueness—those characteristics and attributes that made them different (Hahn, 1985; Murphy, 1987). Simultaneously, the political focus shifted to getting larger organizations and social systems, such as school, corporations, universities, and recreational and social programs, to understand and accommodate the needs of people with disabilities, rather than force them into preexisting roles.

In disability studies, though, the idea of promoting and celebrating differences as uniquely representative of the individual is nonetheless unevenly applied across persons, as the stigma of a particular disability leaves the individual unevenly treated by society in terms of access to jobs, friends, and valued social roles. For example, the experience of having schizophrenia for a young male who is African American might be twice as stigmatizing as either of these memberships would be alone. It is possible to promote positive identity development for people whose disability is compounded with ethnic differences, and the tasks for the rehabilitation counselor are very straightforward: helping people develop strategies to manage the various social and economic discriminations they will face. The task in training rehabilitation counselors is not only to explore awareness of the multiple perspectives and social treatment of people with disabilities in our culture, but to examine the ways people with disabilities are similar to as well as different from the cultural or ethnic groups to which they belong.

COUNSELOR TRAINING

The role of the rehabilitation counselor has generally been analyzed and defined as one that incorporates both counseling and case-management functions (Rubin & Roessler, 1987). Rehabilitation counseling has a very pragmatic and outcome-oriented focus: It was shaped by federal legislation from the 1920s to the present that was specifically designed to train counselors who could help people with disabilities get and keep jobs. Because of this pragmatic focus, rehabilitation counselor training courses are based on building a framework for understanding the social and psychological issues that define the disability experience in American society. For example, finding a job for a person with a disability involves understanding the functional aspects of the particular impairment, as well as understanding the environmental and attitudinal barriers the person will face on moving into social and work worlds. For this reason, the core content in rehabilitation counselor education has always included understanding the social and psychological aspects of the disability experience.

In understanding how this multiple perspective has come about, we can examine the facets of the rehabilitation counselor education curricula in relation to Pedersen's (1988) three-pronged approach (awareness, knowledge, and skills) to developing culturally competent counselors, discussed earlier in this chapter.

Pedersen's first training recommendation is awareness, which attends to building students' recognition of their own cultural heritage while encouraging identification and recognition of cultural differences. For rehabilitation counselor trainees, awareness carries at least a dual meaning: Awareness of the meaning of being disabled and awareness of cultural or ethnic differences that interact with the socially imposed disability role. Depending on the nature of the faculty, the other students, and the surrounding environment, each of these awareness components presents different challenges to the counselor educator. At the most basic level, it is important for students first to understand the meaning of cultural differentness in order to have a context for relating to the disability experience. That is, relying on disability awareness training outside of cultural awareness makes it difficult for students to later interpret or understand the differing meaning that disability has across cultures. International research in rehabilitation has strongly demonstrated the differing meaning that disability does have across cultures (e.g., Kleinman, 1978; Lefley, 1985). Recent research supports the different meaning that disability may have across American cultural groups (Leung & Sakata, 1988; Smart & Smart, 1991).

Pedersen's second stage, knowledge, involves information on both the disability and cultural experiences of clients. A person's reaction to a disability, as well as the social and interpersonal meaning of the experience, is intimately tied to cultural meanings and belief systems. Unfortunately, too much of the rehabilitation research examining adjustment to disability meant adjustment of White males, with minority groups and women mentioned as interesting subgroups. Knowledge of various cultural beliefs informs students' increasingly sophisticated approach to understanding the disability experience, including reaction to disability and individual and family adjustment issues. For example, the goal of many rehabilitation programs has long been independence in living and working. Clients are assessed and plans are derived in relation to achieving independence. But, for instance, Asian-American parents of a young adult with moderate mental retardation may resist independence for their daughter or son. Rehabilitation counselors might label this resistance sabotage, when in fact it is bound up with different cultural beliefs and assumptions. Moreover, rehabilitation counselor educators have a uniquely sensitive role in mediating the boundaries between understanding the dual implications of being disabled *and* a person of color in our society and ensuring that students maintain a positive approach to these clients. With an outcome-oriented focus, rehabilitation counselors are trained to develop plans that lead to employment success. Focusing on the obstacles a young African-American woman who is blind will face in the job market negates the positive aspects of her identity. Maintaining a realistic culture of hope is part of the third stage of counselor training, skill development.

Pedersen's skill development stage involves learning to use and extend cultural knowledge to counseling and other applied settings (McRae & Johnson, 1991). In rehabilitation counselor education, acquiring skills requires that student counselors be able to apply knowledge of cultural beliefs and assumptions to helping people with disabilities and their families define the meaning of the disability experience and design life plans for managing it. Performing this dual role means that rehabilitation counselors have to undertake what Atkinson, Morten, and Sue (1989) called "alternative roles." Anderson and Cranston-Gingras (1991) suggested that the thrust of these alternative roles is becoming engaged in preventive activities in the client's environment, which might include acting as a consultant, change agent, ombudsman, or facilitator in the development of client support systems. This alternative role stance is particularly relevant to the functions of the rehabilitation counselor as he or she is engaged in empowering clients to enter or reenter meaningful social and vocational roles in society. People of color who also have disabilities, particularly severe disabilities, continue to confront implicit and explicit discrimination, which together deny access to quality lives in the community. To address these barriers, multicultural skills training for rehabilitation counselors needs to consist of opportunities not only to apply skills in counseling situations, but to expand the basis of these skills to other aspects of clients' lives. Role-plays such as those suggested by Pedersen (1988) for incorporating skills into actual training encounters should also consist of learning how to inoculate clients against the social and employment discrimination they will eventually confront. Competency in preparing clients to address these barriers requires awareness and knowledge of the meaning of the multicultural disability experience.

RECOMMENDATIONS

Social and psychological indicators suggest that the disability experience for people from racial and ethnic minorities is one that negatively affects the quality of their lives, perhaps in more stressful and significant ways than for any other group in our society. Moreover, counselor educators need to confront the fact that there have been "few initiatives to address the specific training needs of professionals who serve ethnic minorities with disabilities" (Wright, 1988, p. 5), despite the evidence that they will comprise an increasingly large proportion of the rehabilitation caseload in the 21st century.

Midgette and Meggert (1991) presented programmatic recommendations for multicultural counseling instruction, all of which are applicable to rehabilitation counselor training and to transcultural counseling. Additional steps that might be incorporated into the curriculum include the following:

1. Infusing multicultural perspectives into core curriculum courses such as psychosocial aspects of disability, job development and placement, vocational assessment, and foundations of rehabilitation.

2. Expanding foundational rehabilitation courses to include transcultural aspects of the disability experience, relying on international research in rehabilitation to stimulate discussion of different perspectives and meanings.

3. Enriching current text readings with perspectives on the disability experience of people of different cultures through, for example, scholarly readings and personal accounts such as Pape, Walker, and Quinn (1983), Torrey (1972), and Warner (1987).

4. Presenting recent research findings that suggest that adjustment to disability might be culturally understood and culturally bound.

5. Requiring that students select at least one elective course that deals with diversity issues.

6. Encouraging development of a rehabilitation research base in multicultural issues through advising graduate students in thesis and dissertation topics and proposing special multicultural issues in major rehabilitation journals.

329

7. Initiating active outreach efforts to recruit more students from diverse ethnic and cultural backgrounds as rehabilitation counselor trainees.

CONCLUSION

In this chapter, curricular issues in implementing transcultural counseling in counselor education have been explored. The position taken is that such implementation is a multidimensional process, not a simple one. The subsystems of a counselor education training in transcultural counseling have been discussed as a limited or comprehensive process, and as primarily cognitive or experiential or both.

Two examples of emphases within counselor education to which transcultural counseling has been seen as directly related are internationalizing counselor education and rehabilitation counselor education. These examples have been used to illustrate some broad implications of implementing content and practice pertinent to transcultural counseling as well as more narrow implications related to specialties within counselor education.

The examples used have served as frames of reference against which to project training models concerned with the student acquisition of awareness, knowledge, and skills; communication skills that transcend potential cultural barriers to mutual understanding by counselor and client; and staging phenomena in developmental models intended to help counselor education students progress from naïveté and ethnocentrism relative to transcultural issues to a self-identity that embraces transcultural knowledge, skills, and activism.

REFERENCES

Anderson, D. J., & Cranston-Gingras, A. (1991). Sensitizing counselors and educators to multicultural issues: An interactive approach. *Journal of Counseling and Development, 70*, 91–98.

Atkinson, D. R., Morten, G., & Sue, S. W. (1989). *Counseling American minorities: A cross-cultural perspective* (3rd ed.). Dubuque, IA: Brown.

Brakel, S. J., Parry, J., & Weiner, B. A. (1985). *The mentally disabled and the law*. Chicago: American Bar Association.

Carney, C. G., & Kahn, K. B. (1984). Building competencies for effective cross-cultural counseling: A developmental view. *Counseling Psychologist, 12*(1), 111–119.

Coulson, J., Carr, C. T., Hutchinson, L., & Eagle, D. (Eds.). (1985). *The Oxford illustrated dictionary.* Oxford: Oxford University Press.

Crystal, R. M., & Alston, R. J. (1991). Ethnicity and culture in rehabilitation counseling: The perspectives of three prominent counselor educators. *Rehabilitation Education, 5,* 209–214.

Hahn, H. (1985). Changing perception of disability and the future of rehabilitation. In L. G. Perlman & G. F. Austin (Eds.), *Social influences in rehabilitation planning: A blueprint for the 21st century* (pp. 53–64). Alexandria, VA: National Rehabilitation Association.

Herr, E. L. (1985). International approaches to career counseling and guidance. In P. Pedersen (Ed.), *Handbook of cross-cultural counseling and therapy* (pp. 3–10). Westport, CT: Greenwood.

Herr, E. L. (1989). *Counseling in a dynamic society. Opportunities and challenges.* Alexandria, VA: American Association for Counseling and Development.

Hollis, J. W., & Wantz, R. A. (1977). *Counselor education directory 1977: Personnel and programs* (3rd ed.). Muncie, IN: Accelerated Development.

Hollis, J. W., & Wantz, R. A. (1980). *Counselor preparation 1980. Programs, personnel, trends* (4th ed.). Muncie, IN: Accelerated Development.

Kleinman, A. M. (1978). Culture, illness and cure: Clinical lessons from anthropological and cross-cultural research. *Annals of Internal Medicine, 88,* 251–258.

Lefley, H. (1985). Mental health training across cultures. In P. Pedersen (Ed.), *Handbook of cross-cultural counseling and therapy* (pp. 259–266). New York: Praeger.

Leung, P., & Sakata, R. (1988). Asian Americans and rehabilitation. *Journal of Applied Rehabilitation Counseling, 19*(4), 16–20.

McGoldrick, M., Pearce, J. K., & Giordano, J. (Eds.). (1982). *Ethnicity and family therapy.* New York: Guilford.

McRae, M. B., & Johnson, S. D. (1991). Toward training for competence in multicultural counselor education. *Journal of Counseling and Development, 70,* 131–135.

Midgette, T. E., & Meggert, S. S. (1991). Multicultural counseling instruction: A challenge for faculties in the 21st century. *Journal of Counseling and Development, 70,* 136–141.

Murphy, R. F. (1987). *The body silent*. New York: Henry Holt.

National Institute on Disability and Rehabilitation Research. (1989). *Chartbook on disability in the United States*. Washington, DC: U.S. Department of Education: Author. (Contract #HN88011001).

Pape, D. A., Walker, C. R., & Quinn, F. H. (1983). Ethnicity and disability: Two minority statuses. *Journal of Applied Rehabilitation Counseling, 14*, 18–23.

Peabody, D. (1985). *National characteristics*. Cambridge, England: Cambridge University Press.

Pedersen, P. (1988). *A handbook for developing multicultural awareness*. Alexandria, VA: American Association for Counseling and Development.

Pedersen, P. (1991). Multiculturalism as a generic approach to counseling. *Journal of Counseling and Development, 70*, 6–12.

Rubin, S. E., & Roessler, R. T. (1987). *Foundations of the vocational rehabilitation process*. Austin: PRO-ED.

Smart, J. F., & Smart, D. W. (1991). Acceptance of disability and the Mexican American culture. *Rehabilitation Counseling Bulletin, 34*, 357–367.

Sue, D. W. (1981). *Counseling the culturally different*. New York: Wiley.

Super, D. E. (1985). Career counseling across cultures. In P. Pedersen (Ed.), *Handbook of cross-cultural counseling and therapy* (pp. 11–20). Westport, CT: Greenwood.

Sussman, M. B. (1969). Dependent disability and dependent pain: Similarity of conceptual issues and research needs. *The Social Service Review, 43*, 383–395.

Torrey, E. F. (1972). *The mind game: Witchdoctors and psychiatrists*. New York: Emerson Hall.

VanZijl, J. C. (1985). Multicultural counseling: Mission impossible. Paper presented at the International Round Table for the Advancement of Counselling, Lund, Sweden.

Vash, C. (1981). *The psychology of disability*. New York: Springer.

Warner, R. (1987). *Recovery from schizophrenia: Psychiatry and political economy*. New York: Routledge & Kegan Paul.

Wehrly, B. (1991). Preparing multicultural counselors. *Counseling and Human Development, 24*(3), 1–24.

Wright, T. J. (1988). Enhancing the professional preparation of rehabilitation counselors for improved services to ethnic minorities with disabilities. *Journal of Applied Rehabilitation Counseling, 19*, 4–10.

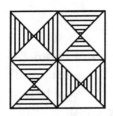

Summary: Bilateral and International Perspectives

John McFadden

Meeting new demands and situations effectively is a focus for transcultural counselors. This style of counseling endeavors to help individuals and groups achieve goals by encouraging effective interaction between different cultures to improve communication. Transcultural counseling introduces individuals to differences with intensity and impact so that exposure to cultural variations can be optimized. The presence of a multiethnic population invariably serves to interpret social systems and articulate apparatuses that frequently assume monoethnicity, monoculturalism, homogeneity, and supremacy or superiority of the culture of the dominant group.

The trend toward diversifying the liberal arts curriculum has introduced questions. In its simplest terms, the battle is over the content of the curriculum. What authors, books, and ideas are most appropriate for students or trainees? Some faculty desire to expand the canon to include a broader range of ethnic scholars. Their opponents argue for a traditional perspective: Great Books. The time has come for today's bibliographies and counseling approaches to be broadened to include the current and future multiethnic nature of the people of the United States.

During the past few decades, American society has come to recognize and accept the fact that its multiethnicity includes racial, religious, and nationality groups and that the experiences of these different peoples have by no means been identical. The legitimacy of such diversity is now an indisputable fact that may remain an essential part of life in the United States. The interaction between our citizens and immigrants is pivotal to understanding societal differentiation and the basis for cultural reconstruction.

By attempting to blend with mainstream American society, cultural and ethnic minorities could find themselves surrendering to those elements of the mainstream who believe that those who are culturally different are inferior. By attempting to assimilate, minorities frequently lose part of their rich and proud heritage of family relationships, history, and language, albeit some persons advocate that minorities cannot afford to separate themselves from the majority. The turbulent 1960s and early 1970s brought about an increased awareness of the plight of people of color and resulted in fundamental changes in the way White America viewed these people. Today we must work toward respect for, if not acceptance of, values of the minority by the majority and vice versa. To attempt to survive without interfacing with the cultural juggernaut is to lead a life of frustration, alienation, and economic subservience.

This book has assembled some of the finest theorists and practitioners, particularly those who have focused their attention on cross-cultural, multicultural, and transcultural issues, to provide their views on contemporary developments in counseling. The central theme is to encourage transcultural counselors to examine the cultural paradigms of their clients. Transcultural counseling sees the world as a community of nations that are continually growing together. With that worldview in mind, counselors work to reach beyond national boundaries and cultures to help humankind understand and respect other ways of life. Such a transpersonal view creates the basis for regional and national as well as bilateral and multilateral coexistence. Curriculum and instruction for the education of counselors must direct special attention to these issues and factor them into programs for undergraduate and graduate study.

Projections indicate that, by year 2000, more than one third of the population of the United States will be racial and ethnic minorities. By 2010, racial and ethnic minorities are expected to be a majority, with White America constituting approximately 48% of the population (Sue, 1991). A huge body of literature indicates the widespread ineffectiveness of traditional counseling approaches and techniques when applied to minorities (Axelson, 1993). This therapeutic inadequacy is a result of a unilateral training system that does not recognize the roles played by race, culture, and ethnicity. The transcultural counseling perspective not only includes counseling ethnic and racial minorities but also addresses gender-based segregation as well as other sources of alienation. Many persons inextricably caught between opposing values could benefit enormously from transcultural counseling, which promotes transcendency beyond cultural differences. In fact, transcultural counselors advocate a celebration of cultural diversity.

As confirmed by numerous research and scholarly publications, the need for multiculturalism in the counseling and mental health profession is urgent for ethical and effective practice, an integral part of our professional work. The culturally competent counselor is one who is well aware of perceived notions about and limitations on human behavior and one who is likely to understand his or her own worldviews as a component of the larger worldview (Ibrahim, 1992) and function accordingly.

In sum, this book has woven together ideas and theoretical contributions of various cultural dimensions, interdependence issues, and the need for maintenance of an ecosystem essential to the lives of all creatures, great and small. Such a broad approach is expected to provide some useful information in the process of development and growth of transcultural counselors, for a barrier to one is a barrier to all.

REFERENCES

Axelson, J. A. (1993). *Counseling and development in a multicultural setting* (2nd ed.). Belmont, CA: Brooks/Cole.

Ibrahim, F. A. (1992). A course on Asian-American women: Identity development issues. *Women's Studies Quarterly, 20*(1), 41–58.

Sue, D. W. (1991). A conceptual model for cultural diversity training. *Journal of Counseling and Development, 70*, 99–105.

INDEX

American Indian and Alaskan Native culture, 168–169
Asian-American culture, 248
disabled persons, 324, 328
Hispanic culture, 232–233
literature review, 11
stylistic model for transcultural counseling, 65, 69, 79–80
Diversity of Arab-American population, 262–263
Diversity of Hispanic population, 214–217, 222
Doubling technique, 126
Dual relationship conflict, 231–232

E

Eastern cultures, 12, 15. *See also* Arab-American culture; Asian-American culture; Chinese culture
Economic issues
American Indian and Alaskan Native culture, 166–167, 177–182
Arab-American culture, 263, 266
disabled persons, 323
Educational and Vocational Guidance Bulletin, 322
Educational issues. *See also* Curriculum trends in counselor education; Textbook review; Training and education of counselors
African-American culture, 78–79, 199–200
American Indian and Alaskan Native culture, 175–178
Arab-American culture, 269–270, 271, 278
Asian-American culture, 240, 242–246
Hispanic culture, 101–102, 219, 227–228, 232
Taiwanese culture, 250–254
Educational measurement. *See* Evaluation and assessment for transcultural counseling

Educational Resources Information Center, 290–291
Emotional cutoff, 119–120
Emotional insight, 139–140, 144
Emotional reactions, 136–139
Emotional triangles, 116–118
Employment issues. *See also* Discrimination
Arab-American culture, 263
Asian-American culture, 248–249, 256–257
disabled persons, 323–324, 326, 329
Taiwanese culture, 252–253
Enactment techniques, 114–115
Ethnic identity. *See also* Cultural identity
African-American culture, 196–199
American Indian and Alaskan Native culture, 164–167
disabled persons, 324–326
ethnic and cultural identity, 97–100
Hispanic culture, 213–217
Ethnic matching, 35
Ethnocentrism, 98–100
Ethnoentropy, 98–100
Ethnosyncretism, 98–100
Evaluation and assessment for transcultural counseling
literature review, 289–294
multicultural scholarship, 294–295
science of measurement history, 295–298
terminology, 287–288
Evangelical Protestantism, 217–218
Existential categories, 30–33
Existential isolation, 32
Existential worldview theory
applications in counseling and psychotherapy, 38–40
counselor-client cultural match, 35–38
cultural identity and worldview, 33–35
defined, 23–24
implications for process and outcome, 40

research reviews and resources, 227–228

stylistic model for transcultural counseling, 72–73, 80

transcendent counseling case study, 101–102

transcultural counseling, 222–224

Historical approaches in transcultural counseling

development of counseling profession, 3–4

goals for counseling professionals, 20–21

literature review, 8–13

taxonomy of terms, 4–8

transculturalism, 13–20

Historical family therapy. *See* Extended family therapy

Holding therapy technique, 126–127

Holistic health counseling goal, 88

Homosexuality, 223

Hug therapy technique, 126–127

Human nature existential category, 31

Human nature worldview, 43–44

I

Immigration and Naturalization Act of 1965, 263

Indian Education Act of 1972, 176

Indian Gaming Regulatory Act of 1988, 181

Indian/Native culture. *See* American Indian and Alaskan Native culture;
Hispanic culture

Indian Self-Determination and Educational Assistance Act, 176

Individualism, 12

Initial client assessment, 90, 229

Intelligence measurement history, 295–298

Interactions, 114–116, 142

Intercultural counseling, 7

International Association for Applied Psychology, 322

International Association for Educational and Vocational Guidance, 322

International counseling, 7, 18

International Journal for the Advancement of Counselling, 322

International Round Table for the Advancement of Counselling, 322

Interracial marriage, 73–74, 252

Introduction to Educational Measurement, 293

Introjection, 202–203

Islamic culture, 262–265, 268–270, 279–280

J

Japanese culture, 12

JCD. See Journal of Counseling and Development

JMCD. See Journal of Multicultural Counseling and Development

Johnson O'Malley Act, 165

Joining technique, 113–114

Journal of Counseling and Development, 289–293

Journal of Multicultural Counseling and Development, 289–293

L

Language considerations

Arab-American culture, 274–275

Asian-American culture, 240, 257–258

Hispanic culture, 215–216, 224–226, 232

Latinos. *See* Hispanic culture

Legal issues, 77, 180–182, 215, 234–236. *See also specific legislation*

Life experiences model, 136–139

Life-style change counseling goal, 87–88

Life-style considerations. *See* Alcohol and substance abuse;
Transcendent counseling

Link therapy technique, 122–123

implications for process and outcome, 40
SAWV profiles in counseling and therapy, 41–45
training and education model for counseling and therapy, 46–49
Scale to Assess Worldviews II, 41. *See also* Scale to Assess Worldviews
Schizophrenia, 116, 119, 126–127, 226
Scholarship in evaluation and assessment, 294–295
Science of measurement, 295–298
Scientific-ideological dimension of counseling, 63–70
Self-control and beliefs, 139–142
Self-definitions
    African-American culture, 194
    American Indian and Alaskan Native culture, 167
    differentiation of self, 117, 120
    Hispanic culture, 220
    transcultural contexts, 26–27
Self-determination, 176, 187
Self-dialogue, 169
Self-hate hypothesis, 197–198
Sibling position, 119
Situational Attitude Scale, 292
Skill development in counseling, 312–314, 328
Smithsonian handbooks, 234
Social cognitive interventions, 184–186
Social issues, 17, 37, 174–175, 232–233, 241–242. *See also* Rehabilitation counselor education
Social relationships existential category, 31–32
Sociopolitical aspects of counselor education, 314–323
Spearman, Charles, 297–298
Special education assessment. *See* Evaluation and assessment for transcultural counseling
Spiritual influences. *See* Religious and spiritual influences
Stanford-Binet, 291, 293, 297
State Department, 234

State government gaming regulations, 181–182
State-Trait Anxiety Inventory, 291
State-trait anxiety theory, 97–99
Status of counseling profession, 19–20
Stereotypes
    African-American culture, 199, 208
    American Indian and Alaskan Native culture, 167–171
    Asian-American culture, 239–241
    Hispanic culture, 221–222
    transcultural model premises, 309
Strong Vocational Interest Blank, 290
Structural biases and myths, 167–171, 239–241
Structural family therapy, 110, 111–116, 129
Stylistic model for transcultural counseling
    anatomy of stylistic counseling, 63–65
    case studies, 71–80
    counseling considerations, 59–60
    cubical descriptors, 65–70
    description of model, 62
    principles of stylistic counseling, 70–71
    scope of model, 60–62
Substance abuse. *See* Alcohol and substance abuse
Supportive techniques of transcendent counseling, 93
Surname significance, 215–216, 222–223, 226
Synthetic-personal behavioral style, 195–196
Systemic counseling, 8–9, 184–185

T

Taiwanese culture, 250–254
Taoism, 247
Teaching techniques of transcendent counseling, 93–94
Tenth Mental Measurements Yearbook, 293–295